An Expat's Life,
Luxembourg &
The White Rose

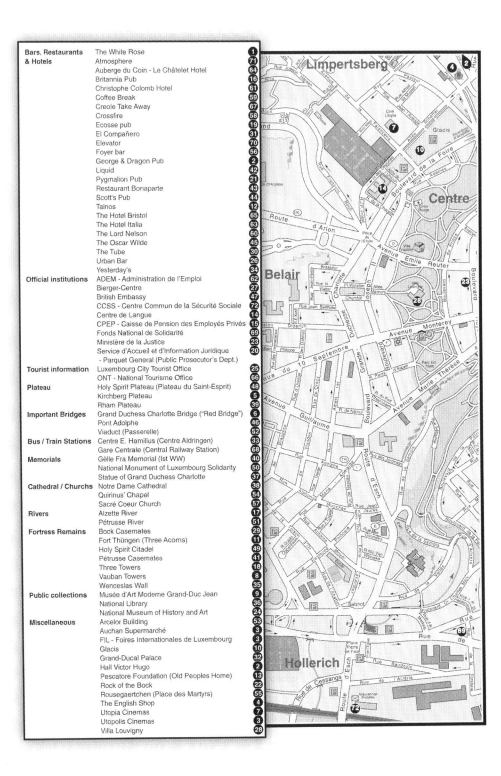

Bars, Restaurants & Hotels	The White Rose	❶
	Atmosphere	71
	Auberge du Coin - Le Châtelet Hotel	64
	Britannia Pub	16
	Christophe Colomb Hotel	61
	Coffee Break	59
	Creole Take Away	67
	Crossfire	58
	Ecosse pub	19
	El Compañero	31
	Elevator	70
	Foyer bar	56
	George & Dragon Pub	❷
	Liquid	42
	Pygmalion Pub	21
	Restaurant Bonaparte	43
	Scott's Pub	44
	Tainos	12
	The Hotel Bristol	65
	The Hotel Italia	63
	The Lord Nelson	60
	The Oscar Wilde	45
	The Tube	30
	Urban Bar	26
	Yesterday's	34
Official institutions	ADEM - Administration de l'Emploi	62
	Bierger-Centre	27
	British Embassy	❸
	CCSS - Centre Commun de la Sécurité Sociale	72
	Centre de Langue	14
	CPEP - Caisse de Pension des Employés Privés	15
	Fonds National de Solidarité	69
	Ministère de la Justice	23
	Service d'Accueil et d'Information Juridique	20
	- Parquet General (Public Prosecutor's Dept.)	
Tourist information	Luxembourg City Tourist Office	25
	ONT - National Tourisme Office	66
Plateau	Holy Spirit Plateau (Plateau du Saint-Esprit)	48
	Kirchberg Plateau	❺
	Rham Plateau	39
Important Bridges	Grand Duchess Charlotte Bridge ("Red Bridge")	❻
	Pont Adolphe	46
	Viaduct (Passerelle)	52
Bus / Train Stations	Centre E. Hamilius (Centre Aldringen)	33
	Gare Centrale (Central Railway Station)	68
Memorials	Gëlle Fra Memorial (Ist WW)	40
	National Monument of Luxembourg Solidarity	50
	Statue of Grand Duchess Charlotte	37
Cathedral / Churchs	Notre Dame Cathedral	38
	Quirinus' Chapel	54
	Sacré Coeur Church	57
Rivers	Alzette River	17
	Pétrusse River	51
Fortress Remains	Bock Casemates	29
	Fort Thüngen (Three Acorns)	11
	Holy Spirit Citadel	49
	Pétrusse Casemates	41
	Three Towers	18
	Vauban Towers	❽
	Wenceslas Wall	35
Public collections	Musée d'Art Moderne Grand-Duc Jean	❾
	National Library	36
	National Museum of History and Art	24
Miscellaneous	Arcelor Building	53
	Auchan Supermarché	❸
	FIL - Foires Internationales de Luxembourg	❸
	Glacis	10
	Grand-Ducal Palace	32
	Hall Victor Hugo	❷
	Pescatore Foundation (Old Peoples Home)	13
	Rock of the Bock	22
	Rousegaertchen (Place des Martyrs)	55
	The English Shop	❹
	Utopia Cinemas	❼
	Utopolis Cinemas	❸
	Villa Louvigny	28

Further information about this book can be found in the Diadem Books website: www.diadembooks.com/luxembourg.htm

Other books by Luxembourg authors include:

Marrying It All by Diana Button. (A story about a woman's journey back to life, set in Luxembourg.) (See more at www.diadembooks.com/button.htm)

An Odyssey of Murder by Frank Binns. (A murder thriller.) (See more at www.diadembooks.com/binns.htm)

An Expat's Life, Luxembourg & The White Rose

◆

Part of an Englishman Living Abroad
Series

by David Robinson

iUniverse, Inc.
New York Lincoln Shanghai

An Expat's Life, Luxembourg & The White Rose
Part of an Englishman Living Abroad Series

iUniverse, Inc.

For information address:
iUniverse, Inc.
2021 Pine Lake Road, Suite 100
Lincoln, NE 68512
www.iuniverse.com

This book is based on true-life experiences. Names however have for the most part been changed.

Published in Association with Diadem Books
(www.diadembooks.com)

ISBN: 0-595-31485-6 (pbk)
ISBN: 0-595-66323-0 (cloth)

Printed in the United States of America

To Lionel

A great friend forever. You will be missed but never forgotten.

David Robinson
5th January 2004

◆　　　◆　　　◆

Lionel Mayling was the treasurer of the ex Finsbury Circus Branch Investment Club. When I started this book, he was having difficulty writing to me. Tragically, whilst on the final amendments of this book Lionel died—on the 4th January 2004. I had sent him in December 2003 four-draft chapters including the introduction to read. He was, according to his daughter, delighted to have a book dedicated to him. He and his family had enjoyed reading the draft. It is now even more of an honour to dedicate this book to him.

Contents

Acknowledgements

Thanks are due to: Agathe Vincent, Alan and Anna Baldwin, Alf and Helen Silverman, André Bruns, Andy Horswell, Angela, Audrey Lewis, Bruce Milne, Carine Mattioni, César Diego Diez, Charles Muller, Chris Wilson, Christianne, Danni, Dave Christian, David Harris, David Ogles, Diana Button, Duncan Roberts, Eric Villiet, Gill Blaydon, Graham Belton, Graham and June Oldham, Gudrun Rumpf, Jasmine Pearson, Johannes Schiederig, John Langsley, John William Thomsen, Kremer Celestin, Liam Higgins, Lisa Shepherd, Louise Fraser-Mitchell, Marc Thissen, Marie-Sophie Collard, Mark Faulkner, Mark Newberry, Marion Bullock, Marta Castillo-Franco, Michel Daloze, Mike and Gwen Brewster, Mike Town, Mike Walton, Monique Durlacher, My friends who are unemployed, Natalia Gasper, My parents, Paolo Agretti, Patricia Schwall, Paul Cummings, Paula, Peter Tonks, Peter Martin, Preyamon Villiet-Ampaporn, Rachel Barnes, Ralf and Julia Tilmann, Richard Molloy, Roger Parker, Romain Bantz, Sabrine, Sandra, Serge Bernard, Siobhann Clark, Stefano Trotta, Steve Carton, Stewart Cooper, Susan Whicher, The girls of Longwy, The late Ken Flaxman, The late Lionel Mayling, The late Roland Pecheur, Tony & Irish Devenish, Valerio Ricci, Valentina Katina, Valérie Schiel, Volkert Behr, and the many others who have assisted me.

ADEM, Adecco, Bank of Bermuda, Bibliothèque nationale de Luxembourg, Centre de Langues—Luxembourg City, CFL, Circ Raluy, Circus Krone, DeLux Productions, Diadem Books, Essex Association of Boys Clubs, Frënn vun der Festungsgeschicht Lëtzebuerg (Friends of Luxembourg Forts Association), Hospital Radio in Chelmsford, Lloyds TSB, Luxembourg Tourist Board, Market Development International SARL, Polyglot club Luxembourg, Polyglot clubs of Belgium, Samsa film, The Carousel Picture Company, The former Finsbury Circus Investment Club, The Four Arrows Team, The Friends of Fort Fermont, The Various Luxembourg Government offices, The White Rose.

Introduction

As an Englishman living abroad, I am in Luxembourg at the time of writing this book. To be precise, living in the Grand Duchy of Luxembourg. Great, you may say! Well yes, it is, actually.

One day in the month of April 2003 I was sitting at the round dining room table in my second floor flat replying to a letter I had received that morning. It was mid-afternoon and the person I was replying to was an old friend of mine called Lionel. Now, Lionel and I go back a long way—more than twenty years, a long time in my life! Lionel is now seventy-nine years young and he wrote to me advising he is now an old man and was having difficulty writing. I was deeply moved by this and it prompted me immediately to sit down and write him a letter.

That letter turned into quite an epistle. I wrote it because I wanted him to share my experiences of living abroad. I wanted him to imagine a lifestyle that was quite different to the normal everyday life that most people live in their lives.

In effect, I wanted him to imagine a different life altogether—a life away from hot, sweaty trains heading into London jam-packed with commuters feeling like death warmed up every morning, some yearning for better opportunities in life, others dreaming of pastures new abroad in the sun. I wanted Lionel as a retired person who used to work in the city to share, together with his wife, my experiences of living abroad.

They say an Englishman's home is his castle. Indeed, it is. However, when you're sitting in your own living room as a pensioner and you're being defeated by old age, routines can get a little dull. Some people no doubt escape in nostalgic memories, reliving their pleasant experiences from an earlier time. But don't get me wrong—I know some very lively old-age pensioners! What I'm trying to say is that everyone likes to imagine a different life, and to get a letter from an old friend abroad is one way of sharing that experience.

In these days of electronic wizardry and touch-button responses and instant communication—I believe this is known as e-mail—there's still the thought that the Royal Mail in England can deliver that one nice cheerful letter.

Now we all get fed up receiving bills! A birthday is only once a year and if you're lucky you may get a few birthday cards. You're even luckier if you get a postcard from a friend. However, to receive a handwritten letter is the cherry on the top, providing that personal touch computer-generated ones just cannot give.

It's a rarity in itself these days to receive one of these handwritten letters! My cousin Jack told me this on receiving one from me. (*His* reply was on a computer typed letter!) I myself still write the occasional handwritten letter, but even I have resorted to that newfangled invention everyone seems to have these days—a laptop! Admittedly it's very good and I'm amazed as to what it does. Indeed, I've learnt so much from it.

Lionel was also sending me some information about an investment club we closed down about three years ago. We closed it because the stock market was going nowhere. The FCB Investment club had been in existence for about thirty years and I had been a member for about twenty. However, it had reached a parting of the ways. Various members were branching out and so it had reached a natural end. We had all decided to call it a day. It was time to move on.

The end was very sad—we had a good drink-up in the West End, reminiscing past binges in the city and the West End of London before going our separate ways.

Members of Lloyds Bank Ltd, Finsbury Circus Branch, originally set up the club back in the early 1970's. Over the years its popularity branched out and it expanded throughout the UK to take in new members who worked for or had worked for the bank. I joined it in the very early 1980's. It was one of the first investment clubs about. These days there are thousands of them.

It was set up to play the stock market using small amounts of money of about two pounds, which the members put in every month with growth being the aim. We didn't know it then, but it turned out to be a good idea as the portfolio grew. It was nothing large, but it did grow until 2000 when it started to hover.

Now most people will know that the UK stock market went into freefall from about mid 1999. Many people have lost a lot of money since then, especially up to March 2003. We got out just at the right time. Of course, if you don't sell anything and you have the right stocks, then they should recover over time. But then again, they may not! That's the joy—and excitement—of the stock market.

The Finsbury Circus branch is no longer there. It closed as part of the bank's reorganisation in London in the 1980's. Lloyds, like all the banks, closed many small branches. Today I think it is either a shop or a hotel. I did go there once in the mid 1990's. I wanted to see for myself the place where my friends had worked. I'm sure there was a small plaque on the wall. It was from a different era.

It's funny, really, that change should bring yet more change. Today's London is different again from the London I first worked in over twenty years ago. I remember Lionel's stories about his life in the bank. For me they were from another era. His City of London belonged to the 1960's and 1970's. Was it *really* swinging or groovy? More like old, dirty and stuck in a time warp! And were there really stream trains in Liverpool Street? I don't remember.

I was told by my father once that as a very small child he put me on his shoulders to see the last steam train leave Preston station in Lancashire. I do remember that as a child growing up in Hertfordshire we would take the train from Ware into Liverpool Street Station. Change at Broxbourne. It was a day out with your mum and dad and to arrive at Liverpool Street was exciting for a kid.

It was the old station then. Even when I worked in the city for over five years, it was still the same old station, stuck with its Victorian architecture of huge arches and glass covering the terminus.

Liverpool Street used to have in the good old days a labyrinth of old tunnels and old-fashioned barber's shops, Victorian toilets and old booking offices where you purchased your tickets for Hertford East.

How many people rushed down that long slope from Liverpool Street to Platform 12 to get the last train home? It was all in an era now long since gone. You know, I remember when it was knocked down around us commuters in the 1980's and rebuilt into the modern buzzing fast moving place it is today.

How many people now rush down the escalators on the Bishopsgate entrance, having dashed into the KFC to eat a chicken burger? Then ringing their loved ones on the train going home? It's a station still living in its own history. Yet it was and still is a home to almost every commuter from Hertfordshire and Essex.

How times change! Lionel's world was a lifetime away from mine. However, our paths crossed with the membership of the investment club.

Overall, our investment club was fun, and we all hoped that the share prices of the stocks we held would go up. We did made some mistakes. Sock shop was a disaster, if I remember correctly. Amstrad was another. BSkyB once hit £21 plus and we held. We eventually sold them around £14. It was a nice little profit, having bought around £4.50.

Lionel retired from the City in the early 1980's. He became a bank pensioner. He was the Treasurer of the FCB Investment Club for many years and I was the Chairman for the final period. Since it closed I have remained in contact with him.

I myself had worked for Lloyds TSB Bank for many years. I left the bank at the end of April 2001, having taken redundancy. The division that I worked for—Lloyds TSB Security Services, was completely shut down, resulting in more than 1,100 job losses. I had a choice. I could change divisions, keep my grade, retain a job and lose my redundancy package—or I could take the money and run!

For anyone who had worked for LTSS for over ten years it was worth their while to take the money. After all, if I stayed I could be demoted tomorrow and have my pension reduced. Of course, I may not have been demoted, but banking these days can be ruthless.

It didn't take long to decide—but not before I had given UK banking a go, working in a new Daily Risk Management department with the option of retaining my redundancy. I wasn't that stupid.

After all, how many people after twenty-two years in one company can seize the opportunity? How many people these days actually stay with one company for twenty-two years? Not many.

The closedown lasted, it seemed, forever. We did have some great leaving parties but the actual leaving presented me with a day of mixed feelings. I had worked in one organisation for a long time. I had made many friends in my years at Lloyds. It was part of my life. Overall, I had enjoyed most of the jobs that I had done.

On the day the closure was announced everyone was a bit glum, so we all headed over to the pub and got thoroughly drunk. It seemed the best idea at the time. It's not funny losing your job, but the opportunity it created for me meant that for the first time in my life I could think of doing something different. Here, staring me in the face, was that one chance we all dream of—a chance of actually doing something different with your life!

I was single, amazingly had no mortgage to pay on the house, had no ties apart from my house, and was ready for a challenge of going into the unknown. I must admit that I have travelled around the world on holiday. If I had been married this probably may not have happened. But I've always said that I would like to do something different in my life. I didn't fancy another twenty years on the train up to London again, being stuck in a dead-end job, or working locally. All of that I would have hated!

Lionel's letter set me thinking and prompted my reply—long but worth the time and effort. God, how many letters have I written to other friends since I've been here! I seem to write a lot of letters to various friends about my experiences. Everyone says that I seem to do more than most people in my life. I don't think that I do. Life is what you make it. Perhaps that's the point! Perhaps being so ordinary is also the point. Various people over the years have said to me that I should write a book of my experiences. I never bothered until now. Lionel's letter prompted me—to make someone happy across the sea. It sounds ridiculous, but why not? Why not indeed write a book and put my experiences into something that others can share!

Over the years many friends and expats I've met on my travels have said that living abroad is completely different to going on holiday. I was faced with the opportunity of finding that out for myself. What better opportunity would there be? To start again and discover what living one's life is really like on the other side of the sea. A life as an Englishman living abroad…

1

Hello Luxembourg

"Luxembourg—where's that?" a friend in England asked me in a letter after I had been here a while. "Is it near Wales? Is it in Europe?"

Bloody cheek! I knew she was joking. (Well, I hope she was!) I actually responded to this comment as I thought it deserved a suitable answer. Ironically, the envelope the letter had arrived in had been addressed to 'Luxembourg, Belgium!' I decided to give her a short history and geography lesson. Nothing serious, you understand.

My reply went like this: "Well, it's *next* to Belgium—but you'll have to look carefully as it's one of the smallest countries in Europe. It's the one in-between Germany, France and Belgium." I continued: "But wait. Had you spelt it 'Luxemburg' you'd be spelling it the German way. By adding 'Belgium' on your envelope it might have gone to Belgium. Yes, a strange fate of history makes it confusing." I explained: "Before 1839 it was a lot bigger than it now is. Once upon a time it was four times its present size. I suppose Luxembourg today is about the size of Essex." The brief history lesson continued: "When at the Congress of Vienna in 1815, the great powers came together to sort Europe out at the end of the Napoleonic wars, they made Luxembourg a Grand Duchy. They created a United Kingdom of the Netherlands with King William I as King, and Luxembourg became part of this. In 1830 Belgium broke away from this Kingdom to form its own Kingdom. In 1831, at the Conference of London, the great powers recognised the new independent Belgium and decided to cede the west side of Luxembourg to Belgium. The southeast corner of Belgium is still called the Province of Luxembourg. In 1890 Luxembourg left the United Kingdom of the Netherlands. This was when the Ducal crown changed to the Nassau family who still rule today..." I finished the letter by saying, "There is also a station in Brussels called 'Brussels Luxembourg', which is about the third one out heading towards Luxembourg! Belgium is what I call a tin pot country made out of

France, Holland and Luxembourg. They can thank the British for that—or was it Napoleon?"

But Belgium is *not* a tin pot country, as I discovered later. Nevertheless, I still prefer Luxembourg! (Incidentally, there are three places in the USA with the name 'Luxemburg'. One is in Minnesota, another in Iowa, and the largest is in Wisconsin.)

I think my friend took the lesson in good jest. Certainly her husband did. You need a sense of humour when you live abroad. It's different. The way you live is just different. Some people may say it isn't, but I can assure you that from my own experience it *is* different. It also has its moments—believe me—plenty of them!

Being a Brit abroad broadens your horizons. It gives one the opportunity to experience a different lifestyle. I've met many Brits who like it. Having sampled a life abroad, they choose to remain in the country of their choice. Some expats might even try another country before they settle down.

Many Brits have absolutely no qualms about living abroad. They become expats and join the many thousands of expatriates who have already left the UK. It seems that once they've lived abroad most choose not to return to a life in the UK.

All countries have pockets of expats living in them. Some countries will have more than others. Most people will choose to live in a country where they have a job. Others will go to a country to retire.

A good example here is Spain where there is a large expats community. Many Europeans including Brits have bought Spanish villas as second homes, either to live in or to rent out for part of the year. Many Brits have second homes in France. Some even have homes in Italy. Tuscany is a favourite, famous for its rolling countryside. Maybe I'll get there one day. A current fad is to invest in property in Florida, in the USA. Nice, especially if you like hurricanes. But the houses there are very good quality and they are cheap and chic.

Okay, so more people are taking the chance now, and doing the same as me. We all also have a bit more money in our pockets than our parents had at our age. I myself want to live in a place that has life, which has people around and has a bit of culture. I also want to live in a place that has local shops, with trains and buses nearby. It's called a town, or, in this instance, a city. As a single person, I suppose I want to live a single person's life. I want to meet other people, go to the cinema and hang out in the local bars. I don't want to live in the middle of nowhere, miles from the nearest Tesco.

I just cannot get too excited about people who go to France or Italy and buy a farmhouse in the middle of nowhere to do it up. I mean, the French and Italians are not stupid. They have long since abandoned them and moved themselves into the cities. Why the Brits have this current fad about escaping from suburbia and living fifty miles from the nearest supermarket, I have no idea. However, each to their own.

Actually, it's not Tesco or Sainsbury's. It's European supermarkets and hypermarkets that we have here in Europe. Continental names like Auchan, Match or Alima spring to mind. These names and others have their supermarkets and hypermarkets all over this region, for starters. They sell an amazing range of foodstuffs. It's truly an experience to go round these giants sampling the delights of these products, and the local produce. Of course, the big ones sell everything else as well. The large European shopping malls are all the rage with their malls being next to the main shop. I love going round, looking at the local meats, seeing the way they are packaged. I like the labels, the imports from France, Belgium and Germany. Even the stuff coming in from Italy. I didn't know there were so many types of pasta or how many different soft drinks you can get here. Yes, I know you can get some of it in the UK. But you're missing the point. You simply won't get the same atmosphere in your local supermarket back home.

So—I'm in Luxembourg. Great! Luxembourg City, to be precise. This is the country's capital. What an earth made me end up here? Ask that of all the expats here and you'll probably get a different answer from each one. We all have our own story to tell. This one happens to be mine.

It's one of the smallest countries in Europe. It's two thousand, five hundred and eighty-six square kilometres with a maximum length of eighty-two kilometres and maximum width of fifty-seven kilometres. Its borders total three hundred and fifty-six kilometres in length. Luxembourg City is three hundred metres above sea level. Certainly, at the time of writing, it is the smallest country in the European Union.

Luxembourg is a country that has its own language—Luxembourgish (*Lëtzebuergesch*). This was until recent times mainly a spoken language. In 1984, Luxembourgish was officially recognised as a language. In its own language Luxembourg is called *Lëtzebuerg*. The other main spoken languages are French, German and English. Portuguese and Italian are also widely spoken here.

Luxembourg is diverse. It's a country where many nationalities live. It is rich in culture and rich in wealth. It's most famous for its banking and financial services sector. The financial services industry here rivals Dublin in Ireland for business.

Luxembourg is also famous for its steel industry. It also has many European Union Offices, including the European Court of Justice. It retains its strong farming community but has adapted to change by encouraging new developments outside the city.

Luxembourg has is own Grand Duke, who is the Grand Duke Henri. His wife Maria Teresa, is the Grand Duchess. They have several children. The Prime Minister is Jean-Claude Juncker. Most expats remain blissfully ignorant of anything beyond this. After all, politics are not exactly high on their list when they've finished a day's work.

Most expats, when they arrive in Luxembourg to live, probably have secured their job beforehand. Some will have flown over before in order to go to the interview. Others will get the job abroad, simply arrive and get on with it. I've met all sorts of workers here.

There's also a huge singles environment in Luxembourg City. There are also expats with their families whose kids end up at The European School or The International School.

Everyone always thinks that the country is not that far from the coast and you'll soon be there. Be warned! It seems to take forever to reach Luxembourg on the train down from Brussels. The journey south seems to go on forever. It's only when you look on a map that its position can be understood. It's indeed further than one realises, which makes it that bit nearer Switzerland and a long way from the UK.

The main expats industry is banking. There is also life assurance and fund accounting. The European Union employs a few people here, as does the European Court of Justice.

You'll be surprised just how many different professions there are for expats. There's the usual bar staff, not forgetting the shop workers. Then we get the engineers and the money brokers. The Luxembourg movie industry also sees a few expats working in it. Don't let me forget the IT Boys—what would our PC do without them! I even know of a Brit who drives a tractor round all day on a golf course. Actually, I know he does a bit more than that. (I believe he's the head green keeper.)

Then we get the one or two nighter's staying here and visiting the bars. These include the lorry drivers, the blokes who set up the exhibition stands, not forgetting those members of the different governments visiting the European Commission. Finally, we get the bosses of offshore companies coming over to visit their staff here.

A great benefit to the country, of course, is a result of the people who, whilst not working in the country, help the economy by spending their money here—the friends and family members of people visiting friends and loved ones. This keeps many others in a job.

Finally, there are the tourists. The Japanese and Koreans visit from about the third week in March, and everyone else arrives about a month later when the weather is a bit warmer. Generally they all stay for one night.

Luxembourg is delighted to receive you, of course! But next time, stay for longer and you'll discover it's really worth that extra night. Ask my visiting friends. They loved it.

One good thing about Luxembourg is that it doesn't attract the yobbo element that heads from the UK over to Amsterdam for the weekend on the piss. Your football yob-yelling 'United' supporters would look very out of place here. It's a much classier place, thank God!

To live in Luxembourg you don't need to speak the language. However, it does come in handy if you do. You can actually get by with just English if necessary. However, it's sensible to give another language a go. French is widely spoken here and it is handy to know, be it only a few words. The more you know the easier life is, literally.

To compare Luxembourg with the UK when it comes to languages is like comparing chalk and cheese. The trouble is, most Brits back home just can't be bothered to learn another language. Most will know a few words of French, but unfortunately, your average Brit has zero-knowledge of a foreign language and is proud of it! It's the mentality of the system. "Everyone speaks English so I don't need to," I hear them cry.

Well, Great Britain might once have owned an empire and these days English is the business language of the world. But—so what! What makes the average 'English speaking only' Brit back home so superior to the person who sits next to them that speaks at least two languages? Think about it. Just who is the master? It helps, too, when job hunting, and we are in Europe, after all…

Some people say that Luxembourg is boring. "There is nothing to do," is the usual moan. These must be very sad people. Okay, this is not London or Milan—both huge cities with a vibrant nightlife. Luxembourg is indeed a very small country and the city is small compared to most capital cities in the world—but hey, wait a minute! I *like* that, and so do most of the people who live here. It's unique. It's special. It's home. And, incidentally, there *is* plenty to do. You just have to know where to go.

Many people are here on contract. When their contract ends they either go home or on to their next job abroad. Not everyone, though. Some people do find different work here. Others hang on. What is intriguing is that those that leave always come back! I know many people that have returned. Why? Because they *like* it here. It's something special, living here. It's quality of life. It's friendships. Maybe it's the old cobblestone streets in the old town. I don't know—but whatever their reason, it's all sorts of different things that the expats just like about the place.

Living in Luxembourg is like a taste of Europe. Europe is on your doorstep. You don't have to see Europe—Europe will see you! I say this simply because of all the different European cultures and people who now live in the Grand Duchy.

Luxembourg has changed dramatically in the last twenty years. In earlier days the country was a lot more conservative and traditional. There were few foreigners, bar the Italians and Portuguese. To get a job you needed umpteen papers. Life wasn't made easy for you as a foreigner. The country then had its own border controls. It also had its own currency, the Luxembourg Franc.

Luxembourg has a rich history going back more than a thousand years that I have found fascinating to learn. Nevertheless, without boring you too much with a long history lesson, I discovered that in the distant past there was already a small enclave here called Lucilinburhuc.

In AD963 Count Sigefroi acquired from the Saint Maximin Abbey in Trier, a rock that looked out on the Alzette valley. The deeds that record the transaction mention the name Luxembourg. This is the first time the name had been used. Sigefroi constructed a chateau on this rock of Bock. The city grew around it and over time gradually increased its defences into large fortifications around the city. It became a fortress. Many centuries later, the city became known as 'The Gibraltar of the North' because of all these fortifications.

Luxembourg is a country that has been invaded by everyone—from the Burgundians in 1443 to the Spanish who were the legal successors to the Burgundians. Austria then took over after the War of the Spanish Succession.

On more than one occasion Luxembourg was part of France. The first time was in 1684, the second in 1794. The German confederation took over the fortress by decision of the Congress of Vienna in 1815. The Germans were back in 1914 and again under Nazi rule in 1940. These days the only people who invade the country are the tourists.

Luxembourg became a neutral and independent country after the signing of the Treaty of London in 1867. Most of the fortifications were dismantled over the next sixteen years. In 1994, UNESCO listed some of the remaining fortifications that remained in the old town as World Heritage.

After the forts were demolished the new Luxembourg rose out of the rubble. In fact, a lot of the city's architecture you see today was largely designed and built around one hundred years ago, twenty years or so after the forts' demolition.

Luxembourg, like other parts of Europe, unfortunately saw the brunt of two world wars. After these, it was a country that needed to change and adapt in order to survive. In 1948 Luxembourg was one of the founding members of NATO, thus giving up the neutrality given to her by the Treaty of London in 1867. In 1952, Luxembourg managed to attract the foreign ministers to choose the country as its headquarters for the European coal and steel community. This developed in time into the European Community.

Luxembourg was one of the founding members of the European Community. This was largely thanks to Robert Schuman who was one of its founding fathers. Born in Clausen, he grew up in Luxembourg but later moved to France and actually went on to become Prime Minister of France. He is recognised in Luxembourg because of his dedicated work in the Grand Duchy for promoting the iron and steel communities and later the European Community.

Over time the membership of the European Community grew. It decided to change its name to the European Union, which is what it is still known as today. Luxembourg is one of the European Union's three headquarters, along with Strasbourg and Brussels. Over seven and a half thousand European officials work in various offices and departments of the European Union in Luxembourg. The country's main function as a centre of banking has probably saved its economy. It has around two hundred banks. It is most famous for its banking secrecy that for donkey's years has been upsetting its neighbours.

Luxembourg, with the impact of the banking industry, grew in the sixties. However, many older properties were torn down to construct modern concrete buildings, some of which look awful. The Place de Paris is a good example. This situation continues today and there are building sites everywhere. New office blocks are under construction. Luxembourg is a happening place. Six storey flats continue to pop up everywhere at a rapid rate. Land, flat and house prices have gone through the roof. But, at the same time, whilst some of the old places are being torn down, there is also a lot of restoration, especially in the old town, which is pleasing to see.

Today the country has open borders. We now have the Euro (though many Luxembourgers and foreigners do miss their Luf's). Change is happening and fast…

Foreigners are welcome. Let's face it, without the foreigners the country wouldn't have survived in the way that you see it today. Certainly, it's a better place to live in as a result. This is true for both the real Luxembourgers and the newcomers. European Union people can stay here on temporary residency. If you get a full time job, you will get a five-year residency permit. A temporary residency is issued to those who secure other forms of legitimate work, for example having a three or six-month contract. A job is needed in order to secure the usual state benefits. Even non European Union people can get ninety days to stay provided they have a job to come to. They can then return home for ninety days before coming back for a final ninety days. Many people do this. It's amazing to see many beautiful Russian girls and many other nationalities married to Luxembourg men because of this. It's a great idea. Why not?

If you buy or build a house, you can apply to your commune for a residency permit. This also requires a police interview, normally at your new house. There are rebates for legal fees, interest on mortgages, cash concessions and t.v.a. for building costs and fixed furnishings is 3%.

Crime may have increased. Nevertheless, the quality of life and the many choices everyone now has here has dramatically improved. You now have a large multinational workforce. There are multinational shopping centres. There is every sort of restaurant. Certainly, a good example to mention here is that years ago Luxembourgers generally ate Luxembourg food in Luxembourg restaurants. Yes, there were Italian and French restaurants, but let me finish. In those days there were no Indian restaurants in town. Now there must be over a dozen of them and they are all highly popular, especially with the Luxembourgers whose change of palate has diversified. This change is today reflected in every other field of life, which is why the country is so special.

Luxembourg does have some very silly rules—but then so does every country. It is just a matter of accepting them or leaving. You take your choice. Most people stay. Why? Because they like it!

However, it is not a cheap country to live in. The rents are expensive. Yes, food, booze, fags, petrol and cars are cheap. Taxes are low—but clothes are expensive compared with Germany.

Luxembourg continues to change and grow. It is a carefully managed project and it appears to be working. Its future, after all, depends on good planning today.

What better place to start in my quest for something different and not too far from home than the Grand Duchy of Luxembourg! And yet the only thing I knew about the country was that in its day it was home to the world famous Radio Luxembourg. Everyone who comes here, though, has to start from somewhere…

2

Getting Started

I arrived in Luxembourg on a train whilst on holiday. I had taken my redundancy and rested at home for more than a week. I had nothing definite planned. Most people in that situation do much the same thing. I had, however, decided to check out Luxembourg on the job scene.

Two friends of mine had previously left the bank. One had worked in Paris, another in Frankfurt. Richard, who had been in Paris for a few months, came home—back to Chelmsford as, ironically, the firm had folded. He ended up working in London. Another friend, Tom, is married to a Belgian lady. They had lived abroad before and had thought about living in Germany. He had managed to get himself a job in a bank in Frankfurt, which is another expats banking centre. The advantage he had was that he spoke fluent German. He loved it. He loved the job, the people and the place. However, he came home after two months and went to work for one of the large UK banks, also up in the City of London.

I went to see him and his wife for a meal. We consumed a few beers and he went on to tell me of his experiences of living and working abroad. I thought it was madness—his coming home when he had had that 'Golden opportunity'. His reasons, however, were logical. "In the UK you pay 22% tax. Then it goes up to 40%. Well, in Germany, you pay, apparently, more tax than you do in the UK. It's much higher than many places in Europe." He also didn't want his wife. who is retired, cooped up all day in a tiny flat with no garden when he was at work. In the UK they had a lovely house and garden, which his wife loved.

In the big cities of continental Europe, many people live in flats and most people rent. This is because it is so expensive to buy anything. I was amazed just how much flats are in Milan when I visited there in October 2002. With the advent of the Euro, everyone can now clearly see the price of everything right across

Europe, which is great. It is a revelation to see the different prices for the same thing in different countries.

In Luxembourg, property prices are very expensive compared to over the border. Here you can buy three bricks for the same amount that you could purchase a house in Thionville in France. All right, I'm exaggerating.

Anyway, we were discussing this and umpteen possibilities when I said, "Okay, I'll try Luxembourg. It's famous for its banking. Maybe I can get something there." I wasn't being too serious when I said it as at the time I knew absolutely nothing about the country. Weeks I think went by during which I did check out the tax side here and at the time, it was on a par with the UK from my point of view. That was good enough for me. Nevertheless, nothing happened for weeks in the final days at Lloyds and even when I had left, I had applied for several local jobs. These, I suppose, could have suited me fine if I had been offered one. However, seeing as I had been going on about doing something different in my life for months, here was that opportunity staring me in the face. And so I decided to give it a go.

Now, I'm a Capricorn, and if you know your stars, then you'll know that Capricorns generally take the safest option! I had talked for months about going round the world, going off and trekking between Istanbul to Cairo, living in the Far East, living in Spain or living by the Mediterranean. I could head off to some deepest jungle or to some beautiful beach. I could go anywhere. It was an opportunity not to be missed. But I couldn't decide what I wanted to do. Finally, I made a decision. I decided to go to Luxembourg on holiday and from there go on to Holland to see a few friends. If I was lucky, I would go to Germany, Belgium, and France as well. Of course, I would technically be going into the unknown on this holiday. Even though I had been to all these countries years and years ago, it was still a little unnerving contemplating looking for a job in these places. However, there is an old English saying: 'Nothing ventured, nothing gained.' It was quite apt as I hadn't a clue what I was about to let myself in for. I mean, I have travelled around a lot but the notion of living abroad permanently was still alien to me.

I decided to go on the Eurostar to Brussels, as having been on the French Eurostar to Paris a couple of times I thought it would be a great way of travelling into Europe relatively cheaply. The service itself is fast. I mean, three hundred kilometres per hour is fantastic in France. Can you imagine that in the UK? Come on!

The UK train system is stuck in Victorian times. What does the UK Government do about it? Well, it moans and groans. It says it doesn't have enough money to invest in the railways. It also huffs and puffs like a steam train trying to leave the station, its brakes on hold. It blows more hot air than 'Two Jags' Jaguars put together. ('Two Jags' is the nickname for John Prescott, the British Deputy Prime Minister who has two Jaguar cars when everyone else makes do with one smaller fuel-efficient car.) Maybe one day the UK Minister of Transport might actually bother to take a trip over to France on Eurostar to see the joy of the TGV system. If you have ever travelled in Europe then you will know that France, the Netherlands and Germany all have double-decker trains. Even Switzerland has them. But does the UK have double-decker trains? Pigs might fly before that happens. You get the old excuses like 'tunnels too small'. This might refer to the tunnel between London and Hastings. Apparently, many years ago when the line was constructed in Victorian times, the tunnel was built smaller than it should have been. This might have been because of problems encountered in the construction due to poor earth subsidence or whatever. But, as a result, big modern trains can't get through, and Hastings remains a poorer town than its neighbours because of this. The solution is quite simple. Rebuild the railways like the continentals have and construct a tunnel large enough for trains in the twenty-first century. That's double-decker trains to you and me. The problem of overcrowding would then surely reduce. Oh, I can dream.

Anyway, from Brussels I took the train down to Luxembourg, arriving late evening at the Gare (station). Now, if you have ever been to Luxembourg station, then you'll know it is not very big compared with big city terminuses. But I think it's very beautiful. It has its own Luxembourg style, which I love. The Gare was built between 1907 and 1913. The station's clock tower makes it one of the city's more interesting landmarks.

I arrived in Luxembourg carrying nothing more than a travel bag, having come here on holiday. Anyway, I wandered up the Avenue de la Gare before discovering the Place de Paris. I was looking for a hotel but hadn't a clue as to where I might end up. I tried a couple of hotels, which turned out to be full. It was a Thursday night and as I discovered later, most Luxembourg hotels are full of businessmen between Monday and Friday, leaving the tourists the hotels at the weekend.

I eventually discovered the Christophe Colomb Hotel and having checked it out once eventually went back there. It was quite expensive by my standards, so I paid for just the one night. It's not expensive at all if you compare it to all the others around, but I didn't know that then.

One of my London friends said to me later, "Christ! You've just been made redundant. Treat yourself for once, you tight bastard. You can afford it." I replied, "Sod off," then added, "But you're right."

Anyway, I had noticed there was a hotel opposite called The Hotel Italia and decided to get a room there for a week. The man on the reception desk said to me, "Sorry, you can only have a room for three nights; after that we're fully booked."

"Oh," I said. "Why's that?"

"Well sir, there's an EU conference on and we're booked up."

'Fair enough,' I thought. The hotel staff were very good and the next day assisted me in my search for another hotel. They suggested I go down to the station and visit the National Tourist Information Centre. What a good idea! I strolled down there and the lady was most helpful. She suggested the Hotel Bristol and rang them to find out if they had a room.

"Yes, they do have a room," she advised me.

Great! So after the three nights I ended up there.

During my first weekend in the Grand Duchy the first bar I visited was The Lord Nelson. This bar stands on the corner of the Rue Dicks and the Rue Ste Zithe, opposite an old cinema. It was a hot Saturday afternoon and as it was en route from the hotel, I decided to call in and sample a local beer.

I was going to go to another nearby pub that I had discovered whilst wandering round town. The name of this pub was The White Rose but as it was Cup final day in England, you couldn't get in the door due to everyone watching the game on TV. As I wasn't too particular on the teams in the cup final of 2001, I gave the bar a miss. Some days later I made my first visit. The rest, as they say, is history.

Whilst in Luxembourg I had rung my friends in Holland to arrange a visit. I decided to hire a car and have a look around. Well, that was an experience! I mean, we're talking left-hand drive over here!

I had driven left-hand drive before. I had the pleasure when I was in Texas in the USA whilst on holiday. My friend was driving at the time with me as passenger. I wanted to have a go and the opportunity arose when we were driving around Corpus Christi.

Now, *that's* a lovely place to visit. We were on a nearby island called Padra Island, which is famous for its white sand beaches and wildlife. On the way back, I started in the hot seat and as there was nothing about, thought it was cool to be left-hand driving in a big American car with cruise control. I kept going and suddenly I was presented with a six-lane highway full of traffic with road works to boot. One learns fast as there was nowhere to pull over to hand back the driving to my mate. I kept going, but I ended up driving all the way down to Brownsville on the Mexican border. But that's another story.

I discovered that Avis Europe have an office at the station. So I enquired further and ended up getting an Opel Corsa for a week. None of your Vauxhall rubbish here. It was a good small car and was just what I needed to run about the area. There was just one small problem preventing me from leaving the station—I couldn't find the reverse on the gear stick. It sounds ridiculous but on my car back home, its gears were different. I mean, whoever heard of lifting the gear lever *up* before you move it across. Come on! I was used to driving a very old Toyota that my friends thought had come out of the dark ages. I had to embarrassingly ask the lady for assistance. After that, it was easy.

Well, that's not quite true. I drove off around the streets of Luxembourg City, but I didn't know where the hell I was going, so I just kept driving. I had no map of any form of description on me, and the idea was to go back to the hotel to put my luggage in my room. I had literally just changed hotels that morning to the Hotel Bristol and, as I had been a little early, I had had to leave my luggage in a safe area. Well, like I said, I kept driving. I was a little nervous in those narrow streets. However, I kept going, ending up over the red bridge and getting completely lost in Kirchberg.

The plateau of Kirchberg is largely where the new Luxembourg is developing. There are all manner of building works going on. Huge new developments are being constructed at a rapid rate. There are banks, insurance companies and hotels. There is also the new national sports centre, the Auchan shopping centre, the Utopolis cinema complex, and the Foires Internationales, which is an exhibition centre. RTL, the television station, is also located here. There are also various European buildings including the European Parliament and the European Court of Justice.

I kept driving, heading eastwards. I discovered later that I had driven along the old pre-motorway road. I actually ended up in Wasserbillig from where I rang the hotel to advise the man that "I may be a little late as I am now near the German border."

"No problem, Sir," said the gentleman at the hotel reception.

So I went into Germany and drove right into Trier. Gosh, it was exciting. But I couldn't stop to look around because you had to pay to park and I didn't have a Deutsche Mark on me. So I crossed back into Luxembourg and decided it would be a good idea to follow the river. As it turned out—and I didn't know it then—I was following the Moselle valley up river. If you have ever driven down there you'll know what a lovely place it is. The vineyards stretch out on the hills around. Germany stares at you from across the river. The old farmhouses are dotted around the landscape.

When I reached Remich, I got out and had a look around. It's a nice little border town with a good few bars and restaurants. There is even a boat or two doing tours up and down the Moselle River. There's also a bridge that connects to Germany. Next to it on the German side is a large campsite. I thought Remich got all the campers coming across the bridge for food supplies. Little did I know then that they were actually all coming across the border for cheap petrol and cigarettes.

Anyway, I kept going, as I wanted to reach the southeast corner of Luxembourg. I reached Schengen, which is the point where there was another bridge crossing into Germany. This I took and then turned right. About one hundred metres later I crossed over the border into France. Oh, how exciting! I followed signs towards Thionville. It's amazing how all the road signs, houses and shops are so different in such a small area where the three countries meet.

Thionville's nothing special. It's a border town. Some people might call it quaint, others a dump. I had had a brief encounter at the station many years before whilst passing through. However, I knew nothing about the town. I stopped to park the car to look around but again I didn't have a French Franc on me to feed the meter. Later, after driving round, I did find somewhere free to park. But this was not in the centre. In fact, I only stopped for a soft drink, thinking that in the shop they might take Luxembourg Francs, being a border town. They didn't. However, when in the shop something struck my eye.

That something was a 'Jobs.lu' paper. I had a quick look at it. It was most interesting. But again, I would have to wait until I got back to Luxembourg before I could purchase it. I headed back up the motorway, back into Luxembourg and back to the hotel car park. I purchased the paper the next morning and whilst reading it found several adverts for different jobs. One of them was an advert for the Bank of Bermuda. Later I rang my agent in London and gave him some e-mail addresses to try.

During my first few days looking around Luxembourg City I visited a job agency called Adecco. I was enquiring about job possibilities. The woman told me, "You want a job, get a mobile phone." She even told me where to get one. When I asked "Why?" she said, "So we can contact you." She then explained: "I've had another client who didn't have one and he has been extremely difficult to contact." After all, he wasn't going to stay by his phone in his hotel bedroom all day, was he! Well, to cut a long story short I thought about it and then decided to take the ladies advice. I went where she mentioned, which was to a place called Auchan and bought the phone. I can honestly say that that was one of the best bits of advice I have ever been given. For that, I thank her.

Now, I don't wish to bore you with the nitty-gritty of one's holiday details, but in brief I was due to go to Holland later that week. Now the number one rule my old boss said to me was, "That if you are ever offered an interview, take it and don't mess them around." Well, having let one of my Dutch friends down twice I was not going to miss this holiday rendezvous. You can guess what happened. I got the interview. I then asked, "Could you possibly rearrange it as I am in Holland that day." Much to my utter amazement, they did. So I spent a few days seeing friends before returning to Luxembourg and attending the interview. I advised them that I was returning to the UK on Thursday.

A second interview followed two days later, after which I found out I had got the job. It was all rather rushed, as they wanted me to start on the 1st June. This meant I would have six days to change my life.

To say it did change my life is an understatement. Had I known then exactly all the 'in's and out's' that this would entail I might have done things a bit differently. However, here was that opportunity and I had taken it. For everyone back home it was exciting.

Not knowing exactly what would happen in the future, I decided to pack up most of my personal things into storage boxes. I booked a flight with Ryanair that flew to nearby Brussels, having discovered I could get a one-way ticket for £23, which my family and friends all thought was a great price. As my father put it, "What do you want to buy a return ticket for when you don't know when you'll be coming home? After all, you'll need time to settle in, then get yourself a return from there."

The Ryanair ticket price was considerably cheaper than LuxAir that flew directly into Luxembourg, which in those days was very expensive. I was quoted over £220 for a return, which is why I opted for Ryanair. These days tickets on LuxAir can be a lot cheaper.

At the time of departing the UK I had some lodgers at my house and, not knowing all the implications I was letting myself into, decided to let them stay. I held a small leaving party with my friends, neighbours and parents before going up to Stansted airport to board the Ryanair flight to Brussels/Charleroi.

Now not knowing Belgium at all, I didn't know that the airport Brussels/Charleroi was actually Charleroi airport, which is miles from the City centre. It turned out to be an hour's travel on one of Ryanair's own buses into the centre of

Brussels. It was also another hour before that whilst they got everyone onto the bus from the plane. The fare was around a fiver. The alternatives looked bleak. I mean, the taxi fare must be huge! I've heard since that should you drive to the airport it is not safe to leave your car up there. This is because of a number of car jacking at gunpoint!

The journey took forever. But remember, it was cheap. The coach drops you off at the Wild Geese Pub that felt like it was in the middle of nowhere, though it's in the centre of Brussels. They do serve good food there. I then had to take a taxi to the central station in order to get the train down to Luxembourg. This whole experience, including lunch, I reckon had taken longer than when I had taken the Eurostar from London originally. Certainly, I could have left home later. But it was another experience, so what the hell. These days the Ryan air coach service goes direct from Charleroi airport direct to Brussels Midi—now that is much better for everyone.

I discovered much later, there is an easier way to get to Charleroi airport from Luxembourg by simply taking the train towards Lille, via Namur. Then with a short bus ride from the station, Charleroi Sud, to the Airport, the journey takes only two and a half hours, for a return cost of around 45€, or 35€ at weekends.

Just make sure you buy the *right* ticket or you could end up in Charleroi-Ouest (West). You need Charleroi Sud (South)! This is much quicker and less expensive than the journey I had done and is much cheaper than a stolen car, eh!

Incidentally, anyone requiring information on how to get from Luxembourg, to the other local airport used by Ryanair, in Hahn, Germany, should check www.hahn-airport.de, and for bookings use www.ryanair.com for the £1.29 flights! There is no useful information available at Luxembourg station even though the bus leaves from outside it!

The bank had arranged to put me up at the Auberge du Coin-Le Chatelet. This is a hotel with studios. As it turned out, this is common practise here. Most people generally get one or two months in a hotel after which they have to find their own place. I was lucky in that my deal was for six months. The deal did, however; reflect the nature of the job that I had to do.

I had a free day before I started work. However, I did have to pop in to see the Human Resources people at the bank. They suggested I register in order to avoid a 38% tax deduction on my salary slip. Naturally, I went to sort this out straight-away. The place to register in those good old days was in a tiny old building, which was located in a narrow passageway near the Place Guillaume.

Place Guillaume, which in English means William Square, was named after King William II of the Netherlands who was also the Grand Duke of Luxembourg between 1840 to 1849. He is famous for granting Luxembourg its first parliament. There's actually a statue of him on a horse in the square. I arrived in the afternoon just before it opened. I joined a few people who were waiting outside. The office opened and I climbed the stairs to the second floor where I discovered myself on a landing queuing behind those in front. Soon after the queue went half way down the stairs. Boy! Was I glad I had arrived early. I later discovered from other queues that if you don't get there early or in good time, you may find that when it comes to closing time you'll just have to come back the next day.

Many expats will remember the queues that went down the stairs! They won't forget this building for that reason—it will have been their first experience with Luxembourg bureaucracy. Everyone has to go through it. The staff, however, were very helpful, and after sorting out my documents, I then had to do a similar exercise in the office below. This was to do with my tax and where I lived. Soon afterwards I received various documents in the post.

These days life is made a lot more comfortable for the new arrivals and people already here. The state has now opened a new office called the Bierger-Center at 51 Boulevard Royal. The building is located next to the bus station in the main town in the Place Emile Hamilius. It incorporates a variety of functions into one space, making life easier for everyone, including the staff. The difference couldn't be more marked. It is modern and open plan. There are modern seats with a TV to watch while you wait. You even take a ticket while you wait your turn.

For any new arrivals in Luxembourg, it can be a bit daunting at first. You have to be able to *adapt* quickly. A married Russian girl I met later at college used this word, telling me it was important for her to be able to 'adapt' her lifestyle. I thought that was a very apt term. Adapting is the key to survival in any environment.

Meanwhile I was now ready to start work. I had now got started. I was ready to adapt…

3

Flat Hunting

The number one rule when one lives abroad is, "Before you buy a place to live in, live there for at least a year before you even consider buying a place." I've been advised this on many occasions by different people.

When you first live abroad, it is hard to imagine why this statement is relevant. However, only after a year of living in rented accommodation could I begin to understand its relevance. It takes a year to understand a country, its people, the culture and its traditions; also, the country's rules and regulations.

You might think that you know it in two months. Nevertheless, step back and think about it. You'll only learn with time. A good deal is not always so. Don't rush into anything before you have really thought it through. Only then does the above statement ring true. I learnt through bitter experience the meaning of this phrase.

When you live abroad, you need somewhere to live. Here in Luxembourg most expats start by staying in a hotel. Anything from a few nights to a month or two months is quite normal. After which they will have to branch out and find themselves a flat to live in.

This is a wonderful experience to encounter and until you have done it, you just won't appreciate what a pain in the arse it can be. On the other hand, you can be very lucky and find what you're looking for straight away. Of course, everyone has their own story to tell about looking for a flat to live in. We have all done it, been there, and if you are here for a while, been there again no doubt.

I get the impression that most people, especially foreigners in Luxembourg, prefer to rent flats as opposed to buying them. This is due to the European thinking of renting as opposed to the British 'let's buy a place' attitude. However, other reasons come into it, the main one being the sheer cost of buying a place.

Luxembourg is not cheap when it comes to buying. Then there's the question of how long you're going to be here. Luxembourg is a place where many nationalities come and go. The way Luxembourg works means that there is always a steady flow of flats becoming available. If you talk to people in the bars, you'll always find someone who is either looking or wants to offload their flat. There are a thousand different experiences and everyone has had their fair share of hassle and fun whilst flat hunting.

In the heart of town and especially in the Gare area the banks own many flats. These they keep their key workers in. This keeps the prices artificially high. However, having said that, I did discover there is some form of set prices as laid out by the Government. Luxembourg is not a cheap place to live and the rents are expensive. We're talking London prices here, you know.

A good start when looking for a flat is to go round the agencies. This in itself is an experience as there are good and bad agencies. Each has a variety of properties for rent.

Most people, when they first arrive in Luxembourg, opt to rent somewhere basic or small to begin with while they get their feet on the ground. Once they get their bearings and learn the system, they branch out, some literally to the areas beyond the Gare.

Here's a tip one friend once gave: "Try living in different parts of the city. Do six months or a year in each location. That way you will see a different part of life and you will get to know its people better." Most people, on finding a place they like, simply stay put. It's easier. Nevertheless, we are all different in what we want.

You'll discover that there are three sorts of expats here. There are the short timers who do less than three years. Then there are the mid-term expats who do around seven years. Finally, there are the long-stay expats. Some of these stay fifteen years or more.

Short-term expats hop in and out of flats like you hop on and off buses. Mid-term expats are more settled. They tend to remain in a flat once they've found a good one. Long-term expats generally opt to buy either a flat or a house.

You can find out the cost of renting in whatever area you choose by visiting an agency, or by word of mouth. Talking to friends will give you many tips. Looking around a few places is another good idea. Don't rush into the first deal. Get the feel of the flat. Look at the area it's in. What are the neighbours like? Ask questions.

Some agencies have price lists in the window. These days you might even be lucky and get a photograph in the window. Don't hold your breath on this, though. But price lists in windows with or without photos will tell you about the agency. Presentation is a key selling point, after all. Watch out for the lazy ones.

How often do they update the window? Some agencies also put their available accommodation on their website.

When I started to look I knew approximately where I wanted to live and I knew the price range my friends had advised me for a flat 'in Town'—the rule of thumb being that it will cost you less as you go further out from the heart of the city. There are exceptions to this rule and 'price' has a lot to do with the 'location' of a flat in certain areas.

The best place to look is in the *agence immobilière's*, as they are known. They are all around town. Also, if you look in the newsagents, there are various Immo magazines that are full of private rents and sales of studios, apartments and houses.

There are also *immobilière* agencies in these magazines that you can then telephone for more information. Then there is the internet that the agencies use. Finally, there are the national papers, *Le Jeudi*, *Le Quotidien* or the *Luxemburger Wort*.

Now, I'm not going to bore you with all the details, but to give you a flavour of the fun that I had, this is how I started.

I was originally offered a flat by someone I met in a pub. It was in The White Rose, actually. Anyway, I didn't take the offer up as I didn't have a job at the time. I later had an interview to go to, then went away on holiday, and after a long weekend I came back. In the meantime I had talked to various people about flat hunting here in the city. I then went back to the person who had offered me this flat to say that I would now like to know more and maybe look around.

"Sorry mate, it's gone," was the reply.

Flats don't hang around. Twenty-four hours later I had got a job together with a studio flat thrown in. When I told this person who had offered me his flat (his departure was imminent), he was certainly surprised. I later did find out that had I taken the flat, which I had not even looked at, there would have been a few surprises thrown in—namely, some unpaid bills to take on. So you have to be careful.

Six months or so later I knew I would have to start looking if I was staying in Luxembourg. I decided to start looking at the lower end of the market as I wanted to see what you got. There's an old English saying. 'You pay's the price; you gets what you pays for.' This is very apt, as I soon discovered.

I decided to begin with to visit a variety of agents. This resulted in a couple of appointments. The first one was when, one night, I went to see a studio just off the Avenue de la Gare. It was on the third floor in a 1960's concrete construction. The lift was cramped and next door to the studio was a dentist surgery. It looked a bit of a short-term place as well.

The studio was around forty square metres. It was okay, but there was just one small problem—the furniture was dire. How the landlord got away with calling the place 'furnished' was daylight robbery. The bed was rough, the furniture was from the sixties, it was cheap and falling apart, and most of it looked as though it had been chucked-out office furniture that was well past its sell by date. A skip is where it all should have gone. Also, the whole place was in the middle of being given a coat of paint. The kitchen was in a very poor state and was old. I gave it two out of ten rating for being available and cheap. The location was a bit dodgy and I didn't fancy being awoken by the shrieks of the dentist's customers next door.

The next place I tried was with another agency. I looked at another studio, again around forty square metres. It was in the Rue de Nord, which is in one of the oldest parts of the old city. The building was very old and desperately needed renovation. But it was sound. The studio was on the first floor and access was gained by going up a narrow circular set of stairs that gave the place character. However, when I saw the flat it was a shock to the system. The walls were bright blue. On one side of the room was an old wooden pub-picnic table, the one where the benches are all in. It had seen considerably better days. The bed you wouldn't have dared sleep on for fear of catching something. The kitchen area was, in three words, simple and dire. But the best bit was the shower.

It opened out onto the room and I couldn't help but think that this place could be lived in by Austin Powers. It was a left over of the sixties and you had notions of someone like him stepping out of this shower, saying, "Hey Baby—swing a load of this!" Needless to say, I didn't take it. But it got three out of ten rating for its novelty factor.

I then started to look at one-bedroom flats, which is what I wanted since they were about sixty square metres. This size of flat is ideal if you are a single person. I looked at a couple, including one at Kirchberg. This was a good exercise in discovering how other people look at flats. I say that because when I arranged it there was me and the agent. On my arrival there were three other interested parties and me. It soon became obvious that if you want it, take action fast as it appears that if you don't others will get in there first. This flat was very modern, about three years old. It was a good price and unfurnished. It also had an underground car park, which offered you instant, safe secure parking. The balcony was nice as well. The thing that slightly put me off was the distance out of town. As a single person who enjoys a good social life it was too far to walk home after the pub had closed. Taxis would be too expensive. If I were with a good woman then it would have been ideal. But as I was on my own, it was not quite what I wanted—yet. But it did get a nine out of ten rating.

Eventually I did get myself a furnished one-bedroom flat, and it was 'in town'. When I went to see it, I had booked the appointment to go round with the agent. On the due day and time I went round to see the flat together with an Italian couple. They were dithering, as it was the first flat they had seen; they had only just arrived in Luxembourg, so they were still learning the ropes. I saw the flat and knew then that it was for me. It got a nine out of ten rating. It lost a mark as it was on a hill, but you know when you have found what you're looking for.

There appears to be different types of tenancy, and the length of tenancy also varies from flat to flat. The 'general rule of thumb' is that when looking to rent there are various types of lease to consider. The first is a short-term lease, for example three or six months. The second type is an 'open ended' lease where after the minimum period either side can then give the agreed notice period. The third type of lease is for one or three years.

Watch out as some agencies stipulate a minimum period of three years for a flat. The question you will have to ask yourself is, "How long are you planning to be in Luxembourg?" If the answer is a year then you will only need a flat for a year. Therefore taking out a three-year lease with possible penalties is not going to be of any use to you.

Charges will vary from flat to flat. Some charges will be 'all in'. In others, you will have extra costs on top. In some cases, you will have the electric to pay. Others may charge you for the washing machine water used. In other flats, you may have to pay for your water. The cable TV could be extra. In some places, it's all in. Some flats have cleaning ladies, which come as part of the service charge.

Do you want a furnished or unfurnished flat? You will probably know what you want. But I would strongly recommend that whilst you may know what you want, do look at both so that you can test the waters and give yourself a 'feel' of what is on offer on both types of accommodation. Life is full of surprises and this can be a huge eye opener.

With furnished flats watch out. There are some dives around that I don't know how the landlord gets away with calling furnished. Some should have the entire furniture replaced, as the furniture is dire. A bit of investment can pay dividends. Others can be a pleasure to view. It's places like these where you'll probably say "I like this" and opt to take it. Just don't leave it too long before making your decision.

If you have your own furniture, then you'll probably be looking at unfurnished flats. Location is important, as is accessibility. Things to consider includes whether you can get the furniture up the stairs—or is there a lift? Some furniture removers offer a novel way of getting your furniture in: up a lift on a ladder and through the window—quite a popular option with larger pieces of furniture.

What type of accommodation do you want? Are you after a Studio, a one bedroom flat, a two bedroom flat, a three bedroom flat—or a house? Do you want a flat of your own or are you happy to share with someone else. Would you prefer to simply share a room?

Location is important. Where do you want to live? Do you want to live in town? Do you prefer the countryside? If you live 'in town' then the most expensive place to rent is in the Centre or Gare areas right in the heart of Luxembourg City. Once you spread out from the centre, the rents go down a bit.

The deposit is generally two months' rent money that is locked into your bank account, which you guarantee in writing to the landlord. There is a proper legal framework that state law requires all landlords and tenants to follow. It's hassle and yet more paperwork. It involves you having to go to your bank to sort it out with them. An appointment may be necessary, which involves the time factor. Most banks, however, are used to it as so many people do it. Added to this is the agency's commission of one months rent. This is paid together with the deposit along with the first months rent generally, before you even move in. It's a real eye opener.

When you do move in there will be an inventory. Check it—because if you don't you'll be shafted at the end when you leave the flat. Inspect the flat as if you're looking for gold dust. If there's a scratch on a chair or floor, tell them. Check for glued together broken plates, or broken mugs. The previous tenant will hide them at the back of the cupboard. Mark all your comments on the inventory. Then get a copy of it. Why? Because, if you don't do this, you'll get a large deduction at the end of your tenancy. There probably will be nothing you can do about it. This is because you didn't do it at the beginning when you should have done it.

In case your job changes and you decide to leave the country, check for a 'get out' clause in your tenancy contract. If you are locked into a three-year contract, you may only be able to cancel it if you're leaving the country, and then you may need to prove this. When you do leave some landlords require that you pay an additional months rent or the cost of getting the flat redecorated—not a cheap exercise as you don't benefit. More of a con on the landlord's part. In fact, if it's in your contract the landlord could surprise you with a very large bill should you have the pleasure of having to get your place redecorated. Beware—don't agree to anything that you're not happy with.

First, get a written quote of the cost of the redecoration from the landlord. Then get a second opinion. By that I mean get a written quote from an independent decorator. You might be gob-smacked by the difference in the price. Remember, if there's more than ten per cent difference in the price, then challenge the original quote. Most people regard more than ten per cent as the trigger level to dispute the original quote. I would challenge the landlord and insist on the lower priced quote. After all, it's in your interests and not his. You could save yourself several hundred euros that way.

If you leave the flat, you have to give two or three months notice. There will be an inspection before you leave and you should get all your deposit money back a little while later, but bear in mind they might take into account any electricity bills due to come in etc…Any breakages or damage will also be deducted. Remember, landlords can be nice, but they never loose out.

Don't be afraid to ask the *agence immobilière* people. After all, they get paid your commission to help you.

Sharing a flat with someone is also a great idea as it means the rent is split in two. Now admittedly the rent will be for a two bedroom flat more than for a one bedroom flat, but when you split it in half you should still be saving an awful lot of euros. If you're sharing a three bedroom flat then you'll save even more—and so forth. There's just one small catch. Should anyone except you move out, and the flat is in your name, the rent will still have to be paid. I've heard a few horror stories where it can cripple someone short term until they get another person in to share. Just be warned!

There is also the scenario of three people sharing a two bedroom flat. One person sleeps in the lounge. Just make sure it's all above board. You don't want to receive a visit from the police, do you? Again, this keeps costs down, which allows you more euros in your pocket.

Most one-bedroom places are around sixty square metres in size. They go upwards from there. Two bedroom flats start around eighty-five square metres. After that, you're entering the large flat league.

A word of caution here. I know of a few people who have come to Luxembourg having got themselves a huge salary. Most then can't believe their luck. They then go out and get themselves a huge, nice, modern flat. The problem comes when they're fired or the contract is not renewed. A short period of panic then ensues during which a serious downsizing may have to take place. What makes it worse for them is the three-month leaving rule than can seriously stuff someone who has been living it up and has been on cloud-cuckoo land during this period. Then they come down to earth with a nasty bump.

One of the most popular options is the Studio flat. It's the smallest option for the single person who wishes to remain independent. It's also the cheapest option, unless you want to share a flat or simply rent a room. Most studios are around forty square metres, but some go down to thirty-five square metres. The layouts are all slightly different but most will accommodate a bed in one room and a kitchen in another.

The difference between a studio and a one bedroom flat is that the studio has a bedroom/living area, a kitchen/living area and a bathroom, whereas a one bedroom flat generally has a bedroom, a living/dining room, a kitchen and a bathroom. Some studio flats simply have one room with a bathroom of sorts leading from it.

You will be amazed how many people live in studios. People do start off in them whilst they sort themselves out. Once they're more settled they'll move on to somewhere larger. Most people who live in studios would prefer to live in larger places but the sheer difference of costs generally prevents this. Studios sometimes can feel terribly cramped and you can feel fenced in. That's why people like to get out and about to escape the claustrophobic feel that you sometimes get by living in a studio. Some people, though, absolutely love their studio. We are all different in what we want.

I must add that there are also 'rooms to rent' available. These go for considerably less than a studio or flat. If you're not flush with cash and here on a minimum budget, then they're ideal. You'll have to share cooking and bathroom facilities. But it does give you that living together experience, which I can only recommend. It'll certainly broaden your horizons and make you a better person for it.

Renting a room is for the more communally minded person. Realistically, this is at the cheaper end of the market. Watch out for unscrupulous landlords who can kick you out after a week. That's a bid naughty. It should be at least a month, but not in Luxembourg. I know of one example where this happened around the Place de Paris. The landlord then increased the price of rooms once a lick of paint had been added, never mind the inconvenience to the tenants.

There is the element of 'trust' to be taken into consideration when sharing a flat or living with someone else. Of course, there has to be trust on both sides in order that the situation works with both parties. The moment this breaks down is when it's time to move on. But a second chance is worth its weight in gold. After that, starting again has its advantages!

People on short-term contracts i.e. three, four and a half or six-month contracts are the most vulnerable. They're uncertain of their future plans and have to take a place where the 'get out' clause is not going to cost them too much. Careful planning is needed by them. For this reason, many people will either live with friends or in shared accommodation. They'll also live in office-paid flats as part of their deal. They could also live in office halls of residence. This is where the office pays for either the flat, with two or three people staying there, or the office owns the place and sublets it to these short-termers.

One other possibility is to live with a family. Here you are the lodger and you can either do your own thing or join in on occasions, living with the family. If you're an Au Pair, then you are living with the family, sharing their facilities. This is real 'living in' and there are quite a few Au Pairs who do it.

Incidentally, I shared my house in the UK for some years and rented one or two rooms out. I met some great people this way. But I also shared with some real sharks. Overall, I still keep in contact today with a lot of the former lodgers. So it can be a great way to make friends.

Here's a thought with which to end this chapter. Luxembourg is a very rich country. When it comes to owning property, the Catholic Church appears to own one-half while the *agences immobilières* (Agency Landlords) own the other.

4

So you really want to live in a flat?

A discussion in The White Rose one night did unearth a few hidden nightmares that some people have gone through living in their flats. Here in Luxembourg every block of flats, or apartments, as they are known here, has a number. They have it since it is the number in the street in which the block of flats is located. However, no flat in that block has a separate number.

Back home in England every actual flat in that block has a number allocated to it. Even if the number stays the same on the street, for example number 49, the flats then become, A, B, C, etc…Then the post is delivered to that flat number, and not the name of the person living at number 49. This is not the case in Luxembourg. Here you get a post-box where you put your name on. You also put your name on your bell. Put simply, you stick your name up, generally with tape.

That's all very well, until your name falls off the post-box. This could be because of bad weather, old age or whatever. The point is that by simply falling off a catastrophe of future problems can ensue. The answer is to make sure your name remains glued to the post-box, otherwise the fun might start…

It will start when your mail fails to arrive. An actual good example here is when your electricity bill fails to arrive on its usual day. The next thing you know is that your electric is suddenly cut off. Why? Well, your name wasn't on your mailbox. Therefore, the mail was returned to sender.

It gets better. My friend to whom this happened had to sort a tax card out at the Bierger-Center. However, you yourself could have a similar reason, be it reregistering or whatever. Anyway, he suddenly found out that 'he' as a person had become a 'Comma' in the system down at the Bierger-Center. Of course, in this situation it took a bit of explaining to put it all right. In this case, it was the electricity bill that was sent back. What had happened was the police had been sent out to confirm that the person didn't live there anymore. Well, they looked at the mailbox and found that there was no name on the letterbox, so yes, that person wasn't there anymore. Ludicrous, but true.

Then there's the electric when you actually move in. For the benefit of the previous tenant, you must make sure that the flat is in your name with the electricity people. If you're moving out of a flat, new tenants will soon move in. However, there are some crafty buggers out there who accidentally and sometimes most deliberately forget to advise the electricity people that this change of tenant has taken place. Therefore, the previous tenant will still get the bills if they are still in Luxembourg. They will still be liable for them together with their new place. The electric people will track them down i.e. the previous tenant so that they pay the bill. Even if the landlord intervenes, it means nothing until the tenant himself or herself decides to advise the electricity people. Putting it bluntly, you're stuffed the way it works here. Talk about unfair or what! Oh, and my friend had to pay for the new tenants' electricity that this new guy refused to acknowledge. The good news was that the situation was eventually sorted out.

A solution to new tenants who refuse to pay their bill and not change the electricity into their name is simple. The example I'll use here is what happened to another friend. He turned the situation round and so put the shoe on the other foot. Put simply: the new tenant in his old flat was using the Napoleonic law that is used here in Luxembourg to his advantage. My friend simply sent him a bill by registered post demanding that he pay him the money. Unbelievably, the bill—the amount owing—was paid to him.

You could also get a bill from your landlord; for example, for your yearly outgoings for the block of flats that you live in. If you do, then read it carefully. It may show the electricity that you used over the yearly period. This could be more, or less, than you used on average in your monthly payments. Then you will either owe the difference, or you might even get a refund. If you're lucky, you'll get a reduction. Watch out for this.

I know another friend who had a broken window in his kitchen. This happened to let rather a lot of the heat escape. The result was a rather large heating bill when the landlord read the meter. Was the window fixed? Do pigs fly?

The other devious thing to watch out for on your yearly bill list from your landlord, is you may get hidden bills that suddenly make an appearance. Another example to quote here is a friend who received a hidden extra on such a 'list'. The extra was a bill for a cleaning lady that covered a number of months. That was all very well, but as he had lived there for several years, he had never seen a cleaning lady. He certainly hadn't been advised of one. His contract of charges hadn't ever stated that there was one. There hadn't been one in previous years on his yearly bills, so why was there this sudden inclusion now? He demanded written proof of this fee and evidence of the cleaning. Needless to say, he refused to pay this part of the bill and, guess what, the landlord never asked for payment and the item never appeared again.

Dustbins are another experience. When you move into a flat, you won't get your own personal dustbin. You'll most likely share a pool of dustbins with the other tenants. One of you might have to remember to take them out on the due day, otherwise you'll get two weeks of rubbish sitting there.

One of my friends, on first moving in, couldn't find his dustbin. It turned up later—he found it together with several others in the cellar. Before that, my friend had sneakily put his rubbish in the bin down the road. As it turned out, in his apartment block the dustbins are taken out onto the street using a lift system. This is actually quite common in Luxembourg. By pressing a button, the floor in the cellar rises to present a dustbin that is taken out on street level. Hey presto! On the surface level, anyone standing upon the area that rises will get a cheap thrill. Actually, that's not quite true, as the device is controlled.

Dustbins in Luxembourg are actually wheelie bins if we are getting down to talking rubbish. I suppose I could add here that I have 'bin' here whilst discussing dustbins. If your dustbins are regularly overflowing, ask the landlord for another. He might moan or, worse, put the charges up, as he has to pay the council for every bin. Recycling is big here. You can fill a blue sack with empty cartons and empty water bottles. Collections are twice a month.

Now the simple everyday things you take for granted. Therefore, you'd expect washing machines to be in most flats or at least plumbed into them. Wrong! Unless you have a new flat, you could experience a few problems. It's not in most landlords' dictionaries here in Luxembourg City to plumb in a washing machine facility. Why? I don't know. Maybe it's too much hassle for them or the expense of putting their hand in their pockets. They may argue there's no space. It's probably all of these. Who knows? Ask them straight as it may solve the issue.

So, for you, this will mean a trip to the laundrette, as it is not their problem. I know of two laundrettes in Luxembourg City. One is in the Rue de Strasbourg, which is the one I used to use and is very good. The other is next to or near the sex shop behind Coffee Break off the Avenue de la Gare.

If you're lucky your landlord may install a washing machine for you. This I know happened to a friend of mine when he moved into his studio flat. The landlord couldn't get anyone to fill the studio, probably, according to my friend, because there was no washing machine or the facility for one. He was offered a discount to move in without one but instead insisted the landlord look into putting the plumbing facilities in the bathroom for a washing machine. Amazingly, the landlord not only had the pipes put in but also installed a new washing machine! Now future tenants will benefit along with the landlord. Trying to get this simple notion through to some of the Luxembourg landlords is like trying to get blood out of a stone.

Incidentally, I have to share my washing machine, which is in the basement of the flats with the other tenants. That is how it works where I live.

A common thing you might have to do in older flats is bleed your radiator—that's taking the air out, especially in cold weather, sometimes once a day, which can be a bit frustrating. Wearing one's Alf Garnett hat, it does tend to put a whole new meaning into the phrase 'Bleedin' Radiator!'

Another thing many people talk about is their bathroom or shower room. In England I was used to a bath in the bathroom. Here in Luxembourg City in my flat I only have a shower. This I discovered is quite normal in most flats due to lack of space. Yes, some flats do have baths, but mine doesn't. Showers are more hygienic but I do miss the relaxation of a bath. Oh the joys of living in a flat!

One day a friend invited me round. "I want to show you something," he said. He lived in a block of flats built, I guess, in the sixties. He took me down to the basement and showed me his lockup or cave as it is called. Inside were rat droppings and dead cockroaches. "The rats climb under the door," he said. I was shocked. Walking along the row of lock-ups, we stopped at an open area.

"This is where the homeless were living," he said, adding, "and here is where they watched TV." It was in an area that had had a broken door, which was now sealed. Another doorway had a metal sheet sealing it to stop the homeless sleeping in it. He lived in a studio. I thought he was joking when, still outside, he warned me of the cockroaches. Once inside, I jumped suddenly as one small one literally ran across in front of me as we went in the bathroom. Inside the main studio area a large cockroach ran across the top of the washing machine. It was scary.

"How could you live in a place like this?" I said, shocked.

Needless to say he had complained to the landlord and this, I gather, was not all the faults of the flat. I was actually glad to get out of the place and afterwards was at a loss for words.

To be fair, though, most flats have no problems and are excellent places to live in. So don't be put off by the few that aren't. I happen to know of some delightful flats that I would love to live in and one day I might.

I did hear the story that if you wanted to purchase any land between Luxembourg and Mersch, then forget it. The farmers who own the land know that one day the motorway will be built. It will go from Luxembourg to up north. It will eventually go right through central Luxembourg. The plans have been in place for over ten years and a part of the route is already built. The land on either side of this belt has shot up and God knows how many farmers are waiting for the right time to make a killing. However, most are not selling yet. They're not stupid. They'll sell at an appropriate time, making them even more money.

Flats will then be built, as it is more profitable for the builder. This is because of the price of the land. The flats will then remain mega-expensive when they later go on sale. Nevertheless, they will be accessible to the city. Therefore, who wins? Well, the farmers, of course. However, good luck to them. That's business. After all, it just makes a larger hole in your pocket.

The builder, when it comes to building the flats, will need to raise the money to provide him with ready capital—to finance the building of the flats. He will then either sell to individuals, or, more likely, sell the entire block to an *agence immobilière* practice. Why, you ask? Well, it's simple. When a set of flats is built, the money has to come from somewhere. Name me someone who has a lot of ready cash? Well, actually, there's one or two rich folk here in the Grand Duchy. However, what I mean is, who understands the market better than anyone else does? Yes, it's the *agence immobilière* people. They come out the winners here.

A good landlord, you see, will buy the entire block of flats and then rent the lot out. It's easier then to manage. Costs are kept down and returns remain high. You will never see them buying the odd one or two flats that are advertised. Why? Well, if you get problems from the other tenants in the flats then all sorts of hidden problems start crawling out of the woodwork.

Of course, individuals also do buy flats and modern new flats are a delight to live in. Certainly, because of the cost factor, they remain a very popular choice. However, the cost could be lower if the landowners sold now rather than later. But that's not what it's all about.

When a new block of flats is built, it is constructed generally with only one layer of breezeblock on the outer walls. I find this incredible as in England most houses have an outer layer of bricks followed by an inner layer of breezeblock. There is a gap in the middle, which allows the air to circulate, or you can further inject polystyrene foam, which solidifies. This stops the heat escaping from the building. It also stops the cold entering the building. Overall, it helps to reduce your fuel bills. I've been told on several occasions that, in 'general' terms, here in Luxembourg they construct using only breezeblock and concrete. Then an outer coating of modern chemically treated polystyrene is added, which is enough to solve the damp issue once a layer of plaster is attached on top. This modern method I'm told works better than the UK method. It might do, but I still need to be convinced.

There is new block of flats near me, which I have watched being built over the last eighteen odd months. Sure enough, it was built of breezeblock. Then one day the entire outer surface on the front had lots of these polystyrene tiles glued on. The polystyrene tile is about two inches thick and covers an area that's about the size of two to three breezeblocks. Anyway, once the glue had dried, a layer of plaster was skimmed over the polystyrene tiles. Once this was dry, the wall was painted and the result looked smart. However, the back of the building where it sticks out to form a patio area above is only built of breezeblock. As the building faces north and, being in the valley, it means that these walls will soon succumb to damp.

I myself had an interesting experience in my flat. I noticed the grouting around the floor tiles in the kitchen flaking and getting worse. Bits kept peeling off, which got bigger. One day, when I was doing the washing up, two of the tiles I was standing on decided to move about an inch lower. This was obviously a little worrying and I reported it straight away to the agency people.

In fact, while talking to the sales lady, the boss walked past. I actually spoke to him, as he happened to be in the office at that moment. I explained the situation, and my concerns. After one week I had heard nothing, so I went in and mentioned the situation again. A telephone call to the maintenance guy solved the problem and he would be around the next morning. Of course this could have been done a week before, but still.

Unfortunately, and I was not to know this then, but that night whilst in the kitchen, I was standing either side of the dodgy floor when I happened to stand on part of it with one foot. Now I'm not a heavy person. However, the floor suddenly gave way and the whole tile descended onto the ceiling of the flat below.

It descended some six inches below. Luckily, I reacted and managed to move my foot pretty smartish as I felt part of myself descend downwards. The mere fact that my left foot was on another tile had saved me from a very nasty experience. Otherwise, I might have paid my neighbour below an unexpected visit. The floor looked as though there had been only hardboard supporting the tile. On further investigation, I discovered the floor that covered the joists was actually chipboard. I mean, where were the floorboards? In England, they lay floorboards over the joists, on top of which is then laid chipboard or hardboard to give the floor a flat smooth feel. Here in my flat in Luxembourg the floor had clearly rotted away, through damp or a leak. The maintenance guy confirmed it was not a leak.

I live in an old flat in a valley that is colder by some ten degrees Celsius than those up on the plateau area. The kitchen faces north and the whole building suffers from damp in the winter. The problem is the damp proofing. *What* damp proofing? Please show me some damp proofing. The place is ridden with damp, hence the rotten chipboard! However, regardless of the damp factor, I still like my flat. It has character.

So, what do the landlords do about the damp? To my knowledge, not a lot. In my block of flats, the walls simply get another coat of paint when the tenant moves out. How do I know this? I looked at the walls when I moved in. I can see where and when the problem occurs, which is during a bad winter. I also speak to the other tenants, who confirm this. In a bad winter, part of the walls and ceiling in my kitchen turn black. Other tenants have themselves had similar problems on their walls. As for me, well, I just happen to be the first person in the flats where the damp caused me to go through the floor.

Many older flats suffer from this problem. The building regulations in Luxembourg are different to those in the UK. I think there are many sloppy methods used, even on the new flats built. I remain to be convinced about the damp problem.

Anyway, the landlord turned up with two other guys to assess the issue. I was impressed with his attitude. After a discussion, I was advised that a temporary solution would be sorted the next day. This would be a thick piece of wood to stand on over the hole. The full work would begin the following Tuesday morning, when the extent of the rot would be looked at.

That is exactly what happened. The floor was indeed rotten in part and the whole of the right corner of the kitchen was suffering from damp. Interestingly it appeared that this had occurred before. I say that as I noticed the floorboards stop at the edge of the kitchen.

I also remember the landlord saying they had laid the chipboard when they took over the place. Anyway, a beam on the far side of the kitchen where the worst of the damp was, was rotten and damp, so a new beam was put in next to it. A new proper wooden floor was laid and the kitchen put back together. This whole process was done with as little inconvenience to me, the tenant, as possible. The result was that everything was how it was before. The job had been done quickly and I was happy. As for the damp, well, nothing was done about that.

5

Le Shopping

Living in Luxembourg is a joy for most expats. We love the country, the people, the shops, the restaurants and the wide variety of food. Overall, we expats love the continental lifestyle. It's a wonderful experience after the urban living of the UK. If you cast your minds back to when you did live there, then you were probably mortgaged up to the hilt, living in your place of heaven, being interrupted only by the neighbour's loud music or by various family rows. You were living in downtown suburbia, which is what it's all about in England.

How many of us after our holiday away would arrive back home to grey old England in a taxi or with the family and say to everyone, "God, its good to be back home"? Which may be true, as an Englishman's home is supposed to be his castle. What we all actually think and don't say is, "God, isn't everything so drab and dull looking," or, "What am I doing back here? I should be back on that beach!" Some might even say, "Oh, that hedge has grown, and is that a new car on Mr Jones' drive?"

Well, you get the idea. Of course, wherever you live, if you live there long enough you'll probably say the same thing. But if you live abroad you'll look at life from a different angle. You'll look back at life in the UK and say to yourself, "I don't miss that at all!"

I apologise to those people who do miss it, though I believe the vast majority of us don't.

Occasionally we English expats do miss the little pleasures in life from England, but they can be found if you know where to go. I'm talking, if you are a Brit, about the joy of going down to The English Shop in Limpertsberg, or Little Britain in Strassen and browsing the shelves for those things you just can't get in the supermarkets. Most expats like a nice lean bit of smoked or unsmoked back bacon, which you simply can't get, like you and I know it, except in the expats shops. Yes, the delight of being able to buy decent bacon is great. It comes down from Jack O'Shea's, the Irish Butcher's shop in Brussels, and other bacon is flown in direct from Ireland.

In Luxembourg, they do sell Heinz baked beans. Great! But that in itself is not strictly true. They are actually Heinz Tomato Beans. The tin looks much the same as the one you buy in the UK, but if you look carefully you will see that they're not the same thing at all. The European version has just half the sugar and salt of the UK product. Once a Brit samples them, they soon find out that they taste awful in relation to a normal can of Heinz baked beans that you buy off the shelf back home. Nevertheless, I can actually buy the real thing. Heinz baked beans from the UK can be found in the English shops here in Luxembourg. They are heaven to most Brits who willingly pay a lot more than you pay back home. We had a Baked Beans war when the Euro came in. One of the English shops had the beans priced higher than the other. The price is now around one Euro for a can in either shop, which, like I say, is still a lot more than your local supermarket in the UK.

The English shop at Limpertsberg sells a wicked cheddar with a nutty edge to it. Little Britain sells a variety of makes and strengths of cheddar. Both shops do sell other English cheeses, including Stilton.

Now, I like my British banger and again you can get some lovely imported bangers from The English Shop, which, like the bacon, they import from Jack O'Shea. The pork sausages aren't bad, quite tasty, in fact. Jack O'Shea has been trying his hand at Cumberland and Lincolnshire sausages. Both are worth a fry up.

There are many different types of English tea that you can get living abroad. The number one favourite brand is PG Tips. Unfortunately many places including most supermarkets don't sell it; instead, you can only get hold of the Lipton Yellow label tea. I can get PG Tips, thankfully, in the English shops. It's imported but again not cheap. When friends come out I say to them, "Bring me some PG Tips, please." And they do, much to my relief!

That's when your friends really come in handy. I'd do the same for anyone else.

I still fail to understand why the Lipton tea company, whose sister company owns PG Tips, pushes Lipton Yellow tea so heavily, when PG Tips tastes so much better. Unfortunately everyone who drinks it thinks it's English tea and tastes wonderful, except the British who know otherwise. They know that Lipton Yellow label tea tastes bloody awful in comparison.

As a friend of mine commented, "I see I am drinking the wrong kind of tea!"

Of course, there are other English teas you can get here including Tetley and Typhoo, which are both not bad. Specialist teas you can get include Darjeeling, Earl Grey and Lapsang souchong. But, as you may have gathered by now, I prefer PG Tips any day.

What else do most Brits miss? I would guess that I could include such delights as steak and kidney pie and cottage or shepherd's pie. When it comes to the desserts, there is treacle pudding with custard. Alternatively, there's chocolate pudding with chocolate sauce. You can get all these here, albeit in a tin. And let me not forget my little indulgence in sampling a bar of Cadburys Dairy Milk. Heaven!

There are some wonderful shops and boutiques. The main shopping area is in the old town in the area beyond Place d'Armes. In the small streets around the Grand Rue, it's a delight to wander around. Luxembourg has some very trendy and chic clothes shops. If you've a bob or two to spend, here's the place to spend it. Bring your euros too.

The ladies of Luxembourg can be seen in the many coffee and cake shops that Luxembourg is famous for. If you've never been to Luxembourg before, a must is to sample the delights in a coffee and cake shop. However, Luxembourg is not Amsterdam. Therefore, I should warn you that the Luxembourg coffee shops are nothing like the ones that you maybe imagining from Amsterdam. There are no drugs in the Luxembourg coffee shops. Heaven forbid! These coffee shops sell coffee and normal cakes for which Luxembourg is famous. There is none of your special chocolate cake here. Incidentally, the ladies in these coffee shops are real locals, of the more elderly type, not be confused with the ladies of the night that you get in Amsterdam.

Something I find a bit strange in Luxembourg is that dogs are allowed to go into shops on a lead with their owners. Now in the UK they remain outside tied up. It's all to do with hygiene, especially in food shops. Nevertheless, here they appear to be welcomed with open arms into shops. Even butchers shops allow the dogs to come in.

Some of the smaller shops do close at 12.30pm on Saturday lunchtime. At first, I found this very inconvenient after what appeared to be very liberal shopping hours back in the UK. However if you know where to go, you can actually find many shops open until 6pm, which is actually better than Germany. These include the supermarkets, some corner shops and the shops in the out-of-town shopping malls. (See below) On Monday morning many shops take a half day. They open at 2pm.

Luxembourg's shopping hours in 2004 are like England's used to be twenty years ago. There are virtually no shops open on a Sunday as it is a religious and rest day. It's hard to imagine this in England on a Sunday these days, what with everyone piling down to their local DIY store and supermarket.

There are several small supermarkets around the city including some that are situated in the Gare or station area where many people live. Alima is one supermarket, located in the Rue du Fort Bourbon, which stocks all sorts of goodies. Alima does also have two other stores; one is in Belair, the other in the main town in a small open arcade off the Avenue de la Porte Neuve. Cactus supermarket is in the Rue de Strasbourg. It does have another store up at Limpertsberg in the Avenue Pasteur. Both these stores are one of the few shops open on a Sunday morning.

Some supermarkets you could easily walk right past without realising they are there. Blink and you may miss them. I say this because some are underground and hidden from view. These underground supermarkets all have small shopping malls on the ground level. I discovered my first one by accident soon after my arrival. It was in the Nobilis Centre at 47 Avenue de la Gare. This supermarket at the time of writing is actually closed, and has been for a while, probably due to the out-of-town larger Hypermarkets now taking the lion's share of the market, but I did hear it might reopen. I found my second one thanks to a girl friend who told me where it was. It's in the shopping mall opposite the Gare. Inside, towards the back, are some stairs on the left that will take you down to the Supermarché Boon.

One good thing about living in this country with its many nationalities is that they all like to eat their own country's food. There are many small corner shops to cater for this and there is nothing like nipping into one and trying something new and different. Although there are many French who live across the border but work in Luxembourg, the largest expat communities are the Portuguese and Italians. Many of them shop at the small Portuguese and Italian local food shops that are dotted around town. They sell everything that you would ever want if you went to these countries on holiday. I shop in them occasionally but used to use them more when I lived near one.

There are many Asian shops in Luxembourg. You'd be surprised just how many Asians are living here. Asian Market is my local and is located up on the plateau on the Rue Fort Elizabeth. When you go through the door, you could be in Asia. Inside there is a huge fresh vegetable counter that hits you as you walk in.

Not your run of the mill carrots and tomatoes here, but every single fresh Asian vegetable you can imagine, including bamboo shoots, banana flower, long bean, water convolvulus (kangkung), kacapi, green papaya and cha-om. (Names kindly supplied by Asia Market) This type of shop sells everything Asian including imported rice from Thailand. It's sold not by the packet but by the sack. You can get everything here and it puts a completely new meaning to the phrase Chinese takeaway.

Other Asian shops include, under the bus station in the old town, the Orient Magasin, and in the Rue 1900 is the New World supermarket. Here they sell many different types of Asian soft drinks, many of which you can't get in the normal supermarkets, including Bird's nest with rock sugar, grass jelly drink, guava drink, soya bean drink, chrysanthemum tea, lychee and goyaves and mango juice.

Just off the Place de Paris in the Rue d'Anvers is a shop called Enco Farm épicerie. It sells food from the Balkans and the orient. Inside is a multitude of goodies stacked up high. The shop is popular especially with the many people who have come to Luxembourg from the Balkans.

In the Rue du Fort Neipperg is a fascinating African International Exotic shop called New Kings and Queens Alimentation. Inside is a wealth of different foodstuffs and exotic drinks from all over Africa.

Round the corner in the Rue de Bonnevoie is another interesting shop called the Eurasie Culturshop that specialises in Russian, Kazakhstan, Ukrainian and other ex Soviet Union states food. It also has other unusual eastern bits and bobs for sale, including videos.

I must mention the Scandinavian shop called Scanshop that's a little way out of town. It's up towards the airport on the left-hand side on the Rue de Neudorf, just past the bridge. It sells a whole range of specialities from the five Scandinavian and Nordic countries.

There are two American shops in Luxembourg, one of which is in the Route d'Arlon. It's actually a fair way out in Strassen and if you're going from the centre by car, it's on the left just past the ING Bank building. It's called The Gallery of America & Country Store and has many things direct from the USA. These include American food, Gifts and Native Art. The shop is a delight to wander around. The second is 'in town' and you've probably walked past it without realising it was there. It's called Red Buffalo and is tucked away in a covered alley that runs from the bus station and the Rue Phillip II. Inside is a host of all things American.

There are, of course, other foreign shops, but I hope I've given you a taste of the diversity out there!

You'll learn in time that here in Luxembourg there's more to shopping these days than just your local corner shop or various supermarkets situated in, under, and around the Gare. There are hypermarkets, which can be found on the outer edges of the city.

Auchan is probably the largest hypermarket in Luxembourg City. It's situated up at Kirchberg and is a part of a huge French hypermarket chain that sells literally everything. You could easily spend half a day in there. It doesn't only sell food; it also has a completely separate floor selling everything else, from televisions to CDs, clothes, computers and even mobile phones. You can wander in front of Auchan around a large shopping mall. There are some good restaurants here as well. During the week, many office workers who work around the area invade Auchan. They pop out to lunch and nip into Auchan to restock. There's a huge underground car park, which used to be free all day. Now you get only three hours free. You do get five hours in the evenings, but this is geared for the cinemagoers.

Auchan used to have its own Marks & Spencer's in the shopping mall. This was great in its time and many Brits used it. The locals used to shop there as well. Regretfully the management in the UK decided to pull the plug on their European operations and it has now closed. This was a sad day for all us when that happened. I mean, where do I get my Y fronts now? Actually, I wouldn't be seen dead in Y fronts. However, I know someone who does wear them.

You can get to Auchan on the number 18 bus. However, unless you have a car the local shops in town serve their purpose well. Humping bags and bags of shopping is not much fun on a bus full of people. If you're new to Luxembourg and it's your first time on the bus, you'll have a good idea that you're there when most people on the bus get off.

La Belle Etoile is the name of another out-of-town shopping centre. This one, again, has an underground car park but you can get to it like I did to begin with on bus number 1, which takes about half an hour from town. It's beyond or on the outer edges of Strassen. It's different to the Auchan shopping centre in that its arch-rival owns it. That arch-rival in the war of the supermarkets is Cactus who are a Luxembourg supermarket chain. This is definitely worth a visit and lunch in one of the restaurants is recommended. There are many other shops to browse in here, more than up at Auchan.

If you have your parents here then it's a good place to bring them if you want to vary their choice of location away from the old town shopping area. Mind you,

I took my mother to Auchan. However, I hadn't then discovered this place myself to be able to show her.

City Concorde is yet another shopping centre that has another hypermarket called Match. I discovered it after being here a while. It was quite a while, actually. Match is Belgium and French owned and is well worth a visit. I have to confess I think City Concorde is the poorer of the big shopping complexes in both size and choice, but it does still have some good shops in its malls. To get to it you take a number 11 bus.

Be careful! The number 11 bus does a huge loop via Bertrange. The bus stops here for a while at its terminus. You might begin to wonder if you're on the right bus at this point. If I were you I would simply sit back and the admire the view of people's gardens. After several minutes, the bus does leave and heads off into what seems like the yonder before turning towards the west of the city. Soon after, the City Concorde flies into view. You can alight and spend a good session glancing around.

Beggen is a village north of the city where you'll find a smaller shopping mall, at the back of which you'll find the Match hypermarket. You can get to Beggen by taking bus number 10. It's the smallest of all the shopping malls but has a wide variation of choice. If you live to the north of the city then it is well worth a visit. Just up the road is another Cactus store.

There are other supermarkets and hypermarkets scattered all over Luxembourg. The best way to see them is to go out and find them. It's called discovering Luxembourg.

Now, most blokes hate shopping! When the wife or girl friend goes out and drags them along, they hate it, especially if they are taken clothes shopping. The men would prefer to be down the pub drinking with their friends and catching up on the latest football results. Women, however, like to go shopping together. Have you noticed that? They like to go girlie shopping. They like to browse and look around the clothes shops much to the delight of the sales assistants. They like to do their own thing and get away from their men folk for a while. They like to be able to show off their goods, later. Why not!

Why is it that when you're out food shopping and you run into a fellow Brit you clam up or pretend to mind your own business? Is it that you don't want to be seen in a supermarket? After all, we all have to shop. I mean, you see the continentals happily chatting away to their friends. Maybe it's a bloke's viewpoint coming into view again. You know when you're in the company of male Brits when you bump into them in your local Gare supermarket and they turn round to you and say, "All right, mate, where do you get the bog rolls?!"

I did hear a story about the small child who was with his mother in a restaurant or coffee shop. The boy had his feet folded up on the chair. The waitress came along and told the woman to ask her son to remove his feet from the chair and put them on the floor as he was dirtying the chair. The woman was furious as there, close by to them, was another lady together with her dog, sitting together at the table. The dog was sitting on its own chair.

"What about the dog?" the woman protested in Luxembourgish, adding, "It's got more dirty muddy feet than my son has."

The waitress was having none of it. The child had to lower its feet. The dog remained on its seat.

The motto of the story? If you're a child in a coffee shop or restaurant, then you'll have to lower your feet; but if you're a dog, then you can remain seated, paws on the seat. I have a sneaking suspicion this may have something to do with the dog's owner possibly having more money to spend in the place than the woman with her child. After all, rich ladies with dogs give tips; their custom also helps pay the wages.

I like to go round the different food shops. I also enjoy going round the different supermarkets here. Maybe it's a bloke's thing, or is it just me? There's so much choice here, not that there's not a choice back in the UK. Far from it. What I mean is that it's just different. Some examples of food…

The cheese counter is always worth a look at. There's a multitude of different cheeses over here to try out. There's the camembert and brie from France. You can get that lovely Swiss cheese with the big holes in it, or the Raclette Suisse. Then there's Dutch Gouda, but I find it so rubbery, but there's always Old Amsterdam. You can also get Luxfromage, a local cheese. It's okay but also a bit rubbery, like Dutch Gouda. Berdorfer is another local brand of cheese. The one of three types they do that I tried I found had a much better flavour. There are actually many different other cheeses from around Europe that I never heard of until I came to Luxembourg. There is an old English saying: 'If you don't try it then you won't know what its like.' True!

Now, meat is meat. Somehow, in Europe it's presented in a slightly different way to how I remember it back in the UK. It's to do with the way it's cut, I'm advised. I didn't know there were literally so many hundreds of different salami's on the market. Here you will get salami in small round slices or in big round slices, depending on the type you choose. The butchers sell a large variety of salami but the best place to buy it is up at the Foire at Kirchberg (see Chapter : 'A day out in Luxembourg').

Luxembourg sausages do have a different flavour to your English ones. Every local butcher does his own particular brand and here I've included a few of the types sold in the places I shop at. The most popular local sausages are the Thüringer and the Mettwurst. The Thüringer is made locally and should not be confused with its German version, which, according to my local butcher, is completely different. There are other varieties of Luxembourgish sausage, including the Grillmettwurst, the Edamer, the Grillwurst, the Wainzossis, the Merguez and finally the Kalbsbratwurst. Also, the Wiennerlies, which is a sausage with cheese in it and with bacon wrapped around it.

Luxembourg only offers streaky bacon. It's not like your Danish or English Bacon. Most people buy it in packets from their local supermarket, but the best places to get it is in the local butchers or corner shops and ask them to slice you some. I find the bacon I've tried quite salty.

Watch out for what looks like a ham sandwich, or like a coarse pate sandwich. The ham here is different. Jambon (ham) fermier is smoked and cooked. Jambon cuit is unsmoked but cooked, and Jambon cru is smoked but uncooked. If you do not specify, you will receive the uncooked variety. The other thing to point out is that 'Filet américain' looks like pate but is actually finely minced raw filet steak, often with herbs.

When you buy frozen foods the two large brands are Arco and Iglo. None of your Birds Eye stuff here. (Iglo is the continental name for Birds Eye.) Vegetables that are in tins and glass are dominated by HAK, Caissegrain and Bonduelle. I also like sardines. That's probably a result of going to Morocco and sampling them for lunch in Essaouira. They were fresh, freshly cooked and melted in the mouth. Here I buy Pobina sardines from Spain and La Chasse sardines from Portugal. I like pasta with my home cooked spaghetti bolognaise. Pasta is popular here and two companies selling it here are Spiga and Maxim. A sugar brand here is called Oreye.

The bread one buys is very different from that in the UK. There are many different types to try. Many have fascinating names like, Kürbiskernbrot, Röggli, Platine, Steenuewenbrout, Roggenmisch, Hunsruecker, Roggenschot and Boerli. I actually like a loaf of Graham, which lasts longer than most others, especially if you don't have a freezer. Fancy calling a loaf of bread after someone! It's not, but it's my English warped sense of humour creeping in again. Sad! You actually pronounce it Graaaam without the h.

Heinz do their bit and you can get their tomato ketchup in the supermarkets, which is good. But I also like Daddies variety. Unfortunately, you just can't get it here. I have to ask friends to bring me over a bottle. However, the Lea & Perrins original Worcestershire sauce is also available, which is great with a steak.

The local milk company is called Luxlait. Their 'Lait Chocolaté' or in Luxembourgish 'Schokelas Mëllech' is addictive as is the chocolate milk called 'Cécémel' made by Nutricia, its Belgian rival. Nothing similar is sold in the UK. A relatively new product that I have come across is the 'Funny Orange' and 'Funny Tropical' that's sold alongside the milk products. It's exactly what the product name suggests and is a clever tasty blend of the two. All the usual fruit juices one can also find here.

Everyone has their own favourite foods and there's a whole world of different foodstuffs out there to try and buy. Still, I hope this gives you a small taster of what's on offer here in the Duchy.

Of course you could always eat out. That's where a little gastronomy and wine come in handy…

6

Gastronomy, Restaurants & Pubs

Eating out in Luxembourg City is a normal thing to do; it's a way of life here, whereas in England or other countries it's perhaps regarded as more of a luxury to eat out. In the UK most people dine at home and occasionally invite friends and family around for a meal. In Luxembourg you would more likely meet and eat in a restaurant. 'It's the thing to do.'

There are many restaurants to choose from, depending on your taste. These range from the local Luxembourgish brasseries and restaurants to American, Chinese, English, French, Greek, Indian, Italian, Japanese and Portuguese restaurants. I mustn't forget the Malaysian, Mexican, Mongolian, Moroccan, Thai, Turkish and Vietnamese restaurants as well. Every restaurant is different; some are more expensive than others, many have an excellent choice of wine. Location is also an important point; some have wonderful views, whereas others are tucked away in very unimaginable places adding to their mystic delight as one walks in the door.

I myself have eaten in many restaurants, brasseries and cafés here in Luxembourg. Most have been a great experience. A recommendation by word of mouth will generally take you to a good restaurant. Of course, there is only one way to find out, and that is to go and try them. I don't pretend to be an expert on restaurants, but a little tour of some of the restaurants and bars right now might just enlighten you further…

I think the most famous Luxembourgish restaurant is Mousel's Canteen in Clausen, which specializes in serving up some excellent local food known on the menu as 'Specialites Luxembourgeoises'. This will get you a variety of pork-based local dishes including 'Jarret de Porc' and pork braised in beer. Watch out for the 'Assortiment de Spécialités Luxembourgeoises'. All dishes are recommended. Go there on an empty stomach as they are very rich with cream and fillings. I found it a great place to go with a group.

Other restaurants in the same area of Clausen include Maybe Not Bobs, an American grill bar. It specializes in beef spare ribs that come in baby, mummy, daddy and grandfather portions, depending on how much you fancy eating. They simply melt in the mouth. The chilli con carne they serve as a starter is huge and is also recommended. The nearby Brasserie Mansfeld is a very plush place that you could try. The local nearby expats pubs of the Pygmalion, Britannia and Ecosse are worth calling in for a few drinks as well. Halfway down the hill from the old town to Clausen on the Montée de Clausen is La Villa, a lovely little restaurant with some great views across the Alzette valley.

In Limpertsberg there's a host of good quality restaurants to choose from. If you fancy a good steak then Stones Steak house is one that my friends would recommend. On the actual Glacis itself I have eaten many times with my language class friends in the Osteria del Teatro restaurant. It says it's a Pizza restaurant but does in fact serve up literally everything and again is a great place to go as a group. Next door to it is the Café des Glacis, which is a terrific little bar that's always busy, especially at lunchtimes. Just round the corner by the Utopia cinema is the popular Il Cantuccio restaurant.

If you fancy a really good meal in a trendy place, then a trip to the old town is the place to go. It's the place to be seen, especially at the start of a weekend when the area gets packed out. This is what could be classed as the heart of old Luxembourg as there are many old caves and old buildings that house some great restaurants and bars, one of which is the Brasserie La Loge which gets busy on a weekend. Further round is the plush Ristorante Come Prima. I've eaten in here a few times and I can thoroughly recommend it. Next door to this restaurant is the hugely popular Prime Time bar. Underneath that is Yesterdays, which is a must if you're a newcomer to the city, as the further you go inside to enjoy your drink the more it will unveil fascinating caves of old Luxembourg.

Tucked away in the Passage du Palais just off the cobbled streets is the To Kastro restaurant. It's a very good Greek restaurant that will take you down into some caves. Just up the curving stairs in this old passageway is the tempting El Cid Spanish restaurant. Go further up some more narrow stairs made of cast iron and you'll find yourself in the Alsace restaurant Goethe Stuff. The whole area oozes with history and the atmosphere will make your meal one to remember.

Around the corner in the Rue de la Boucherie is the delightful Art Scène bar that has a great terrace at the back of it. Next door is another popular expats bar called The Tube, which is shaped like an underground tunnel and gets busy at the weekends. On the corner of this rue at the top of the hill is another 'in' expats bar, The Urban bar, which is very art déco thirties modern in its style.

The heart of Luxembourg is in the main square of Place d'Armes, which though not having the best food has a large variety of restaurants. All the restaurants have tables laid out in the square, which makes for a terrific atmosphere. Popular restaurants include the Café de Paris, and the Hotel Français. Opposite is the plush seafood restaurant La Lorraine and Chi Chi's the Mexican restaurant. I mustn't forget that delightful gastronomic American restaurant, McDonalds, next to which is a French equivalent, Quick!

Just off the Place d'Armes are two very popular and lively bars called Banana's and Sparkies. This one is also an internet café bar. Heading in the opposite direction from these two bars and also just off the Place d'Armes in the old cobbled Rue du Curé is the famous El Compañero restaurant, which not only serves up a great meal but also is a fantastic place to experience a night of salsa. In the same street are some very plush restaurants including the restaurant AM Pays Jan Schneidewind, and the brasserie restaurant Bodega.

In-between Place d'Armes and the Place Guillaume is a very old passageway either side of which you can savour the delights of the Kaempff—Kohler restaurant, which dates from 1922, and the Brasserie Guillaume, which specialises in seafood. In Place Guillaume itself along one side you'll find both these restaurants together with several others including the Hotel Casanova and the Café beim Rénert.

Another famous area to eat in is the Place de Paris. Around here, I was once advised, are over fifty different café bars, brasseries and restaurants. In the actual Place de Paris you'll find on the one corner the Akula café, which has recently been renovated and is now bright blue. All the restaurants on the Place de Paris have tables in front of them, including the Bistrot Place de Paris, which does a good beef stroganoff. On the other corner of the Place is Le Fontaine, with its speciality of ribs. All are worth a try and again are recommended. Opposite is Chez Rafael, a Spanish restaurant that I have eaten in a few times and quite like. Overlooking the Place de Paris is, I'm told, a very expensive restaurant called the Cordial. It's on the first floor of one large building and is the one that has a glass front. One day I might get there.

Just off the Place de Paris in the Rue d'Anvers is the first restaurant I ever tried in Luxembourg, the Mona Lisa. It's quite a reasonable Italian. Opposite is another good hotel restaurant called the Italia. In the Rue d'Andre Duchscher is one of Luxembourg's best kept secrets. I'm talking about Vesuvio, which is an inexpensive but superb Italian restaurant.

Leading off also from the Place de Paris from the corner with the Capital café, is Rue Ste Zithe. Here there are some great brasseries and restaurants including

Brasserie a Capital that is next door to the Capital. Opposite is the Brasserie Due, an Italian café that does some terrific lunchtime food including a great lasagne. Just up the rue is the Arpège restaurant, which again caters to groups and is good.

In the Rue Dicks is the legendary late night Saumur restaurant and bar. Just along from here is the Swedish café called the Crossfire that these days attracts many Scandinavians. On the corner is the Lord Nelson (see chapter : 'Mini Baghdad'). One pub I dare not forget to mention is The White Rose, also in the Rue Dicks. It's an expats joint where you can relax and enjoy a beer on the terrace. Life wouldn't be the same without it.

Along the Avenue de la Liberté is Books and Beans, where you can get a good-sized sandwich and glance at a book at the same time. Adjacent, on the corner, is Café Bianca, which does some great lunchtime snacks, including small square pizzas and some great tarts. Further up beyond the Place de Paris is Namur, a delightful coffee bar that serves up some great cakes. It also sells some wicked chocolates. Just along the avenue is a real traditional place called Scheer & Arens. It also sells chocolates, bread and cakes, and at the back of the shop is a real hidden gem in the shape of a real traditional café. Again, they do some great lunchtime food.

Next door to the bus and train station or Gare in the Place de la Gare is the station café called Au Quai de la Gare Brasserie restaurant. It might be the station café, but it does do some great plats du Jour. If you are single and on a budget but don't fancy cooking, then this is a very good place to try as it's relatively cheap. Above it is the Harmony restaurant. If you are into organic food then this is the place to come. At the other bus station in the old town is the Interview café, a very popular place for youngsters.

In the Grund there are some great restaurants, which have some delightful views of the valley. One such example is an Italian restaurant in the Montée de la Pétrusse called Il Fragoino. Here there's a lovely terrace to sit out on—book early to avoid disappointment. Bonaparte's is another plush restaurant in the heart of the Grund with a courtyard where you can sit outside under the trees. By the old stone bridge is another posh restaurant called the Mosconi. Here there's a lovely terrace where you can sit out with a view of the Alzette River. Another place to enjoy some wonderful views is Scott's bar just opposite. They also have a terrace that overlooks the river. Inside is an open fire that is lit on a cold winter's night. It feels great! Across the old stone bridge and heading just a little up the hill on the left you'll come across a very Luxembourgish café called the Café des Artistes, which has a terrific atmosphere, especially when someone strikes up on the old 'honky tonk' piano.

Two other popular expat joints in the Grund are the Liquid bar where they have jam sessions on some nights, and The Oscar Wilde, which is an Irish bar with character.

Next to the tunnel that leads to the lift in the rock is the Rox bar. This is an interesting bar as it's built into the rock face. They also play heavy metal 'rock' music!

Just off the Avenue de la Liberté in the Rue Glesener is a very popular Moroccan restaurant called Maison Berbère that you sometimes have to queue to get into. In the Rue de Bonnevoie is an interesting Moroccan restaurant called Le Marrakech. Just know something about Moroccan food before you order and you'll have a great meal, or you could be disappointed with what you get—speaking from the personal experiences of myself and my friends.

There are many good Indian restaurants in Luxembourg City. The best Indian restaurant in town is undoubtedly the Namaste in the Rue de Strasbourg. It specialises in Indian and Nepalese food. Its lunchtime menu is terrific—if you like a good curry. Our recommendations to friends for the night-time menu got very good feedback. In the Rue Bender you'll find what my friends and I describe as the second best Indian restaurant in town. I'm talking about the Everest restaurant, which also specializes in Nepalese and Indian food. They also do a wicked lunchtime menu of different curries, which the local Luxembourgers who frequent this place seem to enjoy. A nice touch is the dessert of ice cream at no extra cost to round off the meal. The Tahj Mahal is another Indian restaurant in the Rue de Strasbourg. The curries here I found disappointing as they are nothing like the curries I was used to in England. Try explaining that to a Frenchman who has never eaten a curry in his life before! Many expats do, however, like the place, even if I don't! If you like Bengali and tandoori style, there's the Royal Bengal in the Route d'Esch, and in the Rue Ste Zithe is the popular Restaurant Tibet, which specializes in Tibetan and Himalayan food. In town along the Grand Rue is the Maharaja Indian restaurant that's not bad. Other Indian restaurants to mention include the Himalaya and the Star of Asia.

There are some great Portuguese restaurants in Luxembourg City. The most famous one in town is probably Bacano's in Clausen. Here they serve flamed scampi and giant gambas in a thick garlic cream sauce. They also serve some of the best steaks in town. This place is very popular with expats and locals alike. However, if you can't get in here, try Chez Isobel Bacano on Route d'Esch. I went there with a friend of mine and thought it was great.

In the Rue de Rollingergrund is the popular Santola restaurant. This Portuguese restaurant and bar also has pool and snooker tables that are well worth a game or two on.

Another great Portuguese bar worth mentioning is the Café Académica in the Rue de Bonnevoie. It's a hidden bar, which is a bit like 'a tardis' as it's far bigger than it appears from the outside. Inside is a long bar, and also pool tables. It's a real gem of a place that oozes continental flavour. (*Tardis* means: Time And Relative Dimension In Space—from the English TV programme *Dr Who.*)

If you fancy a classy Japanese restaurant there is the Kamakuq restaurant in the Grund; a cheaper option on the Avenue de la Liberté is the Sushi Place, a Japanese snack bar. In town is the popular Kirin restaurant with its Teppan Yaki food. On the ground floor is a Chinese restaurant that specialises in Chinese and Thai food, which my friends and I all found delicious. Upstairs is the Japanese restaurant that I'm told is an experience to visit. The Peking Garden is another Chinese restaurant in the Rue Phillipe II where all the Chinese staff eat after the other restaurants close, so it must be good.

Other Chinese restaurants include the Garden de Jade on the Rue Ste Zithe and at the back of the Dukes Palace is the Palais de Chine that does fabulous dishes. I have eaten in here with a group of friends to round off the evening after the delights of Yesterdays bar.

In Pfaffenthal is a Vietnamese restaurant called Le Triomphe that also does Chinese food as well. In the Rue de Rollingergrund is the Restaurant Over Seas, which does Malaysian and Chinese food that is recommended by several friends.

If you like good Caribbean and South American food, there's Tainos in Pfaffenthal. This is one of my favourite restaurants. Two other restaurants I must mention on recommendation from friends are the D'Artagnan on Boulevard Général Patton for the best steaks in Luxembourg, and further down at the bottom of the hill on the left is the Italian Villa D'Este, which has a nice terrace to sit out on.

In Bonnevoie is a wonderful restaurant bar called Gutschimontana. This is quite a trendy and modern place. It's well worth a visit as it oozes with style and class and is a favourite with those that know about it!

During the year, the big hotels around town have various promotions and festivals. One of these is the Sheraton Aerogolf Hotel that's near the airport. For instance, every year in February it hosts an Indonesian food festival that is highly popular.

All the restaurants do a bustling lunchtime trade when all the office workers pile out of their offices. Many restaurants offer a Plat du Jour at a very reasonable price that is generally very good quality. The Plat du Jour sounds so continental. It sounds so much better than any of its English translations that I hear, like plate of the day, dish of the day, or menu of the day!

There are many other restaurants and bars in the city and country of Luxembourg. I am merely giving you an overview. Like I say, the best way to find out about the latest good restaurants is to talk to people to find out their current favourites. Trying them is the next step. Bon Appetit!

The most famous British expats' pub with pub food is the George & Dragon and is on the number 2 bus route. "It's about ten minutes from the centre of town," Bob, a Canadian friend, once told me. Of course, it depends on which bit you call the centre of town. The first time I went there he said, "Look out for it on the right. It's the red building." Well, imagine I'm on the bus not really knowing where I'm going, desperately looking out for this pub. There was only one small problem—if you've ever been down the number 2 bus route you'll know what I mean when I say that there are many red buildings on the right hand side, all of which looked like they could have been the building I was seeking! In fact, the bus ended up at its terminus, as the driver then informed me. So I started walking back up the hill past a new development of flats that was being constructed at the time. After half an hour I found The George & Dragon, which these days is painted a ghastly pink on the outside and inside as well.

The George and Dragon Pub is situated at the bottom of a hill. It lies about one hundred metres back from the main road. If you're coming from town it's the first turning on your right just past a bathroom factory or showroom called Villeroy & Boch. Actually, the turning is a crossroads. When getting off the bus from town the bus stop is just past this factory. Again, I hadn't been told this.

The area itself I find spectacular as it is in a valley surrounded by forests. The pub is run by a Richard Andrews, a Brit who has been there for over fifteen years. Most expats have been here at least once as it was one of the early expat pubs here in Luxembourg. The beer garden is a delight to sit in during the afternoon on a summer's day, the sun just catching the patio area in the right way, the flowers looking so lovely in the garden. The food's not bad either. Wednesday is pie day. They do a variety of pies from steak and kidney, steak and ale to pork and apple pie. Friday is cod and chips day and because there aren't many places serving this dish it is a treat for the Brits. Sunday lunch is the big meal of the week. The George & Dragon do a wicked roast. They vary it too. One week you can get a nice bit of roast beef with cranberry sauce and roast pork with applesauce. Other times it's roast lamb with mint sauce or roast chicken. All are served up with roast potatoes and Yorkshire pudding.

Why do many Brits eat Yorkshire pudding with everything? I mean, I was brought up to eat Yorkshire pudding only with roast beef. It's part of that roast beef tradition. Do you think I'm missing the point here? If you were a Yorkshire man (perhaps Yorkshire person would be better in these days of equality) you'd eat your Yorkshire pudding separately with thick brown gravy on, before the meal even began.

For those of you not familiar to the Luxembourgish beer, the main beers include Mousel, Diekirch, Bofferding, Battin and Okult. As is typical in Europe, all are pilsner beers.

7

The Wine Tour

If you fancy a wine tour of Luxembourg, then a bit of time, a car and a sunny afternoon constitute the best advice I can offer you to help get you on your way. It might be a small country, but Luxembourg does produce some exceedingly good wines. These are grown mainly in the south east of the country along the Moselle valley. In fact, there are vineyards all along the Moselle River, but our tour will be on the Luxembourg side where villages and vineyards are synonymous.

So what do you know about Luxembourgish wines? Well, probably more than me, but here goes! There are ten popular grapes that are grown in the region.

Riesling is probably the best known. It's an excellent quality white grape that's dry and full-bodied but has a delicate fruity aroma, which gives it its long lasting taste.

Another type of wine is the Pinot Noir or black Pinot, which has a fruity savour and elegant bouquet. The Black Pinot in the region is regarded highly and is probably the red wine's equivalent to what the white wine Riesling is. It is also an original vine that other vines have developed off. The Black Pinot is used in the making of Red and Rosé wines, the latter of which are growing in popularity.

There is also the Pinot Gris, which is a full bodied, semi dry, sturdy wine with a finely spicy robustness that was originally created from successive mutations of the Black Pinot.

The Pinot Blanc or White Pinot is a wine of high quality that's smooth, elegant and fresh and is derived from successive mutations of Pinot Gris.

Another type of grape grown in Luxembourg along the Moselle River is the Gewürztraminer, which makes a very robust wine that's racy and dry, yet has a spicy and delicate taste with an unmistakable aroma.

The Chardonnay is another wine now produced in smallish quantity in Luxembourg. It's a noble white wine. It is interesting to note that Hogsheads are being used as part of a new wine making process by some wine growers in the region in the production of Chardonnay.

There is also the Auxerrois, which is a semi-dry robust wine, which is cheap to produce. It is similar to White Pinot. It is popular and its cultivation is expanding. Auxerrois also matures well with age and can be stored for more than ten years.

The Rivaner is the most commonly drunk wine in Luxembourg. It's a fruity wine with a mild and soft flavour, which should be consumed within three years of harvest.

Finally, let's not forget the Elbling; this is a very old vine that goes back to Roman times. The white Elbling is a dry light and fresh quality wine enhanced by its typically sour flavour. It's found in many of the bars here in Luxembourg. There's also the red Elbling vine that produces a light and cool red wine, which is used to produce Rosé which is now a popular drink on hot summer days.

Most people like to buy their wine from the local super or hypermarket. Some buy their wine from the sparse corner shops. Others purchase it on a trip out to a cave. In this instance I'm talking about when you decide to go for a drive down to a local vineyard. One enters the cave determined to air knowledge; only a few glasses; after more than a few it loses its taste; therefore it is just a matter of knocking back the free wine provided. You then decide to buy a case or two of wine just to keep the owner happy. Finally, you let your hair down and drink it later on that special occasion. Cheers!

Well, assuming you don't do it quite like that, let's rewind and take you on a quick tour of the Luxembourg wine region…

In the glorious summer of 2003 my friend Andrew and I decided to check out the vineyards and caves of Luxembourg. We set out in his Porsche Boxster after a hearty English breakfast in Coffee Break, driving up to Echternach for what I can best describe as a *pre tour*. The town is situated in the east of Luxembourg and was a delight to drive through. Next time we will allow more time to stop and have a stroll around its picturesque centre.

We headed off following the River Sûre along the German border on the Luxembourg side, heading eastwards to Rosport but signposted Wasserbillig on route 10. All along the German side of the river were many campsites that were full of tents and caravans. Rosport is where the famous bottled water comes from, and we passed the production site en route. About a kilometre the other side of Rosport on the left-hand side we found our first visible vineyards, so we took a minor road that took us up the hill to a beauty spot where these small vineyards were now above and below us. It's a terrific view that looks out on the surrounding valley, taking in the German village of Wintersdorf.

On the day that Andrew and I went it was very hot, which helped to make the drive a great day out; within no time we were in Wasserbillig. The road followed the picturesque meandering river. Vineyards were few and far between.

Our next sighting of many vines was on the corner of the road where the road and river do a giant hairpin turn to the right, about half a kilometre past a motorway bridge that passes across the valley. From the vineyards it was a short drive into Wasserbillig where the Sûre joins the Moselle.

Our *main* wine tour commenced at Wasserbillig where we paused to watch the small ferry crossing the Moselle River from Oberbillig on the German side to where we were parked. Our tour would take us along past the south-facing slopes of vines, some forty-two kilometres along the Moselle valley on the Luxembourg side to Schengen where it would end.

From Wasserbillig we headed up-river to Mertert where one can see en route the different grapevines growing on the slopes above the old road from Luxembourg City. We discovered later that many of the vines grown by the vintners are members of a collective called Les Domaines de Vinsmoselle. This collective now makes up nearly two thirds of the country's wine production and covers some eight hundred and sixty hectares. But there are still some fifty-four domains that are private sellers.

We reached the town of Grevenmacher where the vineyards around the town are famous for their Rivaner, Auxerrois, Riesling and Elbling vines. A well-known brand name in the shops from Grevenmacher is Bernard-Massard, who has caves here. We stopped off and had a look round this rather large complex where, to say the least, there were one or two bottles stored. I wanted to try a glass of Gewürztraminer 2002, which is made locally. It was quite nice and so I bought a couple of bottles. Another large cave to stop off at is the Caves Cooperative des Vignerons Grevenmacher. It was walking distance from our first cave and was well worth the look around. Call it an education in Wine.

Our drive took us further along the Moselle to Machtum where the locals meet at the end of August for the annual tasting. Here the Rivaner vine makes up a third of the vines grown around the village. A delightful cave to visit in Machtum is the cave of Jean Schlink-Hoffeld who was very welcoming. We went through the production area, which no doubt would be a hive of activity when the harvest was ready, to the wine tasting area where I had a little tipple. Some of these private concerns may be small but their wine is good.

We moved on to the small laid-back village of Ahn, which we both thought was one of the prettiest villages en route. It again produces great wines and here there are many independent wine growers, more than anywhere else in the region. Pinot Gris and Rivaner vines are widely grown on the slopes around this village. There are a number of small caves in Ahn, which we visited. These were the caves J-P Steinmetz-Duhr, Jean Ley-Schartz, and Albert Berna-Ley.

We discovered that we were on the road known as the route du Vin. Many people cycling along this route stop off to sample a glass or two to help them on their way. Some people were even on tandems.

Another way to see the vines is by taking the ferry M.S Princesse Marie-Astrid that runs up and down the Moselle. It stops at various points including Trier in Germany, Wasserbillig, Remich and Schengen. It's a much more sedate trip where you can sit back and watch the vineyards go past at a more leisurely rate. (Luxembourg, incidentally, has the largest merchant fleet in the world. Think about it.)

Our drive continued on to Wormeldange, an important village as the production of the drink Crémant de Luxembourg is done from here. Crémant is the crème de la crème of Luxembourgish wine, and is what champagne is to France. There are actually several varieties of Crémant including the Cuvée Demi-Sec, the Cuvée Brut, and the Cuvée Riesling. The Riesling vines dominate the slopes around Wormeldange. Smaller amounts of other vines are also grown. We actually visited the Pundel-Err Cave in Wormeldange and the Cellars of Wormeldange.

Our next stop was in the very picturesque village of Ehnen where we discovered a wine museum. By now we were getting a bit hot and were in need of a drink, so we stopped off at a local bar on the riverfront to sample a local glass of Rivaner. We passed the time of day relaxing, looking out along the Moselle. Nearby was a water ski club that was closed. This was a pity as in the heat of the moment it felt like a bloody good idea to try out. Later we wandered around the village and continued our tour by visiting the Caves of Jean Leuck-Thull.

The journey continued, the road meandering its way down beside the Moselle River towards Stadtbredimus. Before reaching it we stopped off at a very strange building, shaped like a square lump of modern concrete. It was the building of Cep d'Or. We wandered around it until I found the entrance. Inside was a very pleasant, cool wine tasting area that looked out on a large square pond. Again we were made welcome. After a good look round we decided to pass on any wine tasting, otherwise we could have ended up very drunk.

Andrew and I got to Stadtbredimus and parked in front of the château of Stadtbredimus where there is also the Domaines de Vinsmoselle and had a nosey about. I found out that in the second week of August the winegrowers and locals come together in this village for the traditional wine tasting. Rivaner is the most popular vine around this village. However; most of the other varieties are also grown.

Our afternoon drive in the Boxster took us on to Remich, which some people would class as the capital of the Moselle wine region. Here, once again, the slopes are mainly dedicated to the Rivaner vine. A well-known brand name is the Caves of St-Martin that has caves at Remich. We stopped off here to look around and to try a little taster of some Rivaner wine, which wasn't too bad.

As we drove along I loved to look out at all the many vineyards growing their different varieties of grapes. After Remich we found ourselves in Wellenstein, another village just along the Moselle River, where in June the wine lovers meet for the day of tasting in the local cellars. We visited the Caves de Wellenstein where we were warmly greeted.

Just in case you're wondering whether all these places are actual caves, they are not! Some are like a wine supermarket, some are the real thing, and others are newly built while some appear to have been there for years. Each one does, though, have character. One thing I will say is that every cave we visited was different, so you never knew what was coming next. Everyone was friendly and I could put my French into good use when in conversation with them.

Continuing up-river, we deviated off the main road heading through Schwebsange. We discovered there's a wine festival held here during the first Sunday in September. A variety of vines are grown in the vineyards around this village. We headed onto a small village called Remerschen where we found the caves du Sud Remerschen where one can sample a few delights at the wine boat, which is a bar inside the cave. There was one couple who appeared to be buying every bottle in the place. Their car was well laden on departure.

Finally, our tour reached its final destination of the village of Schengen in the far south-east corner of Luxembourg, or, as it's known locally, as 'Dreiländereck' or, in English, 'the land of the three borders'. Around this village are many vineyards. At Schengen we visited the caves of Gloden, where my friend Andrew bought some Auxerrois and Pinot Blanc to share with his girlfriend. Next door to this cave were the caves of Legill et fils. Unfortunately they were closed. Schengen is a lovely little village, which we might discover more about on our next trip as we had run out of time.

We headed back to Luxembourg City on the new motorway, which, after thirty years of waiting, had only been open a week or so, and now connects Luxembourg with Saarbrücken. It had been a hot day, over thirty degrees. It had been a great day out for us.

There are many small villages just off the route du vin that runs along the Moselle River that also have their own caves and vineyards. But our tour had given us a taster and as we had discovered, the best way for us had been to get out there in the car and take a leisurely tour. We had appreciated the beauty of the region and the fine wines that go with it.

8

Living—A to R

Whilst living in Luxembourg we all go through similar experiences. The following are just a few of the more mundane, miscellaneous and occasional things we all hear about, have been through and notice but think nothing of.

Burning of the Stake

The burning of the stake is a religious festival that is very catholic oriented. It happens here every year, generally between February and March, on a Sunday, a set number of weeks before Easter. It's to do with giving the year a clean sweep. All the old winter leaves and dead wood are collected and large bonfires are prepared for the big moment on the set date. The burning of the stake ceremony is held all over Luxembourg.

Within the city in the Pétrusse valley, a festival is held in the park area between the bridge Adolphe and the viaduct. It's nice to go for a walk in the afternoon around the area, also going into the Pétrusse valley to stretch the old legs to see the park in all its glory.

In the valley there are small stalls selling beer, hot dogs and, most importantly, the various decorated special festival cakes. One year I tried a huge slice of one and it was delicious.

In the open grassed area a huge bonfire had been built, a wooden cross adorning the top. About 7.30pm, they lit it. Later in the evening they also had a firework display. Many people were there and it made for a great weekend of celebrations.

Car Boot Sales

The British Ladies' Club of Luxembourg once a year hold 'The Great BLC Car Boot Sale' up at the Glacis. Strangely, it takes place on FA Cup Final day. Now, is there a connection here, or what? Whilst car boot sales are a part of the British way of life, over here in Luxembourg I gather it's very regulated. Apart from the BLC one, I don't think I've seen any others.

Over here, people just chuck things out mostly. Yet over in Belgium, when I was in Namur, I saw a huge car boot sale in a long lay-by off the modernised road, which looked busy. It's possibly not in the thoughts of rich Luxembourgers to host these popular events themselves.

"They don't know what they're missing!" I can hear all you car boot sellers saying.

Census

This is done every year around the 15th of October.

Chitchat

There is a story that does the rounds of the rich Luxembourg family who, in keeping up with their neighbours, went on their annual exotic two-week holiday. One week into the vacation neighbours saw lights on in the cellar at night and alerted the police, thinking there were burglars in the premises.

What was discovered in the cellar was the family who were camped out and had been in hiding from the world and the neighbours. Not having been able to afford a holiday, they had thought of trying to fool their friends, so it turned out to be a very sad story in the end.

Another story I heard was about a large Luxembourg Company which, in a cost-cutting exercise, sent an e-mail to its employees telling them that in order to save money, the company would be cutting back on toilet paper by twenty per cent and could they all use less paper when in the toilet? I've given you the clean version of the story here!

Clean Air

I met some Spanish girls who were fairly new arrivals to Luxembourg. They said to me how nice Luxembourg was compared to Madrid, as the city had so much clean air. When I arrived here I had thought much the same.

Nevertheless, I had to laugh as I had heard a completely opposite story on various occasions from other friends. The story that I had heard was that you get all the factory dirt landing on Luxembourg from the French factories over the border.

Certainly, after this I did notice a black element of dirt that appeared to accumulate by the windowsill area. This is more so when the window is open and the sills haven't been wiped regularly. The dirt definitely appears here from the outside air. Some days it's worse than others. The dirt probably comes from over the border in France in the Vallée de la Fensch where there is a steel works. It could also possibly come from Virton in Belgium.

To be fair, the dirt could also come from Luxembourg's industrial south. Around Esch-sur-Alzette there's a steel works. I've also had the pleasure of sampling the air in Esch-sur-Alzette, which on occasions in certain parts of the city smells like bad eggs.

Earthquake

Did you know that Luxembourg had an earthquake in 2003? Well, it did, and it was quite a large one at that. It happened on the 22nd February on a Saturday night around 10.30pm and registered 5.4 on the Richter scale. Most people missed it or, having felt it, soon forgot it.

I was sitting in my lounge watching TV when it hit. It lasted between five to ten seconds. It felt like a large lorry passing, which they do and you get a rumbling on the mirror when this happens. On reflection, perhaps, it wasn't a lorry passing. The mirror shaking was actually picking up the earth tremors that in the weeks before the event had been building.

This particular night the whole building shook and the room wobbled from side to side. It was a most disconcerting feeling and afterwards I was sure it was an earthquake—or was it me? Did I rush to get out? You bet I did!

The epicentre was somewhere in north-east France. When the mirror shakes now, I immediately think, is that more than just a lorry? Is it an earth tremor? Apparently, the authorities received over two hundred calls from worried residents. There was no visible damage anywhere and luckily Luxembourg survived the ordeal to live another day.

Flea Market

This delightful small market takes place every fortnight on a Saturday morning in the Place d'Armes.

Gestapo

One day a friend of mine called Matthew was in The White Rose when he said, "Have you seen the unusual building that's in the Boulevard de la Pétrusse?" I had probably walked past it a thousand times without noticing, so curiosity got the better of me.

"It's about two hundred metres on the right if you are heading away from the bridge Adolphe," he said.

Well, I found the answer. It was the Villa Pauly. I discovered that this very chateau like building was used as the headquarters of the Gestapo from 1940 to 1944. This is where you were brought to be interrogated, tortured, and sometimes killed by the Gestapo and where People were '*enrolés de force*' during the Nazi regime period.

These days the Villa Pauly is a research institute. There is also a documents library. It is also the offices of the Comité Du Souvenir de la Resistance (CDSR).

Holidays

Now, if you work in a bank in Luxembourg, the holidays are very generous. You'll get around thirty-seven days a year working a forty-hour week. In other fields, most people get less than this, around four weeks.

In the summer holidays i.e. the end of July and the whole of August, many expats uproot and take a month's break in the sun. The Portuguese and Italians head home during this period and the French head south to the Mediterranean.

During the Christmas period, as in most other places, most people head home to be with their family.

The point I'm trying to make is, in Luxembourg City, it's noticeable when the expats leave en mass. However, in the summer, Luxembourg is invaded—by tourists…

Horrors of Sandweiler!

Now, if you're a car owner, you should pay attention. If you're not a car owner, you should also pay attention. Luxembourg is a nation of many expensive cars that range from sports cars to large flash motors including four-wheel drives. It's a rich country so its citizens can afford to buy expensive new cars. You won't see many old cars in the country, as it's easier simply to replace your car every two years with a new one.

Cars are cheap to buy here, which is another reason people buy so often. However, the other reason could have something to do with taking your car down to Sandweiler, either for inspection or to get one's papers in order. In the words of some people I know who have had this pleasure, they would describe this as 'The Horrors of Sandweiler!'

I don't have a car here in Luxembourg. I either hire one or I take the bus, etc. But to anyone who does have a car, then quite simply it's a pain in the arse to get your papers in order and have your car tested when you go down to Sandweiler. It's worse than that, I'm told. Even if you are there at the crack of dawn, you are in for a long wait. If you do get there early, then every other bugger is there as well doing the same trick as you. You also know what's coming as well, which makes it worse. You have to allow three hours, which is not funny, especially if you have to work, as most people do.

The horror stories I've heard about the place don't bear thinking about. One girl I know took her car in and had one of her papers missing—this after three hours queuing! She had to return two days later and start all over again. Worse was what she saw. There was a woman in the queue with a baby on board. After three hours, the mother of the baby was frantic. Nevertheless, she still had to wait her turn. Do they care? Like hell they do.

In the old days, I have been told, when 10 o'clock in the morning came along it was tools down and a fifteen-minute tea break took place. Never mind about the poor buggers sitting patiently in their cars waiting for their turn. These days I'm told the situation is a little better.

Your chassis number of your car has to match your Grey card; if it doesn't, then tough. If they can't find your chassis number, then tough.

If you are a girl it should be easier. But not always. You know, flash a bit of leg and wear a short skirt. It doesn't always work but if it beats the queue, then why not.

You wait for half an hour in the Immariculation—that's the registration queue—before you go into two offices, one to check your car, the other where a girl checks your papers so you get your grey card. After this you spend the next two and a half hours sitting in the allotted queue. There are five queues to wait in. There is a priority queue if you have a valid reason, but most don't so you are allotted your queue. Apparently, if you get queue four it's bad news.

What are you waiting for? The answer is the ten-minute check at the control. That, believe it or not, is what it's all about.

Immatrication is for the first year of the car in your ownership. If you keep the car, the next time you join the queue directly to the test bays housed in the Control Technique building.

Now it helps at this point to have that blonde girl with blue eyes and big tits who is wearing that short mini skirt up to her thighs sitting in the car with you. My friend happens to be going out with a blonde who does have blue eyes. She also happens to speak about five languages.

Having been there before to be greeted with a '*Uuh*' and '*Uuuugh*' and everything in Luxembourgish, my friend had observed one of the controllers being extremely rude to all foreigners, including him. If you have a sports car, it's worse. They don't like those at all, practically attacking them with their feet. Are these people animals, or what?

If you are a local—and by that, I mean a real Luxembourger—then everything is fine. Do you get the picture! Anyway, with the blonde girl able to communicate with the guy in German, Luxembourgish and French, they sailed through. What a difference it made. Remember, if you have anything wrong, then it's tough luck and come back again another day. It's brutal.

Every car not registered in Luxembourg had to be imported into the country. This is called *Agrégation*.

I gather that because of these horrors, people actually pay a company to take their car through the test because they know how bad it can be. That's sad. You can now see why most people change their car before it's three years old! All I can say is, "Why don't they have some form of ticket system?"

Certainly, I could recommend a lesson in manners. After all, it doesn't take a lot to be courteous.

A final point I must mention here is that in the late summer of 2003 I met one of the bosses of Sandweiler in The White Rose. I'm pleased to tell you he was entirely human and out of his workplace, a great laugh. I was pleased to meet him and engage in a beer. At work he told me he was relatively new to the job. When I mentioned some of the difficulties and horror stories I'd heard, he acknowledged some of the difficulties. Communication and language difficulties on both sides are one of the issues, and clear information for everyone to read in several languages appears to be another. The bottom line is, new changes will be coming—that's good news for everyone!

Iraq War

Luxembourg had its fair share of demonstrations against the Iraqi war in the spring of 2003. On the day after the war started groups of students decided to protest by simply sitting down in the street. This caused terrible traffic jams. After a while, the police did eject them but the point had been made. The people stuck in those jams though were not happy bunnies that evening.

Certainly, there were other demonstrations that luckily I missed. The American Embassy in Limpertsberg was also targeted by loads of students yelling 'No to War' and 'Down with the USA'. There remains graffiti scattered around saying 'No war US'. The British Embassy was blocked off. A ring of steel was enforced around it. The road past it was blocked off some two hundred metres before. An armoured troop carrier was stationed outside along with umpteen police cars. Armed troops were on twenty-four hour guard. They were positioned at the entrance of the ring of steel.

During the war and for a period of two months the viaduct that runs across the Pétrusse valley was partially blocked off. It was closed to pedestrians on the side of the British Embassy. Everyone had to cross over and use the other side of the viaduct.

New in town?

Now, when you have been here a while you'll get to know your way around. If you have a friend who can show you around, then you'll be greatly assisted. However, if you're here on your own then any advice that you can gain from talking to friends at the office or in the pub is always appreciated, especially if you happen to be single.

Here in Luxembourg there are many single people. A lot of them hitch up together, but a lot don't. I know an awful lot of single girls aged between twenty-seven and thirty-three who are looking for someone. Don't all rush at once, fellas.

Nightclubs

Most young Brits like to go to nightclubs. However, over here they would go to a Disco. There are many good Discos around the city. The word 'nightclub' has a different meaning. Over here it's a cabaret bar where you'll be asked, "Would you like some company?"

The company is generally a beautiful Russian or East European girl who will suddenly want you to buy her lots of champagne. Be warned! You could easily end up with a bill over €800 for simply talking to a beautiful girl. I've heard of several horror stories where large bills arrive as the person is leaving.

Old Breweries

People who have lived in Luxembourg a while may remember the beer that was once brewed by the Henri Funck Brewery on the Rue de Claussen . Alas, the brewery was taken over some years ago by the Mousel Brewery and the beer is no more. The Henri Funck site was shut down and most of it remains empty. Many people go past it to or from the airport, oblivious to the history of this famous old building en route.

Ironically, the Mousel Brewery has since been taken over by the Diekirch Brewery in Diekirch where the Mousel beer is now brewed. I've heard that the former Mousel Brewery site is to be saved and converted into flats and specialist shops, etc—better than knocking it down, anyway.

Parking

Parking is always a hot subject with anyone who owns a car here in Luxembourg. There's a severe lack of parking spaces in the city. The authorities, as in other European towns and cities, have parking meters to ease the problem. These allow you to stay in some places for two hours or in others for a maximum of five hours—after which you have to nip out of the office and feed the meter all over again. This consumes about €8 a day. The parking meter police scour the city all day long in the hope of giving you the pleasure of one of their parking tickets. I'm sure they await their moment with glee!

Multi-storey car parks are encouraged, mostly underground. There is also the Park and Ride scheme, which is being actively pursued currently to encourage all the car owners from Luxembourg together with all the frontier folks to park their cars out of town and take the bus in. That's all very well, but this adds considerable time to your travelling day. If they double the frontier people then radical new planning will be needed.

Polyglot Club

The Polyglot club in Luxembourg is a club where you can meet people of different nationalities. It meets most Tuesdays at the Foyer bar, which is a European Union Bar, located in the Rue H. Heine. Now blink and you'll miss it! I mean, I must have walked past it for eighteen months before I discovered it. I would describe the place as a bit of class. It's one of Luxembourg's best-kept secrets. The place oozes with atmosphere. You'll feel this as you walk in the door. The guard greets you on the door, and then you follow the stone staircase as it winds its way in a tight circle up to the first floor.

The rounded bar overlooks the Pétrusse valley. It has a posh feel about it. Even the seats have an air of exclusivity. It's a European Union bar, after all.

The club welcomes all nationalities and leaves leaflets about town and on notice boards to publicise itself—for example, at the Centre de Langues. Ideally, someone who is already in the club should introduce you. An Argentinean friend of mine introduced me. We had talked about it but it had taken me a month before I got round to going. I've never looked back. It's a youngish club in relation to other Polyglot clubs in other nearby countries, for example Belgium. It has an age group that averages between twenty and forty years old.

It's not everyone's cup of tea. Either you like meeting people or you don't. You can come and go at your leisure. Like any club, there's the regular clan—but newcomers are always welcomed into the club. Luxembourg being the type of place it is, people do come and go more quickly than some other places, I guess.

The club does various out of club activities, which during 2003 included several bowling trips to Esch-sur-Alzette, followed by a meal and, for those with the stamina, a visit to the Melosina Disco. In the spring the club did a day trip to Namur, and during the summer went on several bike rides including one from Luxembourg to Trier. Finally, some went to the Frankfurt motor show.

Quality of life

Now, if you have the choice of working in London or living abroad, what would you prefer?

In London, for example, you have the pleasure of catching your commuter train each day. You can spend about three to four hours on the train there and back, sitting next to hot tired sweaty bodies. You have mobiles going off every five seconds. There are train delays every other day. The rail tickets cost a fortune. However, to be fair, there is one hell of a good social life.

Alternatively, in Luxembourg you might have a ten-minute walk to work and a ten-minute walk back. A bus journey is minutes rather than hours. You can spend your lunchtimes or after work activities doing a leisurely stroll. This could be to the Place d'Armes, the Place de Paris, or other open areas. You're in the summer sun with a beer and with your friends after a hard day at work.

So which one would you choose? My former agent said on more than one occasion that he could see why I preferred Luxembourg. He himself would like to follow my example though, for the moment, he is content with his office in London.

Remember, I've had five or more years in London. I've enjoyed the social side but, as you get older, one changes and quality of life becomes more important.

Roadworks

Now there are 'roadworks' and there are 'roadworks'. You get them in every country and Luxembourg seems to get its fair share. Certainly, the city centre seems to have had more than most areas in the last few years. Roads have been dug up for months on end whilst new modern deep sewage pipes have been laid. New water pipes have also been put in. It's a massive job causing misery for everyone. Why they don't speed it all up, I shall never know.

Important Note: On the Horrors of Sandweiler.

Since writing this book I now have three important points to add.

1. I've received an anonymous threat regarding this article.

2. I'm advised that Luxembourgers, too, experience the same problem as foreigners.

3. I discussed parts of this book with an English lady in November 2003, whose husband had been to Sandweiler. She said, "Compared to before, he was amazed how 'charming' they were to him when he last had to go there." We worked out dates and it was after my discussion in the pub. Interesting.

9

Living—S to Z

Sickness

Soon after I arrived in Luxembourg, I was amazed by the amount of people who had time off sick. If you talk to anyone in the pubs and bars each will have a story to tell you on this subject. What made it even more unbelievable was that some people appeared to do it on a regular basis. That to me was absolutely farcical.

Here you can take two days off automatically after which you need a doctor's certificate. That sounds reasonable enough. However, what I found alien was the fact that the person who was sick only had to ring in and tell the boss that he or she was sick. The boss is by law not allowed to ask the question, "What's wrong with you?"

Oh no, this apparently is personal and none of your boss's business. The sheer amount of business days lost through this abuse must be huge. So what do the bosses do? The answer is nothing. Legally, they can't do anything.

I've heard of several individuals who regularly take more than six weeks off per half year just on sick leave alone. That sounds incredible. What was wrong with them, you ask? I've no idea, as that's personal. How ridiculous! Back in England, the boss would get the staff to fill in a sick form that would clearly show what was wrong with the employee. Any long-term sickness would be discussed with the individual, discretely if necessary, so the employer has some idea what is wrong with his/her staff. It would help him or her to plan, if necessary. Here the employer can't do anything.

It goes without saying that if it's a genuine sickness, I have no issue with the legal situation—but there appears to be a lot of 'Let's just take two days off' attitude. This can be done quite easily, say, every two weeks. If you work in a bank you get around seven weeks holiday, anyway; if you add on all your bank holidays and then play around with your sick days, this can add up to over sixteen weeks or four months out of every year where you are not working. Incredible!

If the person lives over the border in France, then there's not a lot that can be done about it—and don't the French know it! If you live in this country, the state or someone is likely to check up on you. So, if you left the house and you aren't ill, you could be in trouble.

Sport

Sport in Luxembourg isn't a big thing. Luxembourgers *do* like to play sports, but since it's a small country they are not able to be as competitive in winning like the big boys in the larger countries who seem to win all the important sports trophies. The country does compete, but generally it does what it's best at—simply participating in the sports that its people enjoy most.

Luxembourg does partake in competitions with other smaller countries and is very successful as it has more in common with them. There are several tournaments and friendly games between these small countries.

The Duchy in 2003 took part in the European Athletics for smaller nations in Malta. It did quite well and came second in the tournament. One hundred and nine Luxembourgers took part. They managed to win fifty-three medals, doing particularly well in swimming where they picked up twenty-two of them. Other sports at the Malta games that Luxembourg took part in included basketball, volleyball, judo, sailing, pistol shooting, squash, tennis and table tennis. It was a good result for the country. The team was cheered on by the Grand Duke himself.

Rugby is a popular game that many expats play here. I know of friends who have played for Luxembourg's Rugby squad when they play the other non-professional nations. This includes many eastern European states, including Bosnia Herzegovina, Croatia, and Georgia. The club has also played, Bermuda, Sweden, Norway, Austria and Germany. The Rugby club has recently celebrated its thirtieth anniversary.

Basketball is enjoying increasing popularity in the country. There are quite a few teams playing various levels of the sport. Saturday night is a real crowd puller with the locals. I went to one such night in Bertrange, one of the suburbs of the City. The local teams were playing against teams from Echternach. It was good. Luckily, the home team won so the locals went home happy.

Cycling is a popular pastime here. There are many cycle ways all over the city. Mountain bikes are the current trendy fad. You'd be surprised just how many adults are seen about town on them. Certainly, the more adventurous get active, up into the woods where there are some real off-track places to try out your tricks using your mountain bikes. I prefer a bike with mudguards on so you don't get mud up your bum on a wet day—or am I missing the point?

The Tour de France 2002 started in Luxembourg. In fact, The Tour de France spent three days here. The first day was the time trial in the city centre. That day the city came alive. I've never seen so many people for a sporting event gathered all over the city. The atmosphere was electric and the enthusiasm generated for the riders was terrific. The second day saw the race Tour Luxembourg circumnavigating the country, before on the third day leaving Luxembourg City and heading down to Saarbrücken in Germany.

Throughout the year there are various cycle races spread over the whole of Luxembourg including the Tour de Luxembourg and the Flèche du Sud. Both of these are usually held in May.

September sees a large cycling race in Luxembourg City. This is a professional cycling event with all the big names and teams taking part. The longest race of the day is the Charly Gaul race, named after the Luxembourg cycling legend Charly Gaul. The race takes the riders all over Luxembourg. The afternoon sees them return to the finish line in the Avenue de la Liberté. Later in the afternoon the Gala Tour de France takes place in the circuit around the Avenue de la Liberté.

On the same day and sandwiched in-between the cycling events was another sport that is growing in popularity—roller-skating or roller blading, to use its proper name. The skaters utilised the same course used later by the professional cyclists; racing on and in-between the races, the skaters just had a little fun on it. Several Sundays in the summer have seen parts of Luxembourg City cordoned off for roller blading.

A place where everyone seems to head for to practise is in the park area that runs beside the Alzette River. I was quite surprised by just how many skaters use this route. Apart from the skating, a walk in this park is a must.

Football in Luxembourg is the number one sport. It's played all around the country, but is not a large concern like it is in the UK. If you watch any European football match, Luxembourg doesn't exactly rate in the top five European teams. Most big games are played in the 'Josy Barthel' stadium in the route d'Arlon in Luxembourg City.

If you're a football supporter, this might interest you. If you're an Ipswich Town football supporter, then merely the name will conjure up fond memories. Why? Well, in the summer of 2002, Ipswich Town were playing against one of the local teams here in Luxembourg. The team in question was Beggen. They were drawn, in some round of a European football game. Now Beggen isn't a big place. Ipswich town is. Beggen would be classed as a suburb of Ipswich with its local football club in some much lower division. But hey! This is Luxembourg and Beggen is pretty good, I'm told.

One day in the summer of 2002, the city was invaded by Ipswich Town supporters. The place was full of blue and white, be it shirts, scarves or banners. They arrived at first in ones and twos creeping up from the Gare, gently sipping their coffee outside 'Coffee Break', another English-run café. Gradually the few turned into the rest, blue and white crossing over the Pétrusse River and filtering out into the bars and coffee shops in the old town. Suddenly the Place d'Armes didn't just have the sound of the brass band orchestra bellowing out. Oh no! It was more like, "Ipswich Town, Ipswich Town, we love you!"

The best bit was, and I have to give full credit to the bandmaster for this because I thought it was a brilliant piece of planning, was when suddenly the band broke into, "When the Saints go marching in" followed by "Blue is the colour." It was electric. The whole square lit up with the sound of all the supporters joining in. For those of you not acquainted with this strange ritual, 'Blue is the colour' is one of their football songs. I always thought Chelsea sang this song. As the sun began to set, the supporters were streaming down the route d'Arlon and into the stadium. It was a good game for Ipswich. They won 2-0.

Now, if you've ever met an Ipswich Town supporter you'll know that they've been all over the world with their team. They're extremely faithful to the club and have one of the friendliest supporters clubs around. They are also trouble free. The whole day had been a success, which to me was summed up on a blue football shirt someone was wearing. It said on the front, "Ipswich Town," and on the back, "European Tour—Moscow, Berlin, Beggen!" I thought that was brilliant.

A year later and the City was invaded by a different team. This time it was the turn of the Danes. The match was between Luxembourg and Denmark. The bright red shirts were in town…

Stereotypes

The interesting thing about Luxembourg is that you can go into any bar on your own or with whoever and talk quite easily with the person sitting next to you. What makes this rather special is that the person you're talking to is likely to be of a different nationality, be it black, Asian, white, Hispanic or whatever. There are no stereotypes here. If that was in any other country it just wouldn't happen like it does here.

Sunday Mornings

Should you happen to be up early enough on a Sunday morning with the church goers, you can always see the leftovers of the night before. By that I mean the two bowlegged drunks staggering into the Saumur for breakfast after having been on a bender. Then there's the Biblos crowd who have partied the night away and who are still feeling cool. They fancy a bite to eat and also head to a café. There are also the hotel guests. As you walk past any hotel, if the breakfast room is full on a Sunday morning, you know that the tourists will be out by 10.30am armed with their video cameras.

Transport

When I first came to Luxembourg City I didn't have a clue about how the buses ran. Back home it's fairly easy—you simply get on a bus and pay the fare. But in another country you'll be surprised how that simple feat defeats a lot of people at first. They're put off for any number of reasons, which could be the language or the ignorance of simply asking. Some people are frightened at first. Don't laugh. These things do happen.

But a bit of advice pays dividends and Luxembourg's buses are actually a joy to travel on in the day. After 9pm, services get a little thin, so anyone living out of town needs a car. If you live in town near a bus route, it can be ideal. But, like so many other places, if you want a late night out you'll need a taxi. Most buses stop around midnight; however, the city does have a Night-Bus service at the weekend which, if you know where and when it goes, is extremely useful. *It is also free!*

Luxembourg has modern, clean, single decker 'bendy' buses. Each one, as you may discover, is slightly different from another. There are three doors to get on and off. If you need a ticket, just ask the driver. The driver will give you a ticket that will last you an hour on any bus in the city. Either the ticket has been stamped or you have to 'Kliken Ticket' in the machine on the bus to validate it—just as you would on the Amsterdam trams.

There's even music to listen to while you go on your journey. The buses all have radios in them. Can you imagine that in the UK? How long would they last? They also have two-way radios to communicate back to base. This advises the drivers instantly of any occurrences or traffic problems. CFL the bus company are even introducing on-board video camera's on their buses to give the drivers more protection. If there is any trouble on board the bus then this is no bad thing.

I once encountered a bus with seatbelts! That was a new one for me. Just for the record it was a number three bus. The buses also have on their front sides tiny flag holders. On special event days, like the Red Cross Weeks in March, relevant small flags are inserted which flutter as the bus goes around the city. It's quite a nice idea.

If you're here for a while you can purchase various forms of ticket, as in most towns and cities. The main ones include: an hour €1.20(yellow) or a book of ten for €9.20; or a day ticket, €4.60 (red). You can also get a book of red tickets called a carnet, where you get five for €18.50. There is the City-Kaart (€31), which is for all journeys around the city for a month. Finally, there is the monthly ticket for €41(blue), which will allow you to go on any bus or train anywhere in the country. This is probably the best one to get, even if you live in town as it enables you to hop on and off any bus any time. The blue ticket makes a trip to Trier in Germany very cheap as you only pay from the border. These tickets can be purchased together with more information, either at the train station or in the old town under the bus station at the ticket office in the underground walkway there.

I sometimes wonder, "Where do the buses go that go pass me in the street?"—a solution to this being that some bus stops with a bus shelter have maps on the back of them or inside. These are brilliant as they show you the city. They also show you where the bus routes are. Having a blue ticket means you can hop on and off all the buses at your leisure, discovering places you didn't know existed. Try it—you'll learn a lot about the city and the country that way.

When you're in a country as a single person and you've recently arrived, and you're getting your feet on the ground, it takes a lot longer to find out about things. This can be very frustrating. An example is when an Irish girl friend told me about the cinema complex up at Kirchberg. Well, I knew about bus no 18. I had discovered where the complex was. However, it took me three bus rides to discover the bus stop she had mentioned to me. It was right outside one of the doors and I must have walked past it with my eyes closed. Nevertheless, you always play safe if you're on your own. Therefore, the bus stop I was using was actually two stops down.

Just to confuse things further, the bus, on its arrival from town and once it has gone past Auchan, does a little loop. The terminus is at the Foire, one stop before the cinema. Why is it when you're late getting to see a movie you really want to see, the bus has this nasty habit of stopping for ten minutes or so whilst the driver has a pee or whatever!

Luxembourg in the good old days, like many cities, used to have its own tram service. When buses were developed the trams got left behind. Luxembourg, like many towns and cities, eventually closed its tram service. There's a tram museum you can visit in the summer time.

These days Luxembourg City is served by modern clean environmentally friendly buses. However, there is an anticipated new development: trams will be making a comeback in the city! A new route will run from the Gare along the side of the current railway line and cut up to Kirchberg. The line will serve this new area of the city, continuing round until it reaches the airport. The tramline will then continue onwards back to the city, joining up with the current railway system.

Thus a new circular route is being created. It sounds quite exciting. But most Luxembourgers have heard it all before and, as with most things, they'll believe it when it happens. Somewhere along the line the subject of politics enters the equation, if you get the picture.

A thought did occur to me regarding the new tramline. Why bypass the town centre around the bus station at the Centre E. Hamilius? Many people get on here for Kirchberg. Surely, it would have been cheaper to run the line up the Avenue de la Liberté over to the bus station, over the red bridge and—hey, you're in Kirchberg, or am I missing the point?

The train services run from the main station or Gare. Here you can get local, national and international services.

The national ones (CFL) run up to Ettelbrück, Clervaux and Troisvierges in the north. The train passes Mersch and Ettelbruck and services run to Wiltz and Diekirch. In the south, they run to Dudelange, Bettembourg, and south-westwards to various towns including Differdange, Petange and to Esch-sur-Alzette, the second city of Luxembourg.

International trains run to Trier in Germany, connecting you with Deutsche Bahn (DB) railways; to Metz in France (SNCF); and to Arlon or Liège in Belgium (SNCB). International routes go all over Europe. There's even a day train that arrives from Brussels. It stops in Luxembourg, goes on to Thionville, calling at Metz, Strasbourg, and Basel in Switzerland, and ends up at Milan in Italy.

If you fancy a day out by train in the central part of Europe there's a ticket you may wish to buy. It's called the SaarLorLux ticket, and costs €18. If there's a group of you up to five people, then whilst you, for example, pay the €18, your friends pay €8.50 each. All children count as one person. You can use the ticket to go to the bigger towns and cities of Trier and Saarbrücken in Germany, to Verdun, Metz and Nancy in France or a day out in Luxembourg. It will also take you to any smaller station in the region on the map you'll get when you get the ticket. This is a special ticket issued only on a Saturday or Sunday. Each ticket is valid until three in the morning the next day.

More exciting news. Luxembourg now has double-decker trains arriving at the main station in Luxembourg City from Belgium. They're marked 'B', presumably for Belgium, and they look great.

Is the UK Minister of Transport reading this…?

Water

Have you ever looked closely at the colour of the water that comes out of your tap? I hadn't until an Australian friend pointed it out to me one day. The water from the cold tap, when poured into a clear glass, is indeed cool and clear. However, when he poured the hot water into the glass its colour was a distinct pale brown. I was quite surprised and shocked. Since then I've encountered various shades of brown in the water.

If there's a water problem in one of the other flats in your complex rather than your own flat, the water has to be turned off. When it's turned back on a whole load of yucky brown water runs out through the system. Sometimes it's not just water that comes out of the tap! Indeed, you get all the metal bits in the old pipes spluttering out. Sometimes you physically have to undo the filter bit on the top of the tap to let a wad of this 'yuk' out. Certainly, the plumber likes to get shot of it. After that it's fine until the next time.

Mind you, on winter mornings the water pressure has been low. This could be for various reasons. Either everyone in Luxembourg takes a shower between 7.30am and 8.30am, or the water's frozen in the pipes. The other reason might be that the system pump is playing up and probably needs to be replaced. I've also experienced hours of no water due to road or water works or whatever. However, I'm generally advised of this in advance.

I should just like to add that for the majority of the time my water is fine!

White Rose

The White Rose is a British expats' pub but welcomes anyone. Certainly many Luxembourgers use it. It's a good place to watch the football, rugby and ice hockey. If you fancy a game of darts, there is a darts area where the local pub team plays during their league games.

Some people might call it a dive, others a meeting place. It certainly isn't a palace, but it does have character and is a good place to talk to people. Many nights have been spent here, propping up the bar. It's also many expats' second home.

Contrary to the stories I've heard, The White Rose was not one of the first British expat pubs. The first one was actually on one of the corner's of the Place de Paris and was called 'Pub 13'. It was opened around 1968/69 and was actually above a Wimpy Bar at the time. Funnily enough, the whole site is being renovated as I write this. In-between it was a Pizza Hut, which closed long before I arrived.

The second expat pub to open in Luxembourg was in the Place d'Armes, around 1971. It was called the 'Pub on the Top' and was above another Wimpy Bar whose owners at the time owned both pubs.

The actual history of The White Rose is fascinating. I discovered that before it was a pub it was a shoe shop run by a Luxembourger. He retired and his daughter Petra and her husband took over the shop. He was a jack-of-all-trades and together they decided to turn it into a pub. Hence, in the year 1980 or thereabouts, The White Rose was born.

Sometime later they decided to sell the business. It was bought by a Chris Sykes who at the time was a chartered accountant. He was also a Yorkshire man who decided to get a new sign for the pub. He ordered a sign, which said "The White Rose" with the idea that it would be in 'White lettering' with a 'White Rose' symbol on it. Legend has it that unfortunately for him he was on holiday when the sign arrived. It was put up before he got back. When he returned from holiday he allegedly went ape-shit when he saw the sign! Why? Well, fixed up outside the pub was indeed the sign 'The White Rose'—but the letters and the rose symbol were in *red* letters, not *white*, with a background in *white*.

To appreciate the anomaly of this, you need to understand some English history. The thing is, there's an age-old rivalry between a person from Yorkshire and Lancashire. It's all to with 'The War of the Roses'—red being the Lancashire Rose, not to mention The Labour Party slogan of the time, while a white rose is the Yorkshire Rose and a symbol of peace. Nevertheless, the sign remained and to this day it's still talked about, thus keeping the legend intact.

Chris Sykes ran the pub for approximately two years before selling it to Don and Mary Doverstone who were an Irish couple. They were real characters and gave the place a certain feel. During this time the bar was frequented at the lunchtime and after work by employees of one or two money brokering companies together with many Scandinavians who worked in the nearby Scandinavian banks that used to be nearby.

Don and Mary ran the pub for about five to six years before it was taken over by a Danish couple, Peter and Yarna Gleerup. They got their son Søren to help run it with them. This all lasted for about six years until December 1998 when Tony and Irish Devenish took it over. Tony is English and his wife Irish is Filipino. To date they still run the business.

The pub has seen many great barmaids do a sterling job. Many have come and gone, as in most pubs. Overall, the pub remains a popular joint for expats.

In 2002 the pub gained a terrace thanks to the narrowing of the road. Sitting out there now on a sunny summer's afternoon or evening is a positive delight. In July 2003 the pub underwent some modernisation. (I did mention the word 'some'!)

As for the future, well, the bar's open and if you're buying, mine's a pint…

Worries

One thing I've discovered in Luxembourg is the insecurity of many people who live here. Most people have absolutely no idea what this means. However, talk to any one who has or has ever had a short-term contract and you will see a completely new world unfold in front of your eyes. People don't dwell on it lightly. It's life, and while it keeps the wolves from the door, it's deeply worrying for those not knowing what happens next.

Since I first arrived I've met many different nationalities—all here on different contracts, from a two-week temping stint to a three, four and a half or a six-month contract. You're very lucky if you get a year's contract, and if you get a full-time one you've struck gold. In some places there are even five-month contracts issued. That one's a bit sneaky as it gets the government off paying unemployment money.

10

The Dukes Birthday

The big event of the year in Luxembourg is in June. To be precise, it's on the night of June 22nd every year. This is when 'Summer in the City' kicks off. It's a night not to be missed, being 'the night' when the whole of Luxembourg comes into the city to celebrate one giant party.

What's the reason for this celebration? Well, June 23rd is known as 'la fete Nationale' or 'National day'. It's a public holiday for everyone. The day is also known to be the 'Dukes Official birthday'. Quite when his normal one is, I don't know.

Now, it doesn't matter what day of the week it is, whether a Monday or a Friday. The date doesn't change.

The fun starts the day before when the preparations start early in the morning. I say this because of what I saw…

It started at the bus stop. I was on my way to the English shop for my Sunday papers. I waited there for the number 4 bus. However, I soon realised there were no buses running. I turned around and saw the sign. It told me there were no buses that day from this bus stop due to the National day. Instead, I would have to go to the Gare or the Emile Hamilius bus station. So, I decided to walk. After all, it was a nice day, the sun was shining, and a stretch of the legs would make a change. As I walked along I could hear the various church bells ringing out across the valley. Well, by the time, I got to the bus station I had decided to get my Sunday paper from a shop in Place d'Armes where I bought *The Sunday Times*.

I only buy *The Sunday Times* occasionally from this shop as the owner only gets seven eighths of the paper delivered (the European edition), thus increasing his profit. It's a bit naughty, but what can you do?

Anyway, I decided to have a nosey around to see what was going on. There were delivery vans unloading crates of beer. Stands were being erected. There was a hive of activity all around. The preparation was well underway. From the Place d'Armes to the Plateau of the Holy Spirit, things were happening.

Later in the day, a line of old tractors went past my flat on their way to a display. All were looking terrific, considering their age—each restored, cleaned and looking brand-new. (Once I had seen an old brewery delivery cart with horse. It was going to be used in the parade later that night. It had been restored and looked wonderful.)

In the evening, as the sun sets, a line of hot air balloons are set up in the Avenue de la Liberté between the Place de Paris and the bridge Adolphe. They're inflated and their flames light up the inside of the balloon as dusk falls. As the night arrives, they look magnificent. The girls who work in the nearby cabaret bars loiter in the club doorways watching the action. The crowd watches, fascinated by the grandeur of the scene.

On the Place de Paris the area is transformed into a small fairground. By the edge of this is a speciality of Luxembourg, a delightful mobile kitchen restaurant. These can be seen throughout the spring and summer months at various outdoor events. You just won't find them anywhere else except here in Luxembourg. They're staffed by about one hundred and one chefs and waitresses. The chefs wear their smart white tops and tall white hats. The mini restaurants sell cotelettes, hot dogs, both the Thüringer or Mettwurst variety and burgers. There must be a joke here somewhere. Oh yes, these are real Luxem-'Burgers'. Sorry!

The cotelettes are unique to the pork-based diet the Luxembourgers like. You know what a cotelette is, don't you? You don't? Well, it's a pork chop in simple terms, but a butcher might argue against this. Still, one served with chips with tomato ketchup is well worth sampling. Don't come to Luxembourg without trying one!

Elsewhere in the city, other events were happening. Down by the palace there was plenty of activity. In most years the Duke and Duchess spend the evening hosting the main event in the Place Guillaume. Dancers entertain them. There's a small parade where various groups take part. These range from military bands and fire fighters to children marching and doing acrobats. In addition, other children carry fire torches. The local scouts and guides also take part. The procession is a joy to behold! One year there was even an African tribal dance. All march past the Duke and Duchess. Many different nationalities watch the parade.

The Duke's Birthday lights up at around 11.30pm when the Duke and his wife the Duchess arrive at their viewpoint to watch a giant fireworks display that's started on the bridge Adolphe. No, not that Adolf—please don't insult the locals! This Adolphe was an ex-Duke here in Luxembourg.

Thousands and thousands of people gather to view it. People watch the fireworks from every angle. They stand on the streets around the Place de Metz, which is at the end of the Avenue de la Liberté. They also stand on the viaduct and on the grass slopes by the eternal flame of the National Monument of Luxembourg Solidarity.

Everywhere is jam-packed with people. Anywhere where there is a vantage point has people crammed in, all eager to get that better view. It's a real festivity, fit for all the family. Fit for a Duke, even.

The night skies are filled with every possible type of firework. Their colours and shapes ripple out. Music fills the air and the fireworks magically appear to go off to the sound of the music playing. What makes it even better is the scenery around, which gives it that special touch of fantasy including the pointed chateau-like tower of one of the banks in the Place de Metz. An incredible three tons of fireworks go up in sixteen minutes, the audience going "Oooh!" and, "aaah!" after every great firework. A child might be heard saying in Luxembourgish, "Mummy mummy, I can't see!" and is then lifted up upon Daddy's shoulders. It's a real family event and is the one time of the year when all the kids are allowed to stay up late, and I mean late. The smoke from certain fireworks hovers in the air. The smoke gives various unusual shapes that seem to vary from a wave effect to what looked like a giant hand reaching over to the crowd. To those watching from the viaduct it's thrilling.

I must tell you a funny story here. Well, we thought it was funny at the time. One of my English friends was on his own. Now, there is nothing wrong with watching the fireworks on your own. After all, there are many single people here in the city. Anyway, this guy's actually married but his wife was in the UK. However, on this particular night he was single. So there he was, looking desperately for a spot, as one does, to view the fireworks. He found one and waited. He thought he had a good view. He could see the Adolphe Bridge perfectly from his position. He was standing next to this tent-like construction and before long there was an air of excitement in the crowd. Suddenly the Grand Duke himself appeared and walked together with his wife right past my friend. The thing is, they stopped right next to where my friend was standing, for this was the very place reserved for the Grand Duke to watch the display. The Duke and Duchess had their viewpoint from inside the tent. My friend had his viewpoint from the other side of the canvas. Now you can't get a better view than that! Naturally, my friend was flabbergasted that the 'Top Man himself' was standing right next to him. Now, that would be something to tell his kids back home.

When the fireworks are over the real party begins. Held mainly in the old town, but also in the area around the top of the Avenue de la Liberté, the night of a thousand different beats commences.

'The Rhythm of the night' brings the old town to life. Many thousands of people party the night away all over the area. Now if you've never been then you've missed one hell of a good party! In Place Guillaume, a huge stage is blasting out everything from rock to pop, from soul to techno. In fact, there's a bit of everything for everyone in the packed square of youngsters. In the other main square of Place d'Armes, the brass band is playing to a different type of audience. Everywhere there's something for someone. No one misses out.

Down by the elevator, on the Holy Spirit Plateau (also known as St Espirit), is a whole host of small open-air bars and food stalls. Here you can get every type of drink. I actually discovered a new local beer on sale here. It was brewed by what a friend described as a microbrewery. The name of the beer was Okult, which was okay. The food varied from a curry stand to a burger and chilli stand. I tried the chilli, which wasn't bad. My Peruvian friend served me. In addition were the usual hot dog stalls.

On the occasion, a small stage pumped out the music—loud! The partygoers thronged around the stage. The place was packed. They were in full swing to the sound of the beat. Along the front, alongside the statue of The Golden Lady overlooking the Pétrusse valley, was another concert and open-air disco.

One year, on the Place de Metz side of the bridge Adolphe, I watched, fascinated, a theatre-like production of something very different. A local theatre group performed it. They were putting on a story involving fire. Set in the future and to music, it was a real mini opera. There were some stunning displays of special effects using fire. In the darkness of the night the flames lit up the three hundred and sixty degree open stage. The audience watching were electrified and spellbound with the story, which involved some great music and dance. It was clever stuff.

In the old town, the music blasted out. A Tina Turner look-alike was doing her thing live on stage in one of the cobbled streets. The audience was lapping it up around her. Her regular fans gather to watch her. This year she was back with a vengeance. If only the real Tina Turner knew she had some serious competition here in Luxembourg. It made the night.

Beyond, in another old cobbled street, the music of today was blasting out from the platform that had been specially erected for the night. The youngsters were gyrating the night away. It was fun. It was happening. It was Luxembourg!

In the Place de Clairefontaine, another stage was alive with the sound of techno music. A huge TV screen showed various images. In the centre stood a statue of Grand Duchess Charlotte designed by a Parisian sculptor Jean Cardot.

Around the statue was a circle of benches at ninety degrees to the statue where you could rest and enjoy a beer or two.

In the older twisting street of the Rue du St-Esprit, which is on the edge of the former fortified wall, people partied in the street and in the smaller bars that were open. The open-air beer bars did a roaring trade. At several points during the night, you couldn't move in this street, as it was so full of partygoers. I bumped into several people I knew including some Irish, English and Italian friends, which made the night more fun.

The party goes on all night. If you can last the pace, it goes on until six in the morning. What a night, what a party. And oh, by the way, "Happy birthday Grand Duke" from everyone!

'The morning after the night before' is when most people sleep in, recovering from the party. Most people are oblivious to the next day's events. These are held in the centre of the city. They commence in the Avenue de la Liberté. Beginning at nine in the morning there is a presentation of arms to the Duke in front of the Arcelor building. Here a stand has been erected for the event. This is followed by a service in the Notre Dame Cathedral. Here I once saw all the ambassadors leaving in their posh cars afterwards. After the service and at around 11:45 there is a cannon salute. If you've been sleeping in and if you live in the vicinity you'll get your very own alarm call in the form of the cannon. That, certainly, is different, as it wakes you with a blast. (Get it blast—cannon! Another wasted one-liner!)

The celebrations were not over yet. I was in my flat recovering when, in the afternoon, I was interrupted by the sound of music. It was in the park behind where I live and the music I could hear was traditional jazz with a touch of "Oomph-par oomph-par stick-it-up-your-jumper" thrown in.

Well, it got the better of me and, as I needed to stretch the old legs, I rang my friend Chris and suggested a walk down to the fête. I also suggested a game of crazy golf at the course that was in the Pétrusse valley. Also, I wanted to see what was going on. Later that afternoon Chris arrived and we headed down the hill and deviated down the narrow steps that took us onto a path on the right of the viaduct bridge. We crossed the bridge that goes over the Pétrusse River and found ourselves along the Pétrusse valley where there was a small fête.

I found out later that the event was called 'Pétrusse on the beach.' We found ourselves watching the jazz band I had heard earlier. They were very good, but my—did they look a sight! It made my knobbly knees justice after seeing theirs. They wore a striped costume that added to the style of the band. They played some real traditional music that in the heat of the afternoon was really fun to listen to. The toy-town train known as the Pétrusse Express was doing a special service bringing people there and back from the Place de la Constitution.

The small fête was great. Here I discovered a German puppet show version of what we in England call Punch and Judy. In German it is called Kasper and Seppel. There's also Gretel as well. Oh, and I mustn't forget the crocodile and the gangsters. As it's for kids I didn't go in to view it. However, you could clearly see the characters through the doorway and the youngsters seemed well enthralled.

It was time for the crazy golf, which turned out to be next to the fête. Now, considering I've lived in Luxembourg for over two years it was actually my first time. The course is laid out by the side of the Pétrusse River and is inexpensive. I think it was two euros, which for a bit of fun was cheap. I'm afraid I lost by three stokes, but then there's always the rematch some time in the future.

A walk around the battlements followed. This took us over the Alzette River. In fact, in this area is where the Pétrusse River joins the Alzette River. Don't be deceived by the Pétrusse Rivers trickle. After a heavy period of rain it transforms into a normal sized river that cascades into the Alzette.

On the right side of the battlements (which incidentally are 'the original thing') is the railway bridge. In June 2003, the whole bridge was covered over. It was being modernised to become a larger topped bridge that will accommodate the new tram service together with the train service. The bridge was originally built by the British and normally stands there magnificently as it crosses the valley. On this day, it was covered in some form of sheeting to shield the scaffolding from view.

We climbed the stairs and rested at the top. With all these walks I do, I felt like one of the three men in the English television programme 'Last of the summer wine'. We headed up and had a nosey around the hospice up on the Rham plateau. Here the buildings have been converted from their former barracks into the hospice. These historical buildings look magnificent and the gardens in the huge inner courtyard area looked well tended. At the end of the courtyard was a huge modern tent-like construction. Here it looked as though the residents meet to view the entertainment that's laid on for them. Beyond this was a Mousel beer stand. Well, why not? Even when you reach your twilight years a little tipple and a glass of beer makes the day go better.

After this we headed down the Rue du Rham. This was actually blocked off at the end, as extensive new pipe work was being re-laid in the street and overall in the whole area. Instead we took some steep steps down and reached the Rue de Trèves.

We passed a new opening in the famous Wenceslas wall that runs on your right and now gives access to the new flats that have been installed in the renovated building below. This will certainly save the residents a long walk around the block. But if you suffer from vertigo, I can tell you it's a funny feeling looking down from the bridge that crosses over into the flats. All along we noticed that all the run-down properties that run along here were being renovated. This was probably a government initiative, as after years of neglect they were now saved for the future. This is a great idea as the area is one of the oldest parts of the city. For us, though, it was downhill into the Grund where we headed for Bonaparte's. One of the Ukrainian barmaids greeted us and we ordered a pint of Orange Juice and lemonade to round off the afternoon.

11

Summer in the City

There is nothing like sitting out on the Place de Paris watching the world go by. It's a wonderful experience which, if you get the chance, take it! When the sun is shining, it's the place to be. The scenery is wonderful. You'd be amazed by the number of pretty women that pass the time of day there—especially mid-afternoon.

The Place de Paris is also a great place to eat. At lunchtimes and in the evening it is packed with locals enjoying a variety of foods served from the restaurants that line one side of the Place. The beers are not bad either and there's nothing like spending time with your friends sipping a beer or two. The waitresses are friendly, the waiters polite. What more do you want?

In the summer the other main square to be seen sitting out on is the Place d'Armes in the old town. It's the place to be as it's the heart of Luxembourg. This is where everyone heads for. All the locals, expats and tourists eat here in the summer, sharing the moment together, watching the world go by.

The restaurants are on two sides of the square. Their tables spill over onto the central area, making it a delight to eat there. The people who are sitting at their tables enjoy the delight of the square.

Sitting under the trees in the Place d'Armes is wonderful as you enjoy your meal. One can relax and listen to the band playing from the bandstand. I find the atmosphere in the square improved by this live music that they play for your pleasure. As one of my neighbours commented, "There's nothing better than sitting outside Chi Chi's [the Mexican Restaurant] and listening to the band play, especially when they play Star Wars or Dallas." Well, each to their own!

In the summer months umpteen different bands play. Most tend to be brass bands and each band plays for a couple of hours. Each has a bandmaster. Bands come not just from Luxembourg but from all over Europe. There's even a school band from England that performs here—the Simon Ball School band from Hertford in Hertfordshire where I sometimes used to play rugby in my schooldays.

I must pause here to tell you a funny story—well, a relatively funny story. Over twenty years ago my parents first visited Luxembourg. They brought with them my Auntie Jean and my Nan, who I always called 'Nana'. (Both the latter two have sadly passed on.) They arrived in their taxi on a Saturday night ready for a good evening out in the Place d'Armes near the bandstand. They were already a little drunk and jolly when they arrived. My father paid for the taxi while the others waited. The taxi then drove away but, as it did so, ran over Auntie Jean's foot. Auntie Jean exclaimed in a surprised Manchester accent, "The taxis just run over my foot!" Everyone just burst out laughing, assuming she was joking. As it turned out, she wasn't! Fortunately, there was a restaurant nearby and Auntie Jean was assisted to a table. A waiter was then summoned with a view to bringing a serviette together with some cold water to ease the pain. The waiter rushed to comply. A cold compress was applied to stop the swelling and the pain. They were all laughing so much they became the centre of attention. Luckily, Auntie Jean wasn't too distressed and my parents persuaded her to sample a dish of snails. She put one in her mouth and with much face pulling, ate it. Cheers and clapping came from all the tables around. An American later came up to my mother and said, "Ma'am, I sure haven't laughed so much in years! When she said a taxi ran over her foot and she laughed about it, Gee, that was great!" After the meal, my father summoned another taxi. The taxi driver, on seeing what looked like two drunken women propping themselves up, took off smartish. Of course, my mother was propping up Auntie Jean whose foot by now was really hurting. They managed to get another taxi back to their hotel, and it was not until after she got back to Manchester that it was confirmed her foot was broken. She spent many weeks with her foot in plaster after that. One great thing about Auntie Jean was that she was always a great laugh, and in Luxembourg she had left her mark. The accident certainly made their holiday weekend in Luxembourg one to remember.

You sometimes feel as if you're in the 'Centre of Toy town' in this remarkable country; at other times you could be in the heart of some fairytale Kingdom. Whatever your thoughts, you're right in the centre of Luxembourg.

The Tourist Information office is located on the right-hand corner of the square, next door to the city hall. It's a very useful place to pick up information including city walks (see chapter: 'A walk in Luxembourg'). They sell some good mugs and T-shirts as well. If you need a local map or any other bit of advice, don't hesitate to ask them. They are most helpful.

Next door and the largest building in the square is the Town Hall. Its magnificent architectural design gives the square its edge (another bad pun!). It features on the many postcards of Luxembourg. On certain days, you can go inside.

During the year, there are lots of different exhibitions that go on. These are held upstairs on the first floor. Some exquisite crystal chandeliers hang gracefully from the high ceilings in the building. (They always remind me of the English television programme 'Only fools and horses' where, in one legendary sketch, Del Boy the lead character is taking a very large chandelier down. There were actually two and as the last screw was removed the chandelier was meant to be carefully lowered to enable it to be cleaned. Unfortunately, the wrong one had been unscrewed and it crashed to the ground and smashed. Del boy would probably see these chandeliers and say 'Luvly Juvly.') On the few occasions that I have dared to venture upstairs I've been impressed by the magnificent hall they have up there. It reminds me of a smaller Shire Hall that you get back home. One exhibition I saw was a Polish exhibition featuring the many regions of Poland. Another time, on the stair area, they held an exhibition of Old Photographs of Luxembourg City. These, taken by a local photographer years ago, were wonderful to see. So much of Luxembourg has changed over the years. Yet so much of it is still the same. I like the photographs of the old cars and buses. It's also interesting to see the way everyone used to dress, the hairstyles and the glasses they wore. My, how times change.

The other place to sit out on is in the Rue Dicks. The ideal place to sit out here is outside The White Rose. Its just off the Avenue de la Liberté. In the summer afternoons and evenings it is a joy to sit there and enjoy a few beers. Certainly, the expats and locals who drink there seem to think so.

Luxembourg does have some strange names. The Rue Dicks is one of them. There is also the Rue Bender. Neither have the name connotations that you might imagine. Rue Bender was named after Field Marshal de Bender who became famous during the siege of 1794-95.

Mind you, years ago part of the Rue Dicks where the Lord Nelson is situated used to be a much raunchier and livelier place than it is now. There used to be one or two cabaret bars and the Marivaux cinema was opposite.

In the old days when there used to be 'in town' cinemas, nearby bars used to heave. Now life appears to be more laid back. After ten o'clock at night, whilst some bars are busy, many of the bars around the Place de Paris are like a ghost town.

A big summer event is the 'Blues and Jazz' rally. The event is held on a Saturday night in July, primarily in the Grund but is also on in the Place d'Armes. Now, if you like jazz music, then this is one not to miss. For one amazing night, the whole of the Pétrusse valley from the Grund to Clausen is filled with the sound of good music. The night air is alive with the cool music that jazz brings. The festival is now so popular that on this night half the city appears to turn up, the streets heaving with people. So look out. And if it's a hot night, then the beer goes down even better.

In every bar and open area is a different form of jazz. If doesn't matter whether you are a traditional jazz buff or you simply prefer modern jazz, rhythm and blues or even soul. It's all here, under the stars and in the cobbled streets in one of the oldest parts of the city. This gives it just that edge on many of the other jazz festivals you might have been to before.

Forget the North Sea Jazz Festival. This is the Luxembourg version, unique and somehow special. To wander around the lower castle area watching the flames rising inside the hot air balloons on display in the stillness of the night is awesome. The beer is flowing and there is food to sample. People are happy. To experience the wonder of the night is a must. You can bump into old friends en route. The old city walls stare across at you from across the river. The old cobbled bridge crossing the Alzette River in the Grund is full of partygoer's in-between locations, listening and watching the various jazz artists around.

The food stalls sell everything from chicken curry to beef spare ribs. Then there are the freshly cooked sardines, not forgetting the Luxembourg Hot Dog stalls that help to soak up the beer when the stomach demands attention.

Out of every historic brick in the narrow cobbled streets in the Grund, the music on this night vibrates. The night itself appears to bring the old past of the city and the present together, for one glorious moment. A crowd gathers down at Clausen where a German jazz band plays to its audience, spellbound in the open area opposite Mousel's Canteen. The twinkling of the stars in the night sky seem to reflect the rhythm of the music as the party continues. Yes, the sounds of boogie-woogie through to the Chicago blues are here. There is also original Dixieland and mainstream jazz on this night.

There are open-air stages which, if you can find a bit of space, are a delight to watch. In the pubs, the rooms are jam-packed with bodies all eagerly enjoying the moment as the music plays.

The open-air jazz party goes on till three in the morning. The crowd gradually drifts away, back to their beds after a memorable hot summer night in the Grund.

Various music festivals are held in and around Luxembourg during the summer months. Taking the Carnival of Cultures' place in June 2003 was the third festival of Latin Cultures in the Place Guillaume. It was a night of different rhythms that ranged from plenty of salsa to Miami and New York jazz music. There was plenty of Cuban music, too. The local group Salsabor and Xaman-ek played. Other festivals are held periodically on the Holy Spirit plateau where local bands play.

Around the middle of July in the city is a weekend of 'Rock un Knuedler'—a large open-air free music festival held in the Place Guillaume where the 'Top of the Bill' act plays. In recent years, we've had The Scorpions from Germany and before that was Manfred Mann's Earth Band. Both were packed out and a good night was had by one and all. In 2003, Candy Duffer and Band, together with The Original Blues Brothers, hit the headlines. Certainly, you do get the big bands playing here in Luxembourg. Black Sabbath, Deep Purple, Richie Blackmore, Status Quo, The Rolling Stones, Uriah Heep and Wishbone Ash—they have all been here. In 2003 we saw more up-to-date bands including Massive Attack play here in Luxembourg. If you're into Techno music, a huge one-night gathering was held at Kirchberg in mid-July at the Foires Internationales de Luxembourg. In the summer of 2003 Elton John, Simply Red, Simple Minds, ZZ Top and sixties legends Canned Heat played in Luxembourg.

In August, spread over a weekend, is the annual Anno Domini festival. This is held in the old town and is actually a medieval festival including a medieval market. The locals all dress up in medieval costumes. Unfortunately the first time I saw this festival it was a wet rainy day. So for me it was all a bit of a washout. On a sunny day I'm told it's a wonderful experience. Certainly, the evening I attended on another year was very raucous and lively. There are some great medieval musicians and craftsmen to see and for an afternoon or evening, it makes an alternative day out and takes the area back to its origins.

Other smaller festivals held in the summer period include an annual street artist's day that is held in the centre of town, and a festival down by the Gare features sand sculptures. Both are held in August.

The summer is officially rounded off in August with the Schueberfouer. This is one gigantic fair, which is to be found up on the Glacis at Limpertsberg. It runs from around the third week in August through to the end of the first week in September. In days gone by it was a sheep fair, created by its founder John the

Blind, Count of Luxembourg, King of Bohemia. It has matured and is now a modern real Luxembourgish Fun Fair. "Roll Up. Roll Up. It's all the fun of the fair." Indeed, it is! Watch out for those bumper cars. You can't beat those dodgems, can you? What about the Big Wheel? Throw a dart and win a giant tiger toy. Sample some Luxembourgish hot dogs. Try the delights of the small Luxembourgish sideshows. Stop for a Luxembourgish beer. On a hot night, I can't think of anything better. The fair attracts everyone and it brings the whole family out. It gives them a good night out together.

'Summer in the City' is officially rounded off early in September with a grand finale. Each year it is a little different. In 2003 there was a stunning presentation called 'Viva Brazil' held in the afternoon and evening in the Places d'Armes.

There is also a giant fireworks display held up at the Glacis to end the Schueberfouer. There's nothing like finishing the summer with a bang. How was your summer?

Summer in the City in 2001 saw an invasion all over Luxembourg City of many cows. These were, however, artificial cows made either of papier-maché or of whatever and were a result of a competition called 'Art on cows'—to create and then paint your allotted cow. There was a prize for the best-designed cow. The cows were of various shapes but one particular cow shape stood out. It was of a cow standing up. There were more of these than any other position. However, every single one was different in its painted design. Certainly, they proved hugely popular and everyone had their favourite cow. At the end of the summer they were auctioned off. I would have liked to have had one, but it would have been a bit difficult getting a large cow up the stairs to the flat. The thing I found amazing was that they survived over three months in the elements without being vandalised. If it had been anywhere else they wouldn't have lasted five minutes. I cherished the hope that they would revive the competition.

Perhaps my hope was in vain. In the first week of June during the summer of 2003, some strange objects mysteriously appeared in selected spots around town. They were an exhibition of 'art in steel'. Many of the objects were circular in shape and were the year's modern art attraction, designed by established artists. These steel artistic circles were huge, but there were also other shapes made of steel. Each one was unique in its design and it looks. Their creators and designers must have put in hours of work to build them. Now metalwork was never my hot point, so I have to admire their skills for the finished product. However, I have to be honest—I still prefer the cows!

12

Salsa, Salsa, Salsa!

The climate in Luxembourg is different from that of the UK. It's more extreme. At first, you may not notice much difference. Once you've lived here a while you'll begin to notice these things.

I remember sitting in an internet café bar one day called Sparkies. There was a guy in there obviously waiting for friends. Other people were around and he was happy to talk. He was a real London boy—from the East End, by the sound of him. Somehow the conversation got round to the weather. More importantly, it got round to the winter weather.

"Oh, you haven't lived here till you've experienced the winter," he said. Then he added, "It's harsh, minus sixteen degrees Celsius sometimes."

I didn't pay close attention to the story until one day in my first December in Luxembourg. I'd been to my usual pub before going on to El Compañero, just off Place d'Armes where it's a great place to have a beer.

You can feel the music hitting you as you walk in off the street. It hits you in a rush of hot air that escapes and winds its way down the street. The atmosphere is electric with the rhythm of the salsa beat from the bar and from the dance floor in the cavern below. It's a great experience to go downstairs and into the cave. This is where the salsa action takes place. Huge rusting broken edged mirrors make the place look bigger than it is—the arch of the cave lined with cigarette smoke, the dancers on the dance floor wrapped round each other, the music pulsating with the many salsa beats. Suddenly it's the Merengue beat. Dancers swap partners. New bodies hit the dance floor. Hot, tired and by now sweaty bodies head for the bar.

It's music and dance, dance and more dance, right up to when the action has to stop. It's been a busy night. It's December and the Christmas parties are in full swing. The restaurant upstairs has been packed, the diners enjoying the night of a thousand salsa rhythms. Suddenly it's over and its time to head outside and back home for the revellers.

For my friend Jane and I it was off to The White Rose to meet her boyfriend who is not a salsa dancer. The cold of the night hit us hard in our faces. The last bus had long since left the terminus and there wasn't a taxi in sight. We decided to walk to the pub, down the Avenue de la Liberté in what felt like artic conditions. Boy, was it cold! We were well wrapped up—you needed to be. Only a fool would have gone out without a coat. Here, when it's cold, it's *cold*. In fact, it was almost as bad as Moscow on a winter's night.

This particular night I could feel the frost on my ears and nose. I was wearing a hat, for without it, I felt, I would have become frozen. We stumbled on. It felt like forever on that winter's night. Finally, we made it. We were greeted with a warm friendly welcome on our arrival from our regular drinking friends. I even had a Glühwein to warm me up. The fact that it wasn't a Glühwein but merely a hot red wine as the bar had sold out didn't matter. To warm ones stomach up after nearly freezing felt great. It rounded off the evening nicely.

At this point you join the action seven months after I had had an accident with my foot! That meant no salsa—on doctor's orders. When you have a bad foot, which I did, I can assure you the pain soon stops any form of exercise and that includes salsa. But I did go to my first salsa lesson since the accident, you'll be pleased to hear. I was a bit nervous, as I had not danced since mid October the previous year. I had taken a trip about five weeks before on the number 11 bus to discover exactly where I had to go for a possible future lesson. I say this because in the time since my last course the salsa school had changed locations. Originally they were at the 'Champs Elysées école de dance' in the Rue de Hollerich. Now they were at 'The Centre' up the route de Longwy. It is a great place. The dance floor was larger and so are the mirrors. From the city centre, it's only ten minutes on the bus and the buses run every half hour.

The original location was a great dance school. I went every Tuesday but there were lessons on a Thursday as well. The lessons ranged from beginners to intermediate and advanced. Generally, when one arrives the previous lesson is still in progress. If you're lucky enough you can walk in and watch the advanced or intermediates in action. How they do it amazes me. I have two left feet when it comes to dancing. John Travolta I am not! I'm merely a beginner when it comes to salsa.

The good thing about salsa here in Luxembourg is that it's very popular. Many nationalities of both sexes go to the lessons. There are many Italians, French, Luxembourgers and Belgians, not to mention the many Portuguese, Brazilians, English, Russians and Filipinos who go as well. There was even a Japanese and Malaysian girl in the class. Don't let me forget the Germans, the Greek girl and the Spanish girls. There's always such a rich mixture of people. It's like a sweetshop. Most people tend to be early twenties to late forties, but it goes beyond that for salsa dancing has no age barriers. There is none of this dance age-ism here, which, I think, is a good thing. With salsa, thankfully, it doesn't matter who your partner is.

Over the weeks of the salsa course you get to know your partners and they get to know you. There are some girls who are really good at dancing. (And some are bloody awful! But then there are some men who, according to the girls I talk to, are also awful.) The girls have told me on many occasions I'm terrible. I think a memorable occasion was when a Luxembourgish girl said to me, "You're not lis-tening to the beat of the music." Indeed, I was no doubt lost in my own counting world whilst practising with her in the dance lesson. Nevertheless we remain very good friends!

An English friend I met in 'El Compañero' on one of those wild late salsa nights told me, "If you're a guy and you're a beginner, then it's very frustrating standing watching the dancers in action," and he added: "You desperately want to get up on the dance floor and join in the action." He went on to explain, "With the energetic salsa beat many beautiful girls are wanting and waiting to be asked to dance. To be unable to is very frustrating."

Why? Because the guy has to lead the girl. The girl will go where the guy leads her. This is fine if you're experienced, but if you stand there and watch the cou-ples in action you begin to wonder if you can ever reach their level? To go onto the dance floor and start doing level one or two beginners' movements with the girls is downright embarrassing for the guy. It is, honestly. I know exactly what my friend meant. When you watch these guys glide around the dance floor with a different girl, each time doing one hundred and one salsa movements that you have yet to learn, it makes you more determined than ever to give it a go.

At the beginning of the class we all line up in front of the huge mirror that stretches right across the width of the dance room and reaches from the floor to the ceiling. I don't look a pretty sight in that mirror. (I've got a forty-something beer belly. Personally, I put it down to my sway back.) Still, off we all go, follow-ing the dance teacher who is called César. To begin with he shows us how to stretch. You're taught to use muscles in your body that you've probably never used before. The first few weeks can make you ache like hell afterwards if you're not fit. I'm not fit. Still, it's all part of the fun. We learn to move our shoulders forwards and backwards, keeping them always downwards in the motion.

"You're not doing aerobics," César yells at us all.

We move on, stretching to the right and then to the left, keeping our shoulders and hips straight. Try it. It's not easy. Just to prove the point, we all tried a little exercise whereby you join into a threesome. Two of you then hold the other person's stretched out arms whilst they try to stretch their body to the left and right from the waist up. It's not easy and I have still to master it.

Meanwhile, as an 'Absolute Beginner' in the salsa lesson, you're taught to count to the beat: 'One two three, pause, five six seven, pause…' The lesson I was in was 'Beginners two'—but you'll use this count in all your movements at whatever level you are.

After the exercises everyone is spread out in a circle around the room. You find yourself a partner who you team up with. It doesn't matter who this is, as the dance teacher's policy is, ever so often, to call out: "Change!"

The guys stay where they are and the girls move on one place in an anticlockwise direction. Now here's the good thing if you're a guy—there are generally more girls than guys! To solve this, the dance teacher moves, for example, the three girls that remain on their own and puts them in-between the couples. That way, when he says, "Change," they all get a dance. It's called 'waiting your turn.'

There were weeks, though, when it was the guys who were in this position. César, the dance teacher, does try to even things out. If there's a shortage of one sex and there happens to be a few people left over from the previous lesson, he will ask them to volunteer their services on the dance floor. No one complains, as it gives you a partner. For the person volunteering it's a great way of practising. Even experienced dancers need practice. What is that old phrase? Practice makes perfect. How true. The trouble is that I need lots of practice.

Onto the rest of the lesson. The dance teacher gives instructions to everyone. The names of the movements are mostly in Spanish. Whilst I know the names when the lesson is in progress, can I remember them outside the lesson? Like hell I can!

César, who incidentally is Spanish, speaks perfect English. He's a real gentleman and is also a real ladies man. In the lesson girls seem to just fall at his feet. He can spin them round and make them do things they simply can't do when they're with us not so experienced guys. He's a lucky man! The lessons are in English.

César has a dance partner called Louise, who is English. She's a lovely girl and is always there to help you. Both of them will come to your rescue when things go wrong.

There are some couples who prefer not to change partners and keep together during the lesson. I can imagine a few arguments going on when trying to get the step right. Certainly, when they get home and practise the movements there will probably be a few heated arguments with one-half saying, "It's not like that but like this," etc. It's not always easy, especially if you've missed a lesson or you're not as naturally gifted in picking up the movements as some people are. Let's face it—to do salsa you need to *feel* the music, the rhythm and the beat. It's also got to be a good feeling otherwise there's no point in doing it. Try it and you may surprise yourself.

I met some old salsa friends at the Atmosphere Bar after my first salsa class since my accident. They joked, saying I must be the best pupil in the class. Indeed, in my new salsa class I'm currently 'King of the salsa,'—a status to be savoured to the full since it was the only time it was achieved in the 'Beginners two' lesson! I could actually help my partners out when some of them needed a little more practice than others. I liked that. The class seemed to learn at a different pace. As Louise commented after the lesson, "You haven't forgotten the moves then." I was happy. I had returned and I was content to relearn the basics. It had been a good night.

I used to drink regularly in The White Rose in the evenings during my first few mad months in Luxembourg. It was fun. It was escapism from the office. It was also a good way of meeting people. A friend of mine, Andrew, who I met there, once said to me when I had been here a few months, "Why don't you do something other than keep drinking in this pub every night?" I must just add here that it wasn't *every* night—though it was almost every night! He said, "Why don't you join a salsa class like I did? It's a great way to meet the ladies."

You know what—he was right, and join I did! I never looked back.

Of course, when you learn salsa as I have, you soon discover that there is salsa and there is salsa. In simple English, being the simple Englishman I am, this means there are many different styles of salsa, including 'L.A. Style'—that's 'Los Angeles style' salsa that César teaches in most of his courses, which is danced in linear motion with the girl moving backwards and forwards. In fact, this is the current fad and the more linear style salsa. More 'Cuban' teachers are switching to this.

Cuban style salsa, or Casino, is danced in a circular movement with the guy and girl turning around each other. Then there is also the Miami salsa, which is different, but don't ask me to get technical. Two other styles include Puerto Rican and New York salsa, but I don't know either of these, yet!

César has also been teaching the Rueda de Casino, which is a salsa danced by many couples at the same time in a circle with couples exchanging their partners between the different moves. This dance is suitable for people above the beginners two/three level; the level varies depending on which salsa school you attend.

There are many salsa schools here in the City of Luxembourg, which I find surprising considering the size of the city. All have good teachers. However, César and Louise are rated top of the list in a lot of people's eyes, including mine. They *are* good. They also perform in their own right at salsa dance festivals around the region.

Yes, salsa is danced and taught not just in Luxembourg. If you head over the border into Germany there is a salsa school in Trier and one in Saarbrücken. If you head south into France and go down to Metz then you'll find a salsa school down there. Then there's all the salsa bars in these cities. Even I don't know all of them.

In Belgium, except in Brussels, salsa schools seem harder to find. This also applies in other border towns near to Luxembourg like Thionville and Longwy in France. In Longwy, the girls who come from there advise me that there is no salsa, and not a lot to do. Welcome to Luxembourg, girls!

In the early days of salsa in Luxembourg Óscar Guzmán (known as "El loco de la salsa") was the only one organising salsa events. In recent years DJ Freddie has also organised many events and even created a Luxembourg salsa website which has helped to boost awareness. It is 'www.Salsaspirit.com'.

Without Freddy and Óscar the salsa scene in Luxembourg would be much poorer. In fact, these two respected names are salsa pioneers here in the Grand Duchy. Today they are joined by other DJ's.

The original salsa bar in Luxembourg City is the legendary El Compañero; certainly it was the only one when I started learning. It used to heave on a Thursday, Friday and Saturday night. These days other bars have salsa nights, probably to attract the custom.

I've already mentioned the Atmosphere Bar here in town, situated off the Rue de Hollerich. It was dead handy after the Champs Elysées école de dance school lessons had finished, as it was just opposite. If you want to Salsa these days it is probably one of the best venues in town. Anyway its floor area at the back of the X-Shaped bar is huge enough to allow everyone a dance. It's in the area where there are a host of other trendy bars, like The Cat Club, The Elevator, and The Bronx, which is in a group of bars in one complex, including The Marx bar.

The Full Monty Bar also does salsa classes. Salsa nights run on Wednesdays, Fridays and Saturdays. The bar is at Kirchberg next to Auchan. A car is handy as taxis are not cheap going home from there, and the number 18 bus only runs up to just after midnight. I feel like Cinderella when suddenly you have to leave the action and catch the last bus home. I hate asking for a lift. Whilst some people don't mind asking, it's not me.

Talking of Kirchberg, if you check out Utopolis, the ten-screen cinema centre, there is also a surprisingly large hall at the far end from the main entrance. Every so often they host salsa festivals that are great fun. These salsa nights attract a host of experienced and inexperience dancers into the hall.

I myself have been to a fair few up there and loved every minute of it. I meet many of my salsa friends up there. It's only here that you see the regular clan of salsa goers who attend the dance schools. What better place to show off your dance skills after all the practising you've been doing. (In my case it's more a case of, 'Should have been practicing more.') At these events you get everyone just having a good night out, which is nice as it throws together a melting pot of writhing bodies in rhythm to the music.

The events are colourful, with names like Barrio Latino. You get the feel of it straight away. The music comes from the likes of DJ Freddy (Latin Classic) and DJ Ronaldo (Brazilian Beat). Some of these events host top dance competitions, which attract all the good dancers competing for that top prize. (Somehow I don't think I'll be winning any prizes just yet.) Even RTL, the local television station, turn up occasionally to film the best dancers.

I personally like it when they have a live band on. Be it a Luxembourgish Latin band or the real thing matters not. But I do love it even more when they roll out the Brazilian dancers. 'Oh man!'—heads turn if you're lucky enough to see them. The girls are dressed in full carnival costume—as are the guys, for that matter, though I'm not concerned about them. The dancers shake their bodies to the music. The costumes leave little to the imagination, which is probably why they are so popular with the men. To be fair, they're an eye catcher and it certainly makes them 'the icing on the cake' as far as I am concerned. The fact that it's nice to meet your friends of many nationalities is immaterial when the Brazilian girl dancers come on stage.

Another place that rocks to the salsa beat is the Brasserie de l'Arret. This is located at number 365 route de Longwy. They host Fete Latino-Cubaine nights with Cuban music and live bands playing. Two other places include Boca Chica in the Rue Côte d'Eich on some Sunday nights and Pulp on a Thursday night.

Luxembourg City is not the only place in Luxembourg that hosts salsa nights. Luxembourg's second city, Esch-sur-Alzette, has various Cuban festivals, usually held at the Kulturfabrik concert venue.

Salsa is a big thing here in the Grand Duchy. I get to hear about all these events via the internet. I seem to get wads of 'What's on' flyers, which is nice as it keeps me up to date with what's really happening. There seems to be something going on most weekends throughout the year.

Now I mentioned that Belgium was not a hot salsa spot. Well, to be fair, there are some bars up in Brussels that do it. However, I've not had the pleasure, yet...

13

Dancing on water, practising on land

In the summer of 2002, a few friends and I drove over via the motorway to Trier, in Germany, for a salsa cruise. We were a real mixed bunch of nationalities, which I find nice. There was me, the Englishman, a Swedish blonde, a Belgium chap, an Italian, an Italian Luxembourger, several Luxembourgers, some French, and a Cuban guy. Once we were on the boat there were, not surprisingly, a lot of Germans.

Now, I always love going into Germany, as it's a good day out. It gets you out of the flat and on this particular trip put me in the company of some great people.

Our trip to Germany was the salsa highlight of the summer. This was because it followed a year of lessons together. The boat was actually moored on the Moselle River, about thirteen kilometres downstream from Trier City centre. The motorway literally runs right overhead and there's a large camping site next to the moorings of the boat. The actual place of departure was from a small village called Schweich. It was a gorgeous day and after a slight delay we cast off, heading, I guess, eastwards down the Moselle. It was the first time I had seen that part of the river.

Meanwhile, on the boat, inside on the lower deck, a free salsa class took place. The salsa teacher lined everyone up on both sides of the room. The lesson was generally for beginners. A series of basic moves followed after which we were all paired off and more practise continued. (After all, they do say 'practise makes perfect.') There were a lot of novices on board who had never done salsa before. There were also experienced dancers who were called upon to help the beginners out. As usual, there were more girls than blokes, so for the men there was more of a choice of partner. You'll soon know who is any good at salsa dancing. But then, on this particular cruise, it didn't matter, as it was all just a bit of fun. It's was also a good way to make new friends. 'Guten Tag!'

The small towns and villages came and went as we cruised past. It was fun and the sun was shining as we sat out on deck sampling a few German beers, watching the world go by. We were there to 'enjoy!' There were two dance areas on the top deck. One was undercover; the other out on the open deck, which is where the main action was happening. People were dancing all over it, including me. As we danced along the river the vineyards surrounded us, their vines almost ripe for harvesting, their grapes growing bigger every day in the summer sun, their rows neatly kept in the rolling countryside.

At some point upstream there were some very large hills, cliff-like in places, which looked magnificent. Some vineyards are literally perched on top of these cliffs. Others follow the steep sides of the hills as they climb sharply upwards. The river meanders along the valley.

The boat at some point turns around and heads slowly back to base. En-route we even saw a flying cow. Yes, it really *was* a flying cow. In fact, it was a very large flying cow and it was about two hundred feet in the air. All right, it was a hot air balloon, shaped like a cow. But that's still a flying cow, right? It was yellow and white. Did it have spots? I don't think it did.

The salsa boat was described as a 'Tropical Party on the Moselle'—which I suppose it was. 'Romantic and passionate' is how the trip was also described. I'm not sure about that bit, as I didn't encounter any romance. Still, there's always next time…

Well, the next time was nearly a year later. The word got around that there was 'another salsa boat trip' at Trier. Those that knew about it and had been before were very interested. As for the rest, well, let's say they missed out.

There was a slight mix-up on my part with the rendezvous point, for, not having a car, I got the wrong place for the park and ride pick up point. Thank God for mobile phones! Still, off we went and this time I hitched a ride with my Belgian friend and, together with two Spanish girls and an Italian guy, we headed over to Trier.

Much to my surprise we ended up at the same place as the previous year. Our other friends had gone ahead of us but we had all met up outside the boat. The sun was shining. God, was it hot! It must have been over thirty-three degrees. We all made our way to the boat. Luckily the advance party had got the tickets; otherwise we would have been disappointed. The trip was sold out and people were later being turned away.

As I walked the gangplank the German lady at the boat's entrance recognised me from the last trip. Amazing! I mean, out of all the people who get on the boat, she recognised me. We greeted each other, exchanging niceties. But then she said, "The same procedure as last year." Instantly, I knew exactly to what she was referring, and I added, "The same procedure as last year."

We smiled…

Okay. I'll explain!

Up until I had been in Luxembourg for a year and a half I had never heard this phrase before. In fact, an English friend lent me a video that showed me exactly what it is all about.

Years ago, and I mean early 1950's, or even slightly before, a famous British comic, Freddie Frinton, recorded a sketch with another famous female comic May Warden. It was recorded and performed in Germany on the NDR network whilst they were on tour. Anyway, the sketch was called 'Dinner for One' or 'Der 90. Geburtstag'. Translated, this means 'The 90th birthday party'. Its set in a dining room of a big old English house. Its owner, Miss Sophie, is by now a very old lady, and there's her butler James, played by Freddie Frinton. The guests are seated in the same seats year in and year out. But by now the years have rolled by and, apart from the old lady Miss Sophie and the butler James, the other guests have all died. Nevertheless their places remain set for them, as before. Dinner is then served and the wine is drunk. The butler, not wishing to waste the wine or upset Miss Sophie, drinks the toast on behalf of the missing persons. Hence the stage is set for a very funny sketch.

The whole thing lasts for about ten minutes. I cannot ever remember seeing it on UK television. You see, it's before my time—I'm not that old! My mother and father would know it. However, in Germany everyone from knee height upwards knows it!

Somehow, it has become a German national institution. It's even shown here in Luxembourg on RTL, the local Luxembourgish TV station on New Year's Eve. I suppose you could only compare it with the Morecambe and Wise Christmas shows on BBC 1 in the UK—shows that have become 'classics'. Every year on one of the German channels the sketch is still aired. Millions of Germans watch it, because…well, because "It is the same procedure as last year." And by now I hope you've got the joke.

The actual salsa trip was awesome. It was yet another opportunity 'to salsa' amongst the vineyards. The boat was full, the music played and the party got into full swing. Indeed, it was 'the same procedure as last year.'

The only difference was the variety and number of partygoers. Certainly I met many more Germans on the trip and I find it terrifically interesting to compare the lifestyle in Luxembourg to that in Germany. Even the salsa is done differently. The salsa teacher on the boat seemed to love himself. At least with César it's more structured. César just loves the women. I can't blame him.

Most German girls I spoke to had been to Luxembourg once and most came from the surrounding towns around. However, one girl I danced with had lived in Berlin before.

On the boat I discovered the German view on living with many nationalities is a bit like I found the Dutch view, which I had got the week before when I had visited friends in northeast Holland. Let me explain. In Luxembourg City you cannot go anywhere without bumping into many nationalities. It's what makes the place special. Trying to explain this concept of mixed nationality living is hard work. In Germany and Holland, the people I spoke to preferred to live amongst their own nationality, and I got the impression they don't like other cultures invading their lives.

There was a big contingent over from Luxembourg, most of whom I knew, and the majority of whom were of the salsa clan. I met the typical English lady in her fifties, living abroad. Very prim and British, but also a very good friend. Then there were a lot of ex-salsa people, including a lady with her bad back, a Canadian lady and some French and Luxembourgers. Also on board was a large party of German guys out for a stag party. There was much merriment but no trouble. As usual there were also considerably more girls to guys, which was fine by me.

As it was a very hot day the boat had passed hundreds of people enjoying the day who were camping out all along the Moselle River. They waved as the boat passed. Small speedboats were out en masse, and people were even swimming in the river. There was another small party of blokes fishing. One even gave the partygoers a cheap thrill by doing a 'moony' followed by a 'Full Monty' at them. Nice! You should have seen the girls rush over to watch.

The salsa dance floors were packed. The party flowed. The sweat dripped off the bodies of the dancers. Their clothes wet through due to the heat of the moment. A gentle breeze occasionally passed by to cool you down.

On the return leg the sun descended over the vineyards, its red glow reflecting off the ripple-less river. On deck the lights went on and the party entered a new phase. Then suddenly it was over and the boat was back where it had started. The moment had been reached when the trip had finished and it was time to head back over the border.

It had been a great day out. But it wasn't over yet. No, far from it. We had all decided it would be a good idea to continue the moment and head off for a salsa bar on the Route de Longwy. As it turned out, this was a Cuban bar I had not been to before. It turned into a bit of an anticlimax after the boat but proved to be just the tonic to mellow out. Certainly, the Cuban owner went out of his way to welcome us, which I thought was very decent since some just don't bother. Though the place was somewhat quiet after our trip to Trier, a few good Cuban rums warmed our bellies and, whilst the music played, we chilled out, enjoying the lateness of the night. Before long it was time to head home after what had been a very long, tiring but fun day.

You'll be pleased to know that the salsa classes I attended were a total success, apart from being a lot of fun. The class, which had come on a long way in a short space of time, was indeed a rich mixture of nationalities and I met many new friends. It also had its usual mixture of rich divorcees, girls in their early to mid twenties, married ladies, couples, older men having the night off from their wives, single guys and single women—everyone enjoying the "One two three, pause, five six seven, pause" that goes with the beat of the music. The exercises at the beginning of the class have continued. They developed into further movements of the shoulders going backwards and forwards, to the left and to the right. The latest technique learnt was to move your arms and hands in a certain way, in line with the movement of your feet. César makes it all look so easy. He shows you how not to do it, and then how to do it properly. At the end of the course he said, "Practice, practice, practice, and if you can, practice at home during the holidays."

At the end of the course we learnt the romantic technique when doing the salsa. Of course it depends who your partner is as to whether the dance ends up romantic or just a dance. After all, it takes two to tango…or should that be salsa?!

César once said to the class, "Guys, look at the girl. Look straight ahead at her." This was all very well, except at the time I was dancing with a two-metre tall Russian girl. Now, I'm not so tall so all I could see was her large boobs staring at me. Actually, dancing with a really tall girl can be a problem, since she would need to bend down a little so both partners can turn.

Once we had mastered the basic step, we went on to learn other movements and positions, including the 'abrazo' or, to translate into English, 'the Cuddle', where the man ends up with his arms wrapped around the lady, a rather popular movement with most guys.

All the movements and positions have such colourful names—names that are normally either expressed in Spanish or, if they are of American origin, in English. Examples include Guapea/Stop and Go, Abierto/Open, Dile que no/ Tell her no, Kentucky, and also the Hammerlock, a slightly entangled position that sounds like it comes more from the wrestling world than that of dance.

The list of positions is almost endless and it would indeed be impossible to explain what each name represents on paper. The best way to understand what all this means and to find out more would be to go to a salsa lesson.

Some of the movements we learnt in the 'Beginners 2' class are easier than others. Unfortunately, I do find the Spanish names hard to remember. I know how to do the movement in the class, but if I get it wrong, the girl I am dancing with soon tells me.

Since I started my salsa lessons one thing I have discovered is that salsa schools change ownership on a fairly regular basis. That generally means a new name on the door. Salsa teachers also seem to move locations fairly regularly. So keeping up with who is where and when is a challenge in itself.

Current dance schools with salsa classes include Body Basics in the Avenue de la Gare, Fitness Zone in Howald, The Full Monty at Kirchberg, École de Dance in Hollerich, Boca Chica in the Rue Côte d'Eich, and FlashDance (formerly The Centre) in the Route d'Arlon.

Sometimes a change of teacher is worth considering. You might learn a different approach. My salsa friends recommend a variation of teachers, styles and dance school venues—"To broaden your salsa experience," is what they tell me.

However, wherever you are it's nice to be able to go down to the Atmosphere Bar after the lesson and practice what you have learnt with whoever is down there. On the last lesson of the course, most of the class made the effort to go down there, and everyone had a great time.

Now, I have to admit, some of my salsa friends are way advanced of me. I'm therefore a little wary of asking the relevant girls for a dance when I know they know one hell of a lot more movements than I do. But remember what I was told at the beginning—it's difficult if you're a guy. But wait, as I discovered. If you do actually ask the girls, they'll still dance with you, and even though it's basic to them, it doesn't matter—not really.

Finally, I'll leave you with the thought that one of my German friends mentioned to me. He said, "When a girl leaves Luxembourg, she will remember Luxembourg for one thing—the salsa."

It's probably a very true comment. But to be fair—and to ensure I'm not branded a sexist—let me affirm that the comment applies equally to guys!

14

A day out in Luxembourg

Now, as you may have established, Luxembourg is not exactly the largest place on earth. Nevertheless, there's more than enough to do if you fancy a change from the pub. There are some great places to visit which, if you are here for a while, you should make the effort and try them. You can take the train to some but once out of the city a car is better. This is especially so if you have friends or family coming over for the weekend.

If you need a car, then there are the car hire companies that have a variety of cars to suit your need. Most are situated up at the airport including Budget, Hertz and Avis. There's also Avis down at the Gare. If you don't have a car then a number 9 or the LuxAir bus should get you to the airport to pick one up should you opt to pick it up from there. The Gare (station) is a more convenient pick up point if time is against you.

So where do you go? Well, there's a multitude of places to visit, it just depends on what you want to do and what your guests fancy seeing. Certainly, the comment I hear most is that a lot of new expats haven't been up north, which is a really scenic area. Most who do head for Vianden, where there is a huge restored castle. Some go up to the area known as Little Switzerland. Others head for Esch-sur-Sûre where the lake is. Going south eastwards will take you down to Remich to see the boats on the Moselle River. Whatever your taste, you'll find it here in Luxembourg.

But have you thought of going down a mine? That sounds different, doesn't it? I can assure you it *is* different and because of this, I can thoroughly recommend this excursion to an old disused iron ore mine in Rumelange.

Now, admittedly you won't be arriving at it quite like I did. I went in a friend's Porsche Boxster that cruised down from Luxembourg City heading for the south of the country to a small town called Rumelange. You can get to it either by taking the A3 motorway or, as we did, by going on the A4 down to Esch-sur-Alzette, where we took the scenic route across to Rumelange.

It's worth considering lunch on your trip and there are a few good restaurants in the town. These range from the local Pizzeria to more than one or two Chinese restaurants. We actually sampled the delights of a Mongolian restaurant, which for me was a first. If you're lucky you might even get frogs legs served up as part of your meal. These aren't too bad after all I had heard about them.

The disused iron ore mine is a short drive away from the centre of town and is signposted. On arrival there is parking. There's also a nice little café should the weather not be sunny.

There are various types of tour around the mine. We opted for the full tour, which I can thoroughly recommend. One very important point here—make sure you don't leave it too late to get your ticket or you'll be disappointed. Try and get there and get your ticket well before 3pm, because the last tour leaves at 4pm and if all the seats are allocated you'll have gone a long way for nothing and feel as if you had a wasted journey. I speak from personal experience from my second trip.

The tour will take you around the mine museum that describes the history of the mine and why it closed down. It also displays some great pictures of years gone by, including examples of life in the mine. Next, it's time to be kitted out with a safety hat. This is very important if you're going into a mine. A short walk will take you to the rail platform where you can board the train. This is not your average train. This is a mine train. It's very low, narrow and small.

The train journey starts and after a short overland trip, once the barrier opens up, you're in the tunnel heading for the centre of the mine. It's dark, naturally, but there are lights to see with. I always thought you went *down* a mine. Here you go *into* it. There are labyrinths of tunnels, which stretch over seven kilometres; one even stretches over the border into France.

The full tour will show you around the heart of the mine, which is fascinating. As you head out, the daylight hits you. You may need to take a jumper with you or something warm even if it is the hottest of days. Inside the mine it's not hot. It's a good day out and will show you the importance that iron ore once had for the area in the past.

Another trip to consider is one to the Second World War museum at Diekirch. Here you can see all manner of things connected with the period. Now I studied the Second World War as part of my history lessons, but when it came to the Ardennes it was always a little vague. Here you will learn what happened during that time of the Battle of the Bulge. The John Wayne film of the same

name does no justice to the towns in question, but it does show some of the brav-
ery of the people on both sides who were killed. The museum covers the whole of
the war in Luxembourg during the time the country was first occupied by the
Nazis, during the occupation years, the Liberation by the Allies through to the
end of the war itself.

If you're into old cars and vehicles there are a few classics on display. I personally love the old American Jeeps I think most men of my generation and older
would secretly like to own. It must be all those movies I used to watch. I did find
the excursion more of a lad's trip out but some girls might thoroughly enjoy it as
well. Families are welcome.

One of the most scenic places to see in Luxembourg is The Ardennes. One of
the best trips to take is to the lake area around Esch-sur-Sûre. If you look on a
map you'll find it northwest of the city. Whether you're on a drive round a wider
area or simply on a day out to the lake, it's somewhere to take your parents and
friends. The scenery is breathtaking, the views awesome.

The drive there is a pleasure whatever the weather. The winding lake road will
take you at first through the tunnel passing on the way some spectacular scenery
and onwards up to the dam, which if you will pardon the pun is the high point of
the trip. It is a long way down when you look over one of the sides of the bridge,
which crosses the dam. If you suffer from vertigo then hang onto the railings.
The view from the other side is one of idyllic beauty, the lake stretching out
behind the dam, the pine trees lining the sides of the shore. It's a good place to
picnic as well and there are ample picnic spots all along the side of the lake. Pic-
nicking is a favourite pastime with everyone, especially on a nice day. Further up
you can even go sunbathing on the beach. (If you can find the beach, that is.) Yes,
the beach is the place where you can let your hair down, or in my case not, and
run into the water and go for a swim.

Along the lake there are sports facilities where you can go water skiing and
scuba diving. Luxembourg might be a long way from the sea but that should not
put you off having a go at scuba diving. My friend learnt to scuba dive here, passing his Padi diving course. He did some of his dives in the lake itself. I have to
give him credit for having the courage and stamina to do his course in the
autumn and wintertime. He completed the course by taking his final dive in the
lake in mid December. The visibility down under was murky. It was also minus
whatever with snow on the fir trees. Whilst doing his dive he was nibbled by the
Pike in the water. Perhaps they found him tasty! The good news was that he

passed the course and he got his certificate. We did think about giving him a hot water bottle afterwards, but bought him a pint instead—in The White Rose, of course.

Still in the Ardennes is the town of Clervaux, situated in the north of Luxembourg. You can reach it by train. The journey takes about an hour from Luxembourg City. Once past such towns as Mersch and Ettelbruck, which are equally worth a visit, the train begins the most picturesque part of its journey as it winds its way through the valleys of the Ardennes passing some hidden campsites and scenery you just won't see if you go by car. The train ride is worth taking and when you get there it's a stroll down to the centre where there are some lovely small restaurants to choose from.

The town itself is small but a must on your visit are the museums including the ones in the chateau at the top of the hill. Here you will see among other things an exhibition called 'The Family of Man'—a collection of photographs taken by Luxembourg photographer Edward Streichen. There is also a wartime museum devoted to the Battle of the Bulge. Many hikers visit Clervaux, a good place from which to head up into the hills. Most people who drive there arrive on the main road from the south but there are other options.

When the sun is shining and at a weekend, especially on a Sunday, the roads in the Ardennes region in the north of Luxembourg come alive with motorbikes. These bikers come from not just Luxembourg, but from all over Europe to explore this wonderful region. They themselves are an attraction, making your day out just that bit more fun. I lost count of the sheer number of bikes I saw. Was it over a thousand? I think it was.

Vianden is the place everyone takes their mother to. I don't know why, but it is. It's also a place to take your friends and family for a good day out. Apart from Luxembourg City, Vianden is Luxembourg's chief tourist spot and is located in the north east of the country.

The road down to the river is very steep in some places. All along it are all manner of quaint gift shops and restaurants. The Our River at the bottom of the hill is very picturesque. It's very pleasant to stroll around the town. There's parking but you have to pay for it. However, where don't you these days?

At the top of the hill and overlooking the whole town from its central point is the chateau. It can be reached from a turning half way down the main hill as you arrive in the town. You'll need to be fit to walk up the steep slopes to get to the chateau. Once through the gates you can sample the delights of day's gone bye.

Some of the staff sometimes dress up in the costumes people wore in the previous centuries. This helps to bring the castle's past alive.

Why not hire the castle for a party? You can hire various halls. These can be used for a ball, a disco, a Christmas party, a wedding or maybe even a medieval feast. The choice is yours. One of the rooms does cater for classical concerts and in this room stands a huge grand piano used, no doubt, for those special occasions.

Inside the chateau is a museum where you can get a feel of the place and learn about its rich history. Now I like looking at old maps and I'm sure I recollect several in here. There is one of when Luxembourg was four times the size it is today. There were several other countries which don't exist now on these old maps. Watch out for the knights in shining armour.

The three hundred and sixty degree views from the top of the chateau are worth the hike up there. The view is magnificent. You can see the entire town and the surrounding valley for miles around. When you're standing there, you can imagine you're in the chateau that featured in the film 'Chitty Chitty Bang Bang.' You literally feel like you're King of the Castle (as in "King of the Castle, get down you dirty rascal"). The chateau itself has been rebuilt from the shell it became as a result of a host of neglect over the years. I gather that it wasn't until after World War 2 that the government decided to rebuild it to its former glory. The restoration is ongoing and the results make it a delight to see.

There's a chairlift in Vianden that crosses the river and then climbs steeply up the hill. The forest below reaches out beneath you as you dangle your feet and enjoy the silence of the ride to the top. Once there you reach what turns out to be a wonderful vantage point where you can see the whole town and chateau down below. The view stretches for miles and if you're lucky you may see the wind machines in the distance. Lunch at the top of the chairlift is recommended as you can look out and pass the time of day quite easily.

I've been to Vianden several times. During my first visit, I brought one of my English friends Ian to see the place. On this particular day we strolled around the town. From the bridge that passes over the river our route took us in the direction of the chairlift. We decided it would be a good idea to give it a go. Ian volunteered to get the tickets at the ticket office at the bottom of the chairlift.

"Two singles please," said Ian.

"Don't you want a return?" said the astounded ticket man.

"No thanks," was Ian's reply.

"A return would be better," I prompted. The walk down looked a long way from where I was standing!

"Don't be an old woman," Ian said to me, adding, "It'll be fun!"

Actually, it *was* fun. The descent was through the woods down some sharp slopes, sometimes with stairs going most of the time through the rough of the woods. We passed some intrepid folk going in the opposite direction. 'Now they would gain some extra muscles on their legs climbing up that slope,' I thought.

We actually arrived near the edge of the chateau and it was not far to the slope up to the entrance of the chateau.

Vianden is also accessible on a tourist coach trip out. A Canadian friend of mine took the coach during his stay here. However I think that it's only available to go on in the summer months.

Vianden is a destination everyone chooses for a day out in Luxembourg.

A lot of people, when viewing Luxembourg, see the country in their own car, or a hired car. They drive round the various routes that you can create for yourself. You can certainly split the country up and cover the various options during the time you have available. Here are a few possibilities:

Luxembourg—Mondorf-les-Bains—Remich—Grevenmacher—Wasserbillig—Luxembourg

Luxembourg—Little Switzerland—Luxembourg

Luxembourg—Vianden

Luxembourg—Esch-sur-Sûre—Wiltz—Clervaux—Luxembourg

Luxembourg—Esch-sur-Alzette

Luxembourg—Bettembourg—Dudelange—Luxembourg

Luxembourg—Wasserbillig—Echternach—Vianden-Luxembourg

Luxembourg—Diekirch—Ettelbruck—Mersch—Luxembourg

Mondorf-les-Bains is in the southeast and is famous for its hot springs, herbal spa and its casino. The spa is a vast modern complex of open air, enclosed hot and cold baths, some normal, some herbal. There are saunas, gyms and a massage centre as well. Outside in the huge grounds there are some lovely gardens. There is also some forest that is within the grounds. Both the gardens and the forest have some lovely walks through them, which can be visited in all seasons of the year.

The centre also has some large function rooms where conferences, celebrations, parties or Christmas parties are held. In summer it's a delight to come here. Many office workers head for here after a hard day at work. During the weekends the centre is normally packed.

I first came here during my first summer in Luxembourg. The bank had a summer party. It was free! Yes, everything was laid on and a good time was had by one and all. It's better if there's a group of you, for then you can try out the saunas and the swimming pools together. These are all fun. There's nothing like a hot and cold dip to bring you back to reality. Many people do come here on their own.

You'll see some sights whilst there. These can be in all shapes and sizes. However more of the older folk use the centre than the young do. If you're feeling fit then the gym is worth a session. There's nothing like working off a few pounds sweating your socks off on all those gadgets, after which you can soak off the day and relax in a bubbling Jacuzzi. I joined the club for a month—in a December, of all months. I used to come down to Mondorf-les-Bains on the number 175 bus that runs at least an hourly service. The road to Mondorf-les-Bains at first heads south over some rolling hills, passing forests on the way. In wintertime they are like being in Narnia (the fantasy land in *The Lion the Witch and the Wardrobe*) and are a real experience to see.

It certainly makes a novel experience to come here in the snow. Walking to and from the bus stop with six inches of snow underfoot is fun and makes it an experience to remember, especially after having had a sauna. The sauna itself was a blast; in fact, there were several to try out. In one of the hot water pools I used the snow was falling on top of me, after which it was nice to stop off in the Jacuzzi areas where the hot bubbles were blasting out.

Of course all this swimming in hot and cold water is meant to be good for you. The herbal bit must also be healthy. The experience is good and you do feel much better for it about two days later, after you've recovered from the day before when your body felt terrible as it wasn't used to all the goodness you had just given it.

At Mondorf-les-Bains is Luxembourg's only casino. You can go and gamble your Euros in there. But wait! It's not Las Vegas, so if you were thinking it might be, think again.

The room below caters to tea dances in the afternoon on certain days of the week. These are always full but newcomers are always welcome. I did go once with a friend who fancied a waltz, or was it a quickstep? Anyway, it was a good experience but I did feel just a bit too young for this one. However, everyone here is young at heart.

If you want to be a devil you can nip over the border into France. There's a bridge that crosses the tiny Gander River. Once past the disused border post you'll find yourself in France in a tiny village called Mondorff. However, you'll soon discover there's bugger-all to see. Actually. there are one or two houses and a lot of fields. Nevertheless, development is coming thanks to the borders coming down and Mondorf-les-Bains in Luxembourg currently being so popular.

Remich is another small town, which is situated facing Germany. It borders the Moselle River and makes a great stopping off point for a coffee or a beer en route to somewhere else. It's a nice place to have a nosey round. You can enjoy a walk along the riverfront and perhaps take a riverboat along the Moselle River.

Wasserbillig is another small town that borders Germany on the Moselle. It also borders with Germany along the Sure River. Wasserbillig was described by *The Times* correspondent as the "most boring place on earth" when the Euro came in. Personally, I challenge this as there's more here than most places. If you don't believe me, ask the Germans. They use it for the purchase of petrol, cigarettes and duty free bits and bobs that are far cheaper than in Germany. You'll discover a whole stretch of petrol stations. Wasserbillig is actually a nice little town worthy of a stop, even if it's only in the Match supermarket.

Little Switzerland is an area to the north east of Luxembourg City. You'll need a car to see it and it's well worth a drive around for an afternoon. It's called Little Switzerland because of its shear beauty that resembles Switzerland. The local name for it is actually the Mullertal.

Many forests make the area ideal for a hike in the hills. There are fast flowing streams and interesting rocks to clamber over, as your walk passes by dense woodland. There are pastures that descend into the many small villages that are all over the area. In the summer it's a delight to see the small fêtes taking place in these villages. It's fun to stop to sample the way of life for a moment before dashing to your next destination.

Diekirch is a town north of Luxembourg City. It's where they make the beer called 'Diekirch'. The town has a square and the shops are centred in the streets around it. I spent a very pleasant time here showing my parents around. The little cafés to stop off at are a joy and when it's sunny it's even better.

Esch-sur-Alzette is Luxembourg's second city. It's located in the south west of the country bordering France. The shopping centre is worth a trip round. You can take the train there, which is handy. Flats are also a lot cheaper here. The town is full of Italians and Portuguese, and this adds to the European feel it already has.

Two other small towns in the south of Luxembourg worth a visit are Bettembourg and Dudelange. These are typically Luxembourgish in their style. The towns are a delight to wander around, both having some lovely local shops and bars. Dudelange is where Samsa films are located—in part of the old steel works.

Staying in the south and an interesting journey to take is a trip on the train from Luxembourg to Rodange. The train goes through some of the towns in the south of the country, including Petange, Differdange and Esch-sur-Alzette. It's a fascinating journey through some of the industrial zone and countryside and takes about an hour.

The Foire is Luxembourg's large exhibition centre and is situated up at Kirchberg. When there's an exhibition it's best to go to it on the bus as parking can be difficult. Take bus number 18 to get there.

During the year the exhibition centre holds all sorts of exhibitions, fairs and bazaars. These range from the hugely popular International spring and autumn fairs to the holiday and gastronomic fairs. There's also a huge antiques fair that would delight certain friends of mine, and there is a separate property fair. If you like cars, then watch out for the car fair. There's an old car fair as well. In December, an International Bazaar takes place over one weekend. The theme is Christmas, with all sorts of Christmas goodies on display, making it is a delight to go to, especially if you like different cultures. (See chapter: 'The Centre for Different Cultures.') The double-glazing and home improvements fair seems to be there permanently. Food is served inside and there are various restaurants and snack areas to stop and eat in.

The Spring Fair is a popular event and attracts many people. There's a bit of everything here. One hall is full of sports cars and other unusual cars. Watch out for the dancers who put on a great display at certain times around the different cars. There are halls that will flog you every gadget you never needed: from property to Australian hats, industrial kitchens to pizzas—it's all here.

If you like good wine, then this fair is a must. You'll find practically every wine that's grown in Europe—from the many vineyards of Luxembourg to the wine growing regions of France, Germany and Italy; they are all here, along with other countries as well. Sampling the different wines could take all day and the salesman will relish the thought of you buying a case or two or three.

If you like cheese then you'll be able to sample the different cheese flavours of Europe on display here. There is nothing like having a nibble as you wander around.

You can also see just how many different types of salami there are. From every corner of Europe, it rolls up here. Okay, most comes from Italy, but you get the idea. There's every locally produced variety from the farms on display. It does look quite ugly sitting there—I mean, a dried up sausage is not exactly beautiful, is it? But it's the taste that counts and, again, the only way to find out what it's like is to try it. After that, you may be hooked.

Luxlait also have a large stand with chefs concocting various delights as give-aways. CFL, the train and bus company in the spring of 2003 had a large stand at the spring fair, shaped like a tram. Inside was their vision of the future. You could view a short video of the new tram service that's coming to the city.

I've been to the Autumn fair a couple of times now. This varies from The Spring Fair. For example, 2003 saw many sofas on display, a large children's area and a handicapped area, each promoting a multitude of advice and fun. (You can try the sofas out if you want me to define fun on the sofas.)

In September I went with some friends up to the Foire to see the 'Britain in Luxembourg' trade exhibition. There were all manner of British goods on show, including the latest cars ranging from the new Mini's to Bentleys. There was everything from lawnmowers, whisky and books. The George and Dragon pub had a bar selling Boddingtons. Cactus had a stand selling British products including, surprisingly, PG Tips, as did the Little Britain shop. There were business people promoting various products including Horsburgh and Co, an accountancy firm and the staff of the '352' expat magazine. Oh, I mustn't forget the various clubs that were also there.

The best bit, I thought, was outside at the bus stop where an old London bus was giving free rides between the Foire and the Park and Ride. The old 'Routemaster' we couldn't resist and like a bunch of naughty schoolboys sat on the top deck at the front and back. We took the round trip before returning to the real world of the single decker number eighteen bendy bus back into town.

On another occasion I went up and saw the Gastronomy Fair. Well, why not! I fancied the idea of sampling the delights of whatever I may find. Actually, I was pleasantly surprised by what I saw. There were different themes in each of the huge halls. In one hall I went to there was a huge fresh fish area, while next to it was a massive display of mouth-watering vegetables. On one side of one hall they had a butchery, which was sectioned off. There were windows one could look in and see the butchers preparing the carcase meat into the different cuts. I found this interesting as it showed the modern methods that are used when preparing meat for wholesale consumption. You could also see how clean everything was in the surrounding environment.

The standards were very high on all the stands. One of my favourite pastimes was looking around the hall where the chefs of umpteen nations had taken part in the gastronomic competitions and the results were on display. They were mouth-watering to see. Another favourite of everyone's was the chocolate stands. Now I like chocolate and what these chefs can create out of liquid chocolate is incredible. The chocolate is nice to sample as well.

In January there's a massive 'Holiday Exhibition' at the Foire. Luxembourg's central geographical location attracts many of the surrounding countries to attend the fair. It also attracts exhibitors from the Mediterranean countries like Italy and Spain. Portugal is also represented. There are all types of holidays to choose from, from beautiful beaches to grand cities, a walk in the hills, or a tour. Every type of vacation is at the holiday exhibition.

It's not just the big tour companies that are here. There are also many small tour companies and tourist boards from various towns around Europe. I discovered places in Italy and France I had never heard of before promoting their destination to the punters visiting the faire. And why not?

There are also large camper wagons on display that appear to be very popular in Germany, and one mustn't forget the national airline LuxAir who had naturally one of the largest stands in the fair. When I went on holiday using them I got a free beach bag, which isn't bad either. Just look out for their special offers.

In the late winter I went to a Property Fair at the Foire. It was the first one I had been to and therefore I didn't know what to expect. Inside I discovered many different exhibitors, the majority of which were selling flats here in Luxembourg—all very expensive for what they were.

The choice of style was severely limited if you didn't want a flat. Even the flats on offer were very much the same in their design and shape. There were no three-bedroom houses or semi-detached houses like those you get in other countries. Yes, I know Luxembourg has its own style, but even so. Land prices might be expensive, but there seems to be a severe lack of choice or imagination in what was offered.

There were two exhibition stands flogging houses in Spain. These were doing a bustling trade and stood out from the other stands as their presentation style was impressive and the style of the houses and flats were different. The properties for sale in Spain on these stands were also considerably cheaper than the properties for sale in Luxembourg. I was expecting the Property Fair to be much better than it was. Overall I found it all very disappointing and severely limited. It was interesting to look around, but I just couldn't get too excited.

One of the things I did here in Luxembourg was go to the circus. I hadn't been to one for ages and the last time I went was in England. A good opportunity arose when my parents were over during a weekend in May. The name of the circus was 'Circus Krone', which is a German circus and was on tour in Luxembourg. Circus Krone's base is actually in Munich, Germany, where they have been performing since 1905 when Carl Krone created the Circus Krone.

The circus was huge. The tent took up a large area of the Glacis car park where it was sited. All around the tent were the circus's wagons and animal enclosures. As we entered the circus arena, it was all the fun of the circus to watch during the afternoon that we went. The acts were terrific, coming from all round the world, from Russia to Mongolia, from Armenia to the Czech Republic, other performers coming from Spain and Germany. They included some super clowns who did some great slapstick comedy. There were Elephants that did some amazing tricks. The high wire acts kept everyone on tenterhooks. We also watched a giraffe and some zebras, also a fine display by some Arabian Friesian horses and golden coloured Palominos that I thought were fantastic. The dangerous lions thoroughly entertained the crowd and quite how their animal trainer can get them to do the tricks they did was beyond me.

The dancers, artistes and performers all wore a variety of colourful costumes. It was thrilling to see them perform a variety of acts that ranged from the traditional to the modern. Some great ballet dancers brought us a taste of Las Vegas in their act. I also loved the trapeze artists who made flying through the air look easy.

Naturally, I got the best seats for my parents who thoroughly enjoyed the trip. In fact, I'm sure it was the highlight of their weekend as it took them back to their youth, when in the good old days there was a grand circus and giant fun fair in Manchester at a place called Belle Vue, which sadly was pulled down years ago.

These days in England you just don't see this type of circus anymore. The reason for this is that animals are not allowed to perform in circuses. In Europe it's different and animal performances are allowed. People do have very strong views when it comes to the cruelty of animals. Circus Krone is highly aware of these views and keeps its animals in the best possible care. At the end of the day, if you are not for this type of circus, then you don't go. Having been to see the circus, I thoroughly enjoyed the performances though I still have mixed views on the subject.

By strange coincidence, about one year later, I discovered there was another circus in town, also located up on the Glacis. I couldn't resist it and decided to pay it a visit. This time I went with a friend of mine. The circus was a Spanish one. I thought it would be interesting to compare it with the German circus I had seen the previous year. The circus was called 'Cirque Raluy' and was considerably smaller than the German one. In fact, it was tiny in comparison. However, it didn't matter as the whole point of a circus is to sit back and enjoy the different acts.

The thing that I liked about the Circus Raluy was that it has kept its tradition. By that I don't just mean the acts, I mean the whole circus has maintained its roots whilst living in the modern world. For example, most of the wagons used to live in are the original wooden wagons. Some date back to 1927 and 1942. They're decorated outside the wagon with traditional Spanish paintings. I imagine they must be equally fascinating inside. Some of these wagons are lined up at the front of the circus by an old style fence, creating a wonderful effect as you walk along the front to the entrance.

Another interesting place I found myself in was the café and bar area. Again, this was in an old wooden wagon, inside which was finely decorated with old photographs of circus acts and guest stars in days gone by. At the end of this wagon was the bar, which had woodcarving all around it. An old gramophone sat on one side, its cone sticking upwards at an angle. The whole wagon oozed with nostalgia, which helped make that magical circus atmosphere.

The actual circus acts were a joy to watch. There were the usual clowns who messed around during the performance. Also, I watched some fine jugglers, one of whom could juggle on top of a ladder that was incredibly balanced only by himself. It was enough to bring the sweat to the palms of your hands. There were also some acrobats, dressed in Georgian-type costume. They climbed their way towards the ceiling with a story of a balloon, keeping the audience on the edge of their seats with their balancing on a pole act. Right at the top of the tent was where the lady performed her balancing skills. Inches above her was a delightfully painted circular cloth, which formed the top of the tent. Its style was very old and traditional Spanish, adding to the enjoyment of the night.

I thought the knife thrower was great. His knives looked razor sharp as they were thrown at terrific speed at the girl who must have a nerve of steel. Every act had a Spanish flavour, even the sea lion at the end.

The finale brought us all the acts joined together where we were entertained by some Spanish flamenco dancing, the dancers wearing traditional Spanish costume. The circus had been well worth going to and I look forward to the next one.

15

A walk in Luxembourg

There are some lovely walks you can take here in Luxembourg. Whether you fancy a walk around the city or out into the countryside, the variation in the scenery is stunning. Getting out into it is worth the effort. Whether you want to get into the real countryside or just see the countryside that surrounds the city, the choice is yours.

The Tourist Information Office has a list of walks that it recommends tourists to take. These include the city detective, the city promenade, and the circuit Wenzel. There's also the Schuman, the Vauban, the Mansfeld and the Circuit Goethe. You even know how long each walk will take you. That's actually quite a good idea, especially if you're on a tight schedule. Sometimes, though, it's best to do your own thing…

One summer's day my friend Chris called me to ask, "Do you want to stretch your legs and go for a short walk down towards The Black Stuff and relax on some bar terraces?" The weather was hot but a little cloudy. It was, however, a little cooler than the previous few days, so why not? After all, it would get me out of the flat.

As it was, it was a national holiday here in the Grand Duchy. It was Pentecost or Whit Monday. I was expecting an outdoor market to be going on along the Avenue de la Gare but I must have got the dates wrong as there wasn't. Certainly they do have an outdoor market here, on about three different dates during the year. This outdoor market is not to be confused with the Farmers' Market, which runs twice weekly on Wednesday and Saturday mornings in the Place Guillaume where you can sample some real local delights.

Our stroll took us past the Pulp Club disco along the Boulevard Général Patton. Further down along this stretch of the road there's a small crescent of houses, which deviates off on the left hand side. This street, oddly, has almost the same name but is the Boulevard du Général Patton. We strolled down it to see what had happened to the fate of a famous pub.

In its time it was called The Cockpit Inn. Sadly, as we discovered, the site is now another block of flats. The bar used to be run by Icelanders and was famous as it had half cockpits of old planes and fifties style American Cadillacs cut in half.

Years ago there used to be a flight from Luxembourg to America via Iceland. Icelanders came here because they worked for Iceland air and this was their local. There are many Icelanders living here because of that flight with Iceland air. Alas, the service is no more.

One reason for the popularity of the Cockpit was the fact that Icelanders, being Icelanders—the guys, that is—went there to drink themselves into a stupor, leaving the women in desperate need of some TLC from any bloke crafty enough to stay sober after about eleven at night.

We continued our stroll, stopping to look at some wild gooseberry bushes in the hedge. They were full. I said, "It might just be worth checking them out when it's harvest time."

Further down were some wild blackberry bushes. On the side of the road we were walking along was a very steep slope descending into the valley below. Lower down is a road, which we took, that crosses a bridge. Here the Alzette River goes under the bridge in two places. On the left is a massive weir where the river flows over to give a terrific waterfall. The weir is there to control the river water. It looks spectacular.

The two of us decided to take a right turn and head up towards the main road. At the junction we had a choice of what we could do. We could go left to the Blackstuff, which is an Irish pub just up the road, or we could cross the road and continue, looking for some park. We could also go up this very old road that was now behind us that neither of us knew.

We chose the latter, so we turned round and walked back about one hundred metres where we decided to stop at a bar called The Blue Moon. Inside there was a beautiful Italian woman serving. The place had four customers—Italian men—propping up the bar talking to her. There was a resident band's gear set up at the far end. We downed a pint of orange and lemonade before continuing our trip.

Sometimes the best trips are unplanned. This trip was most definitely unplanned as neither of us had a clue as to where we would end up, let alone where we were actually going next.

Chris and I took the old cobbled road that climbed steeply up towards the railway. It curved round, continuing its steep climb upwards, crossing the railway further up. Here you can see the railway to Trier pass under you. From the bridge on the right-hand side you can see the railway pass through a man-made blasted out gorge. The high rock walls rose more than seventy feet above us. There was wire mesh on the rock wall to stop any falling rocks. In addition there was sprayed concrete in places to stop the rock eroding.

We continued upwards admiring the magnificent view that looked out across the city, continuing up until we hit the plateau. This plateau, as I discovered later, is called the Plateau du Rham. We followed the road round and discovered an athletic track on our left. There appeared to be some form of building works going on in the centre of the arena inside the track area. At the junction we turned left and found ourselves at a bus stop called Fort Dumoulin. We both wondered if the running track had been built over this fort. I found out later that it hadn't, but was built close to it. However, it was built over some former out-buildings that were near the old fort.

Had we looked, which we didn't, we would also have discovered that the name of the road we had just walked up was called the Rue du Fort Dumoulin. At this point I would like to say that had we turned right at the junction, we would have come across a real traditional Luxembourg pub just up the road and a short way on the left. It's called the Zeutzius. I've since been in it as a result of this chapter and I mention it now purely on its merits. Inside are many artefacts from the former Mousel and Henri Funck Breweries. The food is real Luxem-bourgish and it's well worth a social visit!

Meanwhile, back on the walk and a short distance from the bus stop down this rue, which was the Rue de Trèves, we saw what looked like a park; so, being nosey, we crossed over and ventured along a narrow path. We found ourselves in a small park area. There was a small football pitch that sloped. If you missed the lower goal then you could have a long way to get the ball. Beyond this was a wooded area with what looked like an adventure playground. Great for kids, I thought—but actually it wasn't for kids, it was for Adults. Yes, really. Each wooden construction had a purpose. Each one was for you to do your own exer-cises, be they gymnastics, aerobics, push-ups or side stretches. Every wooden area had its own sports purpose. Needless to say I didn't take the idea up in my non-fit state.

Chris and I decided to take the path that headed down to the right. This was a steep decline down a dry muddy slope. Keeping right, our short walk then took us along a fairly vertical path—crossing round from one part of the city into the next. All along the route there were strange signs of people doing exercises.

At some point there were about ten wooden poles rounded on the top. These were for you to leapfrog over—as if I wanted to do that. The path itself turned out to be a nature trail. It's also a fitness path specially designed for you to try these little novelties out. The path is also used as a cross-country run by various clubs. A lone runner passed us en route. We exchanged greetings.

The two of us saw a couple of birds on our trip. These were of the feathered variety. There was also a tree that had some nests in. You could hear the baby birds crying out for their mother.

Somewhere along this path you will see something rather special—a huge statue. It rises up at a strategic point somewhere on the opposite side of the valley. The tall statue could be religious. In fact, as we discovered later, it is very religious. The statue I was told is a statue of Christ. From where we saw it, it looked as though it had probably been built years ago. The thing that makes it so special is that you have to be at a certain point and a certain angle in order to see it. Otherwise you won't. In fact, from most places the statue is not visible. Another thing we discovered later is that most people don't know it's there. So if you get the chance, do check it out.

The wooded footpath ended at the top of a road. Then we followed the road up and round a little to see what was there. In fact, we came to a football field where a small football tournament was in progress. There was a portable beer bar where the beer was being served not far from where we were standing. How refreshing! It was just what we needed as it was hot work doing all this energetic walking in the heat of the sun. There was just one problem. There was a fence in the way that blocked our entry. Blast!

So we descended and checked out a new housing estate of posh houses that were being constructed. Now, I must admit I love nosey parkering around houses. I like to see the variation of styles. Here in Luxembourg the styles are pretty unique. Nevertheless, they don't appear to know how to build normal three bedroom houses like those in the UK estates, or even in Holland, for that matter. To be fair, they might not want to. In Luxembourg you have either flats or very expensive houses. There doesn't appear to be much in-between.

Our walk continued. We retraced our steps to the forest. Chris and I could either go down the road or we could take the forest path that went in the opposite direction and was heading along a route heading downwards. We took the forest path and followed it along, ending up on the main road, which was the Rue de Neudorf. The two of us headed back towards the town and The Britannia Pub until we saw some steps, which were going up the other side of the valley. This looked like a public footpath so we crossed over the road and started our ascent. The steps went up and up and up! It was incredible. You had to be fit to climb the bloody things, as they were not for the faint hearted. We rested at several stages to recover our breath. I thought we were at the top when, to my horror, the path merely went on the flat for about one hundred metres before recommencing the climb upwards with yet more steps.

At the top we found a stone step to perch on to rest our weary souls. The sweat was running down my face and neck. It had been a hard climb. If you weren't fit before you most certainly would be now. We had arrived at the side of a private Luxembourgish catholic school. We walked towards the road ahead of us and found ourselves at the back of Kirchberg. We decided to turn left and head off down the hill. This would take us back towards town.

Descending the hill, we found ourselves looking at a large modern building built in such a way that as it rises it sticks out in an upwards triangular fashion over the road. At this point I wanted to show Chris an old Luxembourg road that was no longer being used by cars. In fact, the road is not on any tourist map. In the old days it would have been one of the main access roads into the valley from the plateau. We had visions of old farm carts heading into town. I hope they had good brakes, as it was a steep descent.

There was an old graveyard on the right that must have been over four hundred years old. I have since discovered that it is a Jewish graveyard. At the bottom, there were some steps to take us into the current road. This road, the name of which is Rue Jules Wilhelm, just takes slightly longer to walk down, as it meanders down the valley. We had arrived at a tollgate I had visited once before. Here a big archway crosses over the road and I can only imagine a large wooden gate may have once stood here.

The road did a fork. Either we could go left or we could go right. I had been to the left once before so I chose the right fork. All right! We walked on and continued down the road—literally! A little while later we arrived at a German War Cemetery, which was located on the left-hand side of the street.

Here we stopped and had a look around. The cemetery was split into two parts. As you looked at it from the road on the right side there were the dead soldiers from World War 1. On the left side were the dead soldiers from World War 2. Sadly, many of the soldiers that were buried here were killed in the early part of the Great War. They had mostly all died in the year 1914. In the other war grave, many of the German soldiers had died in the period 1940 between the middle of May and the beginning of July.

There is actually another much larger German war cemetery in Sandweiler where ten thousand, nine hundred and thirteen Germans who perished during the winter of 1944 to 1945 are buried. There is also a large American cemetery outside the city in Hamm where five thousand and seventy six Americans who died in the same winter of 1944 to 1945 are buried. Joining them is their commander in chief of the third U.S. Army Corps, George S. Patton, who expressed his wish to be buried here. These men died in the offensive in the Ardennes that became known as the 'Battle of the Bulge'.

We continued on our walk and ended up down by the Alzette River where we turned right and headed towards Pfaffenthal. Now there is a walkway that you can take that lets you bypass the road. The walkway takes you into a large open park that borders the river. In days gone by the area was flooded to provide water and defence for the city.

Some kids were playing football in the park area and just as we got there, their ball went into the water. The river was fast flowing so I didn't envy them trying to get it out of the water. Some Portuguese and Italian pregnant women sat in the park gossiping. It was a lovely day. The gardens on the opposite side of the river looked magnificent with their summer flowers.

To the left was a weir where a small boy was playing with the water. A separate gulley has been constructed allowing a separate passage for the fishes to go down. The sluice gates were at the other end to this, to be opened when the river is surging.

We were aiming for the Caribbean and Latin bar Tainos, which is right in the middle of Pfaffenthal. But to our dismay we found it shut. By now our tongues were hanging out and we needed a drink. Luckily we found a nearby Italian bar where we downed several more orange drinks and lemonades. After the pause for the cause we headed along the road that ran along the river on the opposite side to where we had been walking though the park area. We walked along it past a newly renovated Catholic Church hospice. The whole thing was brand new and the hospice gardens had only just been completed. They were huge. It must have cost a fortune! Nevertheless they do look magnificent. Still, the Catholic Church isn't short of a few bob, is it?

We ended up going down past the youth hostel. Big renovations and modernisation was taking place at the hostel. There was also a large new development being constructed, which would improve the facility in the future. We crossed over the river and followed it round until we reached the Britannia Pub. As we were both hungry we decided to head towards Maybe Not Bobs, the American Spare Rib joint. Regrettably it was also closed, as it was a Monday.

As I needed food we decided to take the bus up the hill into the old town. Here we alighted and looked around a few restaurants to see what was on offer. Unfortunately most restaurants here in Luxembourg outside the tourist places only open at lunchtime and in the evenings at 7pm. So we decided to call in at Yesterdays bar in the old town while we waited for the magic hour.

Yesterdays is in one of the oldest parts of Luxembourg. The bars and restaurants here serve some of the best food in town. They are allegedly also some of the most expensive. The locals tend to eat here away from the tourists. It is a place to visit to experience the good food, the atmosphere and the history. A drink's not a bad idea either.

After descending some stone steps we entered the bar where we sampled a few bevies. After all this walking we deserved a drink. After all we must have covered over sixteen kilometres over some very varied terrain. Incidentally, the walk with stopovers took us about five hours.

Chris's idea of a short walk had obviously walked out of the back door. Our sitting on a nice sun terrace passing the time of day couldn't have been more opposite to what we had just done. Still, doing what we did on the spur of the moment had turned out just fine. We had seen a hell of a lot of Luxembourg City that you just don't see. We had each covered some new territory, and the important thing was we had enjoyed the walk.

Inside the bar we got talking to the blonde barmaid. It turned out she was French and came from Paris. Unfortunately for us she was living with her Icelandic boyfriend. However, this is where we found out a few more interesting bits about Icelanders who live here and about life in France. It's called pub talk!

I was then coerced into going for a meal round the corner at a famous Luxembourgish Greek Restaurant called To Kastro, which sounds Cuban but I'm told is very Greek. In fact, it was all Greek to me! (Sorry, had to put that one in.) The meal of lamb chops was delicious and was washed down with some excellent Greek red wine.

After all that it was time to head back to where we started or near to. The White Rose was beckoning…

A Polyglot club trip to Namur. Belgium. May 2003

Students from the Centre de Langue on a French trip to Nancy.
July 2003

The Grand Duke Henri and the Grand Duchess Marie-Teresa
at the Duke's birthday firework display. June 2002.

A jazz band plays at the beach party in the Pétrusse valley
on the Duke's birthday. June 2003.

Pont Adolphe with the Place du Metz in the background.
October 2003.

A view from Pont Adolphe towards the Place de la Constitution.
October 2003.

View of the Grund. July 2001.

The Chapelle Saint-Quirin in the Pétrusse valley. October 2003.

Fort Thüngen, Luxembourg. July 2003.

A smaller replica version of Fort Thüngen in one of the
round towers inside Fort Thüngen. July 2003.

The Station in Luxembourg City. October 2003.

Administration de l'emploi (ADEM). October 2003

Avenue de la Liberté on the front line during the first Arcelor
demonstration. April 2003.

B23 squad in the Rue Dicks go in during the second Arcelor
demonstration. April 2003.

The burning of the stake ceremony in the Pétrusse valley.
March 2003.

Steel workers demonstrating on the Avenue de la Liberté
during the first Arcelor demonstration April 2003.

Salsa cruise at Schweich near Trier. Germany. July 2003.

Vineyards on the Moselle River, Germany. July 2003

Fort Berlaimont—Inside the basement of the former *reduit*.
September 2003

Fort Fermont, France. Inside part of the kitchens.
May 2003

Fort Lambert—An unusual view in one of the tunnels with the Monterey underground car park beyond. September 2003

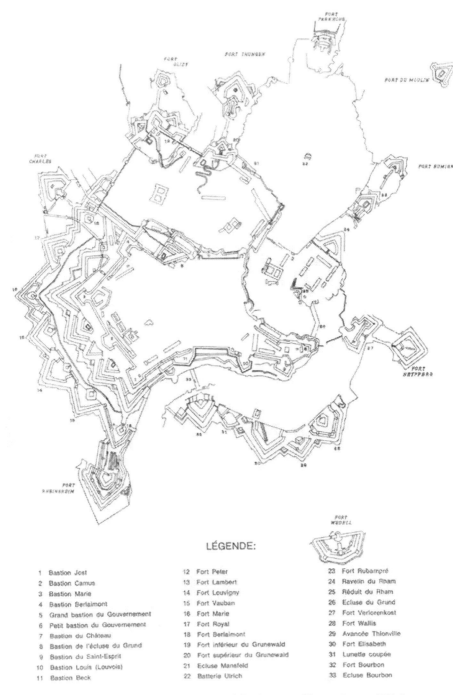

LÉGENDE:

1	Bastion Jost	12	Fort Peter	23	Fort Rubampré
2	Bastion Camus	13	Fort Lambert	24	Ravelin du Rham
3	Bastion Marie	14	Fort Louvigny	25	Réduit du Rham
4	Bastion Berlaimont	15	Fort Vauban	26	Ecluse du Grund
5	Grand bastion du Gouvernement	16	Fort Marie	27	Fort Verlorenkost
6	Petit bastion du Gouvernement	17	Fort Royal	28	Fort Wallis
7	Bastion du Château	18	Fort Berlaimont	29	Avancée Thionville
8	Bastion de l'écluse du Grund	19	Fort inférieur du Grunewald	30	Fort Elisabeth
9	Bastion du Saint-Esprit	20	Fort supérieur du Grunewald	31	Lunette coupée
10	Bastion Louis (Louvois)	21	Ecluse Mansfeld	32	Fort Bourbon
11	Bastion Beck	22	Batterie Ulrich	33	Ecluse Bourbon

Plan of the countermine system of the fortress of Luxembourg (1814)

Plan of the fortress of Luxembourg in 1867

16

The Centre for Different Cultures

Luxembourg, as I have said, is a small country. It's in the centre of Europe, the Germanic countries to the east, the Latin countries to the west. It sits right in the middle. (Don't tell this to the Austrians! If you're ever in Vienna and you look on a map, they'd probably argue that *they* are in the real centre of Europe.)

The name Luxembourg and its language Luxembourgish is derived from an offshoot of its Germanic language base. However, Luxembourg's rich history, that goes back over a thousand years, will reveal that the country has been invaded by everyone under the sun; as a result Luxembourgish has picked up words from just about every language. The main source of the Luxembourg language stems from the German language, with many additions from the French, Dutch and English languages.

When I first came to Luxembourg on holiday I sat in a café in the street opposite the Gare one day having some lunch. Next to me, a couple sat down. Well, at first, everything appeared normal. Nevertheless, my ears then did a bit of ear wigging as, sitting there on my own next to them, I couldn't help but listen in. Were they speaking German? Wait a minute, I'm sure I recognised a Dutch word or two. But were they Dutch words? To me they sounded similar to Dutch. And yet there were definitely French words, then some English crept in! It sounded most odd, but I thought nothing of it until I realised what I had just heard was indeed Luxembourgish. It sounded like and in my humble opinion was a cross between French, German and the Dutch languages.

There's a certain way to speak Luxembourgish. It has its own tongue. Its own accent. The language is unique and not many people speak it outside Luxembourg. Quite a lot of people speak it in the country itself.

The Luxembourgish language and the overall small amount of people who speak it worldwide remind me of that film with Nicholas Cage—'Wind Talkers.' In this film, the Navajo Indians who spoke their own tongue were recruited by the U.S. The Indians worked with the U.S. marines for the war effort in the

Pacific against the Japanese during World War 2. They were recruited to become code talkers on the front line in the battle of Saipan where their Indian code was adapted to be used as a secret military code. As not many people in the world spoke the lingo, it was very useful in frontline code talk.

The promotion of minority languages should be actively encouraged anywhere. After all, if we all spoke English, wouldn't life be boring?

Now, I must tell you about a real minority slang language, or dialect that is here right under the noses of us all. Yet most people, including many Luxembourgers, don't know it exists. This language or dialect I am referring to is called Jeinesch. No, it's nothing to do with Denmark. It's a very old dialect I have since discovered was used by the prisoners in the former jails in the Grund area. It was spoken by the prisoners so the warders couldn't understand them! This is probably more like the original Luxembourgish language of over one thousand years ago. You can actually check it out by heading down to the Pfaffenthal district. Pfaffenthal is located in the valley just upstream from under the Red Bridge.

When one of my friends first told me about this language, I thought he was joking. Some time later I went down to a bar in Pfaffenthal with some friends to sample a few beers. One of the locals was an old man who was sitting there jabbering away in Jeinesch. I thought, 'Wow this is original, man!'

You know, it would be a tragedy if this language or dialect died out. I just hope a few other people continue to speak it.

Some considerable time later I decided to check the national library out to see if they had anything to help me find out more about the dialect. If you've ever been to this library then you'll know what I mean when I say it must rate as one of the most boring libraries I've ever been in! However, the staff soon made up for that and surprisingly I found only two references on their computer that mentioned Jeinesch. One was a small booklet, last published in 1993 in German, called *Das Weimerskircher Jenisch auch Lakersprache oder Lakerschmus genannt* by Joseph Tockert. In it I found the following:

Jenische verse (nach Jos. Feller)
Den Hautzdenhockt e Stapp
An d'Moss déi hockt eng Klont
Den Hautz dee bott de Bossert
An d'Moss déi bott de Schont

I also found an old newspaper article on Jeinesch published in a local paper of the time in German back in 1978. That's twenty-five years ago and since then little has been published about this dialect. That's pretty sad actually and does beg the question, why? Luxembourg is in the heart of the European Union whose commissioners like to promote this, that and the other, yet this is a dying dialect or language right under their noses.

What I discovered was that the Jeinesch language consists of around three hundred words, which are not really enough to use as a full-time language without using other languages interspersed. This, I believe, is what must have happened. However I do find it a bit strange that the language has not been promoted in any way as Luxembourgish has. Perhaps they could run a course at a language school? Or a correspondence course on the internet, like other small languages are now promoted?

I've since discovered that in many towns and villages in Luxembourg, they seem to have their own spoken dialect. Trying to find out more about these dialects is hard work, as it is word of mouth. Still, it is one of my challenges for the future.

A good example of how different languages work here is to pick a couple of words and compare them. When you say, for example, *yes* or *no* in Luxembourgish, you get *jo* pronounced 'jaaah' and *neen* pronounced 'naay'—which always reminds me of Frankie Howard and his one-liner, 'nay nay, thrice nay,' in 'Up Pompeii.' I'm digressing again.

The Germans say *Ja* and *Nein* in a military fashion and the French say *Oui* and *Non*. An interesting point here is that real French people, when saying *Oui*, tend to say it fast, almost as if they're blowing down their nose at the same time to give it that 'wegh' sound. Of course, when it comes to *non* then the French President is the best person in the country to quote here. How did he say it? Wasn't it, "Non, non, non," if I remember rightly?

Luxembourgish as a written language is far newer than you might think. It became officially recognised only in 1984. Before that, it was mainly a spoken language. It was a written language but until 1984 most Luxembourgers spoke it rather than wrote it. They wrote in French and German. They also spoke French and German. These days the locals still speak and write in French and German, but Luxembourgish now takes centre stage.

There are now dictionaries, which in the old days were probably hard to find if the language was learnt on a word to mouth basis. The Luxembourg language has been 'developed' considerably since it became recognised. You can buy a dictionary with over six thousand Luxembourgish words in six languages including Portuguese, French, German, English, Spanish and Italian.

This is all useful stuff for the new generation of Luxembourgers, but to anyone over thirty it's a different story. Why do I say this? Well, speak to the real locals and a lively discussion among those people over thirty will soon make this evident. Some of them still only speak Luxembourgish and writing it and getting the correct spelling can still be a problem. Some locals will also dispute the textbook words that have been 'invented' by some scholar. The locals after all know best on how to speak their own language. These days, if you are under twenty and most definitely under fifteen, speaking and writing Luxembourgish is second nature.

Luxembourgish today has developed considerably. In everyday life, you can see it all around you. There are newspapers, books, documents, web sites, advertisements, television and radio channels, which all use it.

If you are foreigner from outside the European Union and you eventually change nationality to become a Luxembourger, then to qualify for citizenship you will have to learn Luxembourgish. Yon don't need to do this if you're working and living here short time.

Many people have told me that you only need six words to help you here in Luxembourg. These are *Moien*. That means 'Hello'. Then there's *Äddi*, which means 'Goodbye'. 'Please' is *Wanneggeliwt*. *Merci* is 'Thank you'. Finally, there is *Jo* for 'Yes' and *Neen* for 'No.' Other useful words include, *Gudden Appetit*, for 'Bon appetit,' which itself is French in origin. 'Beer' is *Béier* and 'Dance' is *Danzen*. *Schwätzen* means 'speak'. 'Do you speak English?' is *Schwätzt du Englesch?*

A useful romantic phrase is *Ech hun dech gäer*, which literally translated is 'I love you' or, *Ech sin frou mat dir*, which means 'I like you'. But they don't sound very romantic, do they! Not like the French *je t'aime*. I much prefer *Een gudden Humpen (mh mh)*, which is 'a good beer', or *Wéi geet ët* ('How are you').

There you are. You can now practise a few words of Luxembourgish at your leisure.

Luxembourg is a small country of only four hundred and forty-eight thousand three hundred inhabitants. The country has two hundred and seventy-seven thousand six hundred Luxembourgers living in it. There are also one hundred and seventy thousand seven hundred foreigners also living in the country, which is over thirty-eight per cent of the population. Luxembourg City has over eighty thousand inhabitants.

There are many many nationalities living and working here but by far the largest is the Portuguese who make up sixty-one thousand four-hundred and forty. It's almost a mini colony of them. Then there are the Italians who have around nineteen thousand. Both of these nationalities in days gone by came to Luxembourg generally, I heard, for two reasons—one being for the men to work in the steel industry here, the other for the women to breed and improve the breeding stock (the Italian women especially because of their good looks).

There are a fair few people living in Luxembourg from the surrounding countries. There are twenty-one thousand five-hundred and fifty French. There are fifteen thousand nine hundred Belgium's and ten thousand two hundred Germans living here. Other nationalities include the English (four thousand six hundred and fifty), the Dutch, (three thousand six hundred and ten), followed by the Spanish (two thousand eight hundred and seventy) and the Irish (one thousand and forty). There are one thousand one hundred and seventy Greeks, one thousand nine hundred and ninety Danes, five hundred and ninety Austrians, one thousand two hundred and twenty Swedes and eight hundred and forty Finnish people living in Luxembourg.

There are also twenty-four thousand six hundred and thirty people of other nationalities living here; individual figures are not available. These include many Russians and Brazilians. (Source: Luxembourg statistics—from internet, census-recorded information as at 01/01/03.)

A host of other nationalities live here including people from the following countries: Algeria, Austria, Azerbaijan, Belarus, Bulgaria, Canada, Cape Verde, Chile, China, Columbia, Cuba, Czech, Dominican Republic, Egypt, Estonia, Faroe Islands, Greece, Guadeloupe, Hungary, Iceland, India, Indonesia, Japan, Jordan, Kazakhstan, Kenya, Laos, Latvia, Lichtenstein, Madagascar, Maldives, Mongolia, Malaysia, Morocco, Nigeria, Pakistan, Peru, Philippines, Poland, Rumania, South Africa, South Korea, Spain, Sri Lanka, Switzerland, Syria, Thailand, Tibet, Togo, Turkey, USA, Ukraine, Vietnam.

Every nationality mentioned in this chapter I have met here in Luxembourg, most on a fairly regular basis. It just goes to show the real cosmopolitan mixture there is in such a small area.

Luxembourg has taken in its fair share of refugees. I have many friends here from the former Yugoslavia. These days each nationality that comes from this now sub-divided region hates referring to it by its original name of Yugoslavia. They insist, for example, that they come from: Bosnia, Croatia, Macedonia and

Kosovo. My Kosovo friends are either Serbian Kosovo or Albanian Kosovo. So much for unity. I mustn't forget the Albanians, either. Again, they regard themselves as different to the Kosovo Albanians. All the refugees are very proud people and have all been through a hell of a lot. Living here gives them a second chance.

The advent of an increase in population from four hundred and twelve thousand eight hundred in 1996 has led to other social issues expanding.

There has been an increase of births outside marriage from six per cent in 1980 to twenty-one point nine per cent in 2000. The likelihood of getting a divorce has also gone up from twenty-seven per cent in 1980 to forty-seven per cent in 2000. In 2002, there were one thousand and ninety two divorces, which have gone up from five hundred and eighty two back in 1980. These figures, whilst for Luxembourg, will be much the same in any other European country. They reflect the social change that the world has gone through in the last twenty odd years.

There is no other country in the world quite like Luxembourg and the country is proud of it. It is a country of different nationalities, which is why it is so interesting. The number of conversations I have had with these people never ceases to amaze me.

Many people who work in Luxembourg are called frontier people. These are made up of the many French, Belgium and German workers who commute each day into the Grand Duchy. Over one hundred and ten thousand people cross the border on a daily basis. Over sixty-five thousand cross over from France alone. Over fifty-five thousand come up from Thionville and area. The motorway is chock-a-block with one-way rush hour traffic in the mornings coming into Luxembourg. The outward journey during the evening rush hour is much the same. Quite why the French and Luxembourg governments don't build another lane or two of motorway to cope with rush hour traffic is beyond me! Another surge comes in from France in the Longwy area. From Belgium, there are over twenty-eight thousand frontier crossers. From Germany over eighteen thousand. The rest come from other countries like Holland. There are also all the business people who arrive via Findel, the main airport and from the other airports that border Luxembourg.

The Government wants to increase the number of frontier people to two hundred thousand a day. It also wants to increase the resident population to seven hundred thousand from the current figure. Maybe it's to help pay for their pensions or simply help improve the country. Nevertheless, if you increase the population, then the infrastructure must also be improved. This is happening slowly.

The Luxembourg language must have been in decline. However, some bright spark came up with an easy answer. All schoolchildren would have to learn Luxembourgish as their first language followed by French, German and later on English. From the language perspective overall I'd say it's been a success, but pushing everyone to learn the languages has resulted in Luxembourg coming bottom in the European education statistics. Other studies have suffered because of the learning of languages.

The education system in Luxembourg, whilst good on languages, could do a lot better in other areas. It only teaches kids up to a certain point, enough to get them, for example, into a government job. This policy does appear to suit the current government.

The education system compared to that of England is most certainly different, one example being that you do appear to study for longer. In addition, if you want to be a doctor or do a university degree, then, unless you have rich parents, these options may not be possible for you. In fact, if you want to study anything beyond languages then you could have a problem. For example, you as an individual may want to do a particular subject, perhaps a science, but you discover that it's dropped in favour of a language; as a result you may not find it easy studying towards a career you may have wanted to do in your early teens.

Another interesting point to do with language is that if you want a job, especially in the government offices, you need to speak Luxembourgish. This simple rule keeps the foreigners out, for sure. But then the same applies to most government offices in other countries, if you think about it.

This is surely one of the few countries in the world where most people speak at least three languages fluently. I know of a few people who speak six languages, with English, Portuguese, Italian and Spanish making up this next wave. All the smaller minorities of course speak their own languages, so the overall number of languages spoken here is huge.

With so many languages spoken and so many different nationalities now living here, it encourages a fantastic diversity of different cultures. As a result, there are many events held in the city during each year to help you experience this.

One large event is held generally in mid-March. The event is the Migration Festival and is held at the Hall de Victor Hugo in Limpertsberg. (Bus no 4.) I went last year and thoroughly enjoyed myself. I did again this year…

The Migration festival was well worth looking around. There were different food stalls to try out. I wandered round and found myself drawn to an Indian stall, which had some wonderful displays. There was also a delicious looking curry which took my eye, so I started by sampling an Indian chicken curry. Later on another stand, I discovered some Italian cheesecake, which I sampled. It was more like a variation of baked custard but extremely nice. Another delicacy to try was the fresh sardines and bread on the Portuguese stand. However, feeling a little full, I gave it a miss along with the Spanish food stall. After all, there's always next time. Everything could be washed down with the local countries' wine or beer, not forgetting the local beers made here in Luxembourg.

The stands were varied and every type of small organisation was there along with many different small country stands—from Lithuania to Estonia, from charities helping in third world countries abroad to youth groups here in Luxembourg. The African Union in Luxembourg and the Cultural Chinese association of Luxembourg were both here, as well as the Polish cultural association. There was even a gay and lesbian stand. Every type of minority people and organisation in Luxembourg was there. I met some friends there including a Brazilian girl I know from salsa and a Kosovo Albanian friend whom I do German with.

The afternoon events were varied. They included on the huge main stage area various dancers and singers. The first were some Portuguese singers and dancers. Then I watched a Luxembourg twirled dance company followed by some Albanian singers. There were also some Cape Verde dancers and some Nigerian bongo players who were fun. Other events on stage during the weekend event included some oriental dancers. There were also some Italian singers, Peruvian dances, some Brazilian dancers with stunning costumes and dancers from Cameroon.

A large tented area had an International book fair in it. There were also discussion rooms and a variation of statistics. I mustn't forget the international pictures on display, which showed the different cultures.

There was a lively line up of night-time entertainment at the Hall Victor Hugo. The first night included some salsa bands from both Cuba and Luxembourg; the local group was Salsabor and the Cuban band Bamboleo. The second night featured the big event of the festival, a Portuguese classical guitar player called João Pedro Pais and his band. The Hall Victor Hugo was packed, mainly with Portuguese women. João Pedro Pais was very good. There were two encores and the night was washed down with several beers. I thought the singer was great. Certainly, his guitar playing skills were fantastic and his singing wasn't bad even though I didn't understand a word of what he was singing about. The night was rounded off with a real Italian spaghetti bolognaise.

Now, if that's not International, then what is?

In mid-June 2003 in the Places d'Armes, the square came alive with a festival called Discovering some Cultures, mainly southern African and south American cultures. However, the rest of the world was in there somewhere. There was music, dance and festivities taking place in the afternoon and evening.

There was food, some from Ethiopia. Other special features, which you could try, included the weaving of a girl's hair, which is a speciality in Africa especially before a wedding. Yes, I know, blokes get theirs done as well. I mean, look at David Beckham. He got his hair weaved. Fat chance I'd have since my hairline is somewhat receding.

The festival was meant to bring the rich and the poor countries together. There was a mixture of music from Africa and some great music from Brazil; with them were also some Brazilian dancers. The African music featured was the work of pupils from the various schools or Lycée Technique, as they are known here in Luxembourg. They had practised for two months, learning via workshop study.

If you want a preview of this event then the best way to do this is to head down to the Grund area in the Pétrusse valley, to the area right of the Viaduct. Down in this valley you can hear the sound of a local band practising. They do it at least twice a week generally on a Wednesday and Friday evening between eight and ten. Their drums are deafening against the valley walls. Their cries and chants pierce the hot June and July evening air.

I tell you this as I sit here and listen to it all night, night after night during the summer. I sit here with the windows open, the heat of the night making the air sticky. I have the radio on low, which is drowned out by the sound of the live music. The whole experience is quite something.

I actually find the music quite exciting and so different from all the rubbish that makes the charts these days. There's none of your computer generated musical instruments here. These people can sing as well. This is real original live music that's sadly lacking these days.

Mind you, if you wanted an early night before 10pm, then forget it. In fact, I often wonder if I'm not in central Africa up some deepest jungle with the sounds I hear. The music certainly conjures up wild exotic tribal dances. I just hope there's no large cauldron nearby!

Just for the record—before I knew why they were practising I got so intrigued as to who was playing this music that I took a walk down into the Grund to where they were practising. I discovered some Luxembourg teenagers of mixed colour doing all this music. They seemed to be enjoying themselves and I wish them luck with their music.

Another popular Festival in Luxembourg City is the Carnival of Cultures, which is normally held in July. However, it's not held every year and the next one is in June 2004. It commences in the afternoon when there is a mini-carnival. This starts down by the Gare and continues along the Avenue de la Gare; the entertainers bring the city alive with their different dances and costumes. They then snake their way across the viaduct, heading towards the old town. The Carnival of cultures is a colourful event. The procession arrives in the Place Guillaume in the old town. Here the party then begins.

Suddenly the whole event appears transformed into a giant International open air food festival and is a mecca for all food buffs who may wish to try out a bit of home cooking. There were many different types of food for sale. The whole event is the one time of the year when you might want to try out a bit of Russian, Indian, Brazilian, Thai or Filipino food. What about trying some Moroccan tea? There are also different knick-knacks from the different cultures for sale as well. To sit in the Place Guillaume, sampling a nibble of this and that with your friends is fun.

The night comes alive with the sound of a thousand different rhythms and beats. Again, the music is varied, coming from the Luxembourg bands right through to some Indian bands. It is the chance for the community to come together and enjoy themselves. The chances are that you'll bump into friends and even if you're on your own the night offers you something different.

The tail end of the year sees the International Bazaar up at Kirchberg. This is an annual event held in Le Foire exhibition hall. Held normally over one weekend in late November or early December, it's a wonderful chance to buy something different for your friends and loved ones. It's inspiring to see the way different cultures celebrate Christmas. It's also very interesting to see the types of decorations used. Truly, it's a revelation, especially if you're new in town.

The hugely popular event is voluntarily run by the different nationalities who live in Luxembourg. The money raised is for various local and international charities. Stands are by country, and the diversity is huge and fascinating. One will need a good couple of hours to go round and savour the delights on each stall. It makes your average UK bazaar look very plain. I must say that with all the different countries participating makes it a truly worldwide and wonderful experience.

From just about every country, you can sample the delights of their Christmas goodies. There are stands from all over Europe including Austria, Belgium, France, Germany, Holland, Luxembourg, Scandinavia and Switzerland. Mediterranean countries include Greece, Israel, Italy, and Lebanon. From Africa is South

Africa and in 2002 Kenya had a stall. Central and South America were represented in 2003 with stands from Guatemala, Argentina and Chile. Australasia is also well represented.

The bazaar is not just about buying something for Christmas. There is food to try. Lots of it, which is out of this world. In fact, go on an empty stomach as the food is delicious and varied. There's real American Chilli Con Carne served up by the Americans, ostrich on the South African stand, various Filipino foods and different kebabs on the Lebanese stand. There are also curries and other delights in the Indian, Pakistan and Sri Lankan areas. On the European stands foods to sample include ham from Spain, grilled Swiss cheese, cakes from Portugal and fish from Scandinavia.

If you get thirsty and fancy a change from the local beers you could try the Belgium or Kenyan beer. I mustn't forget the Irish stand where one year you could sample a pint or two of Guinness and in another year they had Irish whisky and Irish coffee. You can also try the tea from Morocco or from the Lebanon.

The British have a stand as well which is well supported. It gives the American stand some friendly competition. They both have a prize draw, which have some wicked prizes. Look out for it. Other stands like the Japanese, Greek and the Scandinavian stands also have tombola draws, as they are actually known.

On the Australian stand in 2003 they had a notice directing all Rugby enquiries to the British (including English) stand. Think about it!

Every year sees a couple of second-hand bookstalls, one of which sells English books like hot cakes. It's a great place to pick up some good cheap books and the prices are not to be sneezed at.

The bazaar will open your eyes and show you how other countries celebrate Christmas. The gifts that one can purchase are so different to the run of the mill goodies and tat which you normally get in your Christmas stocking. A variation of a pair of socks is worth thinking about, eh! What about an Indian or Australian tea towel? Alternatively, what about some Lichtenstein Christmas table decorations or some Icelandic hats? Mind you, socks do come in handy.

17

The Centre de Langues

The young son of a friend of mine was heard to say, "Mummy, Mummy. Why don't you speak Luxembourgish? It's easy."

For the youngsters the earlier they start the easier it is for them to pick up several languages. It's normal here. Some of them can switch languages just like that. No, not like Tommy Cooper! Some of them speak bits of six languages.

The chances are that mummy does indeed speak Luxembourgish, especially if she's foreign and comes from outside the European Union. Then mummy *has* to learn it if she wants Luxembourg nationality. Many foreign girls do marry Luxembourg men, and indeed the same can be said for Luxembourgish women who also marry foreigners.

One place to learn a language is at a language school. Here in Luxembourg there are several. These can be split into two sorts—the private ones and the state. The private language schools include Prolingua and Inlingua. Both these schools are great places to learn another language. (They also have a nice price as well, being about ten times the state school price.) The private schools tend to cater to more of an employers' market, the employers actually sending their employees there. However, it must be said that they do cater for anyone, so don't be put off by what I say.

The Centre de Langues is the state language school. It's probably more of a college than a school, but let's not get pedantic. The Centre de Langues is on the number 3 bus route and is situated next to the Glacis. Its entrance is on the Boulevard de la Foire. The language school is based in the old European school. Previously the Centre de Langues was situated down by the Gare but that was before my time. The European school is now up at Kirchberg.

Currently it does have that 1960's feel to the building, but having said that there is a lot of refurbishment going on throughout the whole building. This includes a lift, new windows, new edgings round doors, new doors, new coat stands, new lights, rewiring and new extra handrails which are soldered onto the old ones. Bit by bit the whole place is gradually getting a facelift.

I like the fact that the classrooms are named after different European cities. The language that's taught in the class generally reflects the room name. For example, in 'Toulouse' and 'Paris' French is taught. In 'Wien' and 'Berlin' German is taught; 'London' is English, 'Luxembourg' is Luxembourgish, and in 'Madrid' and 'Barcelona' Spanish is taught. It doesn't apply all the time but you get the idea. New signposts help the students find the rooms and once in the classrooms the maps and items on the walls help the student associate with the language and country in question. Everyone has their favourite city and don't tell me they don't.

The Centre de Langues is where you'll be able to see just how many cultures there are in Luxembourg. It's 'the place' to learn a language. The chances are that at some point during your stay in Luxembourg you'll end up here. The trouble is, there's a waiting list a mile long—so apply early.

My suggestion would be to get down to the reception desk no later than the third week in June for the September enrolment. For the February enrolment check out the position by the first week in December. Even if they tell you to come back, you'll at least be wised up on the latest position. The point is, don't leave it too late. I speak from personal experience as I had to wait half a year because of arriving a week late to sign up. So you've been advised! Even if they're full, ask to go on the waiting list. Be prepared to pay up front or via your bank, which is the procedure here.

If you're new, the actual procedure to get into the college has changed. New entrants now have to take an entrance exam or test so that a computer can assess their actual level. This probably makes it easier for the school to slot people in who are not just beginners. Once you're in, it's like anywhere else—it's just a matter of making that first move.

Due to people coming and going from Luxembourg because of all sorts of different reasons, generally work related, there's a high drop-out rate. So people on the waiting list get a chance. In every class I've been in, I've seen the class change practically on a weekly basis—someone leaving, and someone new arriving to join the class.

The centre is very strict on attendance so if you don't have a valid excuse and you don't bother turning up, then you're out. In fact if you don't phone in and advise them it will go against you, and if you're missing for more than a week you're automatically out and your place goes to someone on the waiting list. It doesn't matter whether you've paid for it or not. There was rumoured to be a waiting list in early 2003 of over two hundred people from ADEM alone. In June 2003, I heard that over eight hundred and fifty people had applied for the next year's re registration, for French alone. You'd think they'd employ more teachers to cope with the demand, wouldn't you? Maybe it's all to do with the budget or space.

However, it could also be the problem of attracting the teachers in the first place. That's always a difficult thing to do here in Luxembourg (is it not the same in any country?). I've heard that even in the private schools they're always recruiting.

If you're unemployed, you can study here for a much-reduced fee of five euros a term. (See chapter: 'Looking for a Job?')

I always thought that the Centre de Langues was for students during the day and adult students at night. It generally works that way back in England. I thought this for months. It wasn't until I went there a few times in the day to do some studying in the library that my views on this began to change radically. I found out that my thinking on this was all wrong. Yes, there were some young students there, but this was a college rather than a school. Therefore, not only did the adult students go at night; they also went there in the day. As I soon realised, people work different work patterns, including shift systems. Some work part time. Others don't work at all. Some people study there during their lunchtimes. Their employers are extremely helpful in this, as the lessons last for an hour and forty minutes each time, which is two hours in book terms. Still, it's in the employers' interest to encourage their employees to study, especially here in Luxembourg.

At the Centre de Langues, the lessons start at eight in the morning, which I don't fancy, as it's early. The next lesson time is at ten. This is followed by a midday session. In the afternoon, there's a class at two. This is on top of the lesson time starts of five fifteen and seven in the evening that I myself knew.

One day in the summer term the German lesson I was attending ceased and we all had to change classes. Half of us changed to midday, the other half to seven in the evening. The latter time clashed with my French class, so that was out. The teacher was taken off the class so that she could take a summer school of students who would be doing an intensive class of German during the summer vacation. It was all to do with the number of hours she worked, I gather.

It was a pity for everyone in the class to split up as I had made some great friends. As a result, some of us met up for a Spanish card game. I played the card game with a Spanish girl, and a Belgian girl and guy. We made a foursome and the Spanish girl Carmen taught us how to play the game 'Mus'. It's a popular game in Spain—all the men play it in the bars. The cards are not like any other that I've used before, and they're not like your average pack. The cards don't have jacks, queens and kings, and the rules take a bit of learning. Still, we enjoyed the cultural experience over a drink outside a bar up on the Glacis.

If you're keen to learn a language, then the Centre de Langues is a good place to learn. There's a lovely library to practise in and you'll meet many fellow students. The canteen's not bad either.

During the day there are many girls from Eastern Europe studying here. In the evenings there are a high percentage of bankers attending classes. I can't think why!

Some people will stay friends for life by meeting each other at this college. Indeed, I know of a few people who have ended up in a relationship with each other as a result of meeting here. In one example, one of my friends is a German. He married a girl from Cape Verde. She speaks Creole, the local language used in Cape Verde, Portuguese, a little English and French. He speaks German, English and French. The common language here is French. The relationship flourished and they got married, which I think is terrific. They also continue to do the language lessons and are living very happily to this day.

There are various levels to study. There are currently eight levels per language. If you're a beginner then you start at level one going onto level two, etc…Levels one to three are for beginners. Levels four to six are intermediates. Level seven to eight are advanced.

To give you a taste of the different levels I'll rewind to one of the end-of-term dinners I attended. At the time I was at level four French. After the class we all made our way up the Glacis to an Italian restaurant there. It's a big restaurant and when we got there, we discovered a huge long table had been reserved for us. Our group of level four French sat at one end of the long table. There were about eight of us. Joining us in the middle section was the teacher's other class of level two. The teacher sat in the middle of level two and four. Finally, at the other end was another class of level six. The meal commenced. We all spoke French. However, the point of the story is whilst level four could hold a conversation, level two really struggled—whilst at the far end level six were jabbering away like there was no tomorrow.

Now, having started German level one and now level two, I know that it just won't click until I get to more than half way through level three. I can make short sentences—just; but hold a conversation—forget it! So I can see why the French level two folk were struggling that night, with moments of silence halting the conversation. You have to remember that we're all different nationalities and the common language of the night was French. The irony is that when we went on level one and level two meals in the German class and found we couldn't get our heads round a full sentence or 'paragraph' of verbal sentences in German we spent most of the night speaking French! This was great for me as I needed the practice.

We've been advised that the current eight level system here in Luxembourg is to be replaced in 2004 with a Europe-wide level of study. This new system will use just six levels. These will be level A1 and A2 followed by level B1 and B2, and finally level C1 and C2. This will benefit anyone moving cross-borders and who has been studying the language in another country before. So if you've been learning French in Barcelona and you're level B2, then when you arrive in Luxembourg you can continue at level B2.

The Centre de Langues currently teaches all the main eight languages spoken here in Luxembourg, which are Luxembourgish, French, German, English, Portuguese, Spanish, Dutch and Italian. Now let me ask you, how many languages do *you* speak?

If you're lucky, you'll get a good teacher. Then learning is fun. Some give homework, others don't. In the classes that do, don't forget to do your homework. Gosh, I could be back at school when I say that! The homework, however, will help you to learn. If you don't do it then you're liable to feel a prat in the class when everyone else has. This is made worse especially if the teacher goes round the class on a random basis or from left to right going over the homework! When it comes to your turn what do you say—"Sorry, I haven't done my homework miss"? Well, maybe not the 'miss' bit, but you get the idea!

There's an exam to take at the end of every term. If you pass it you'll generally go on to the next level providing the teacher is happy with you. If you fail or your in-class work needs improving, you'll have to redo the year again. Worse, you could actually go down a level! This is no bad thing, however, for it could actually be good for you. Why? Because then you have more opportunities to practise the language you're learning. There's an old English saying 'Practice makes perfect'—and right now I need more practice!

I'm actually learning German and French, which I find hard. Nevertheless, compared to when I started, I feel—and this is the important bit—a little more confident now. I can also hold a conversation in French. Speak too fast and it's still over my head. Complicate it and I'm thrown. However, they do say you only need five hundred words to speak a language, basic though that is. After that you can build on what you know.

There are different styles of teaching as there are in any place. Some are modern while some are old fashioned in their approach. I'm afraid I prefer the old-fashioned teaching methods. I prefer to be taught on a blackboard or marker pen with an overhead projector. I also like a desk as opposed to everything being on my lap, which some teachers opt for. The argument of a desk being a barrier to learning I find preposterous. Most importantly, I like the lesson drummed into me with the element of 'You might be next', so I don't dare fall asleep! I'm afraid I can't get into these modern trendy teaching methods of beanbag throwing to each other in a group in front of the desks. I suppose its okay at the beginning, but I need words on the board and old-fashioned methods are the only way to get me through it all. To be fair, many people thrive on these new methods. What do you prefer?

I've had some terrific arguments with one of my friends over this in The White Rose. We nearly came to blows! (Well, not quite.) We agreed to differ and to this day still do. My friend is all for these modern trendy methods and explained the learning techniques they are meant to do for you. They are meant to enhance your learning abilities and memory.

What I do like in the classes, I have to admit, are the group activities. Here you're split into small groups and you do an exercise together. It's a clever 'communicative' way to learn and gets everyone involved.

The visual aids are useful. We use both cassette, CD, and the television to help us learn. There are also computer rooms where, as part of your lesson, you can use the DVD ROMs and the internet. The information gained can then be used back in the class. I have done this on umpteen occasions.

Another good idea was when the local television station RTL made available to the college an unedited tape of the Grand Duke's birthday celebrations in the city. The German class was where we watched a part of that evening events unfold on the eve of the national holiday, which followed the next day on June 23rd. Naturally, we discussed it in German. The class learnt a bit more about the cultural history of Luxembourg. It gave us students the opportunity to discuss the programme and discuss our own national days, all in German. I learnt a lot of European history on those days.

I can also understand the importance of learning a language here in Luxembourg, as everyone who lives here generally speaks at least three to four languages. If you only speak one language then you can get by, especially if that one language is English. However, don't kid yourself. Make the effort. After all, it helps not only on the job scene but in the office as well. It's also useful in out of work hours, like when you're down the pub. It's called socialising.

In my own circumstances both past and present I would far rather be learning a language than learning some boring banking exam, which once I had left the relevant division and moved into another division, meant it wasn't worth the paper it was written on. I would also have to start again and I would have to take a completely new set of exams. Again, once I left that division they were worthless outside the job I was doing.

I'll stick to learning a language or two. At least with a language you can forever communicate with other people, which to me is important, be it that the words may not be the exact words you would normally have used. You can always work your way around a conversation and get there in the end. After all, you can always use sign language if you're stuck!

A final thought: Many people have told me the best way to learn a language is with a person of the opposite sex in bed on the pillow. It's called a 'sleeping dictionary' and I've heard that there's a huge waiting list!

18

Across the border

The good thing about living in Luxembourg is that if you fancy a change of scenery then you can pop over the border into nearby France, Germany or Belgium. These days with border controls down it's easy and hassle-free to cross over the border and enjoy a good day out in the nearby towns. Certainly being in central Europe will give you a great opportunity to see the sites of the area.

Most people who live in Luxembourg, once settled in, eventually cross over the border to see what's on the other side. Most head for Trier in Germany, some go to Arlon in Belgium, whilst others may venture over to Thionville in France. However, there are other towns and cities to visit and there are other places to see. You might fancy a trip to Saarbrücken in Germany or a day out to Nancy in France. Then again, you could head north up to Liège in Belgium. It depends on what you want to do. Also, on how far you want to go, and on how much time you have. There are numerous possibilities and since I've been in Luxembourg I've tried a variety of them.

A common thing I hear is, "Oh, I didn't know about that!" Or, "Oh I didn't have the time to go anywhere on Saturday as I got too pissed last night." And again, "I was out till six o'clock that morning." So a whole day is wasted and you've missed all the joys of the region! Mind you, we've all done it once or twice. I mean, you've got to, haven't you? It's part of life, after all. The hangover is not fun, though. You can spend a day in bed cursing the fact that you had one or six too many in whatever bar you ended up in.

Many newcomers like to venture out. Also, a day across the border is part of the experience. Its part of the tour you take when your friends and family are over. It's an exciting experience for them to visit several countries at once. When they return to their own country, it's a good talking point when their friends ask, "What did you do last weekend?" And they reply, "Oh, I popped into Belgium, then France and finally we nipped into Germany before spending the evening in Luxembourg."

How many people must have said that over the years?

Christmas Markets

December is the month of the Christmas markets and here in central Europe they are a very popular custom. If ever there was an excuse for visiting the region out of season, then this is it, as it provides a good opportunity to see these cities with all their Christmas lights. Each Christmas market sells many local Christmas goodies that you just can't buy in the shops back home.

To stroll round the markets is fun, especially if you round off your trip at one of the many *Glühwein* bars. (*Glühwein* is hot mulled red wine just in case you didn't know. Incidentally, in French they call it *Vin-Chaud*.)

Of course, if there's snow on the ground, which there is likely to be, then it makes it just that tad more festive.

The Christmas market in Trier, which is just across the border in Germany, I love. Apart from the strong tasting Glühwein to warm your stomach on a cold winter's night you can buy a mug as a souvenir. These are definitely a must and make a great Christmas present either for a friend or for you as they make very good coffee mugs. They're also a collectors' item, if you collect mugs, that is, as there appears to be a different design each year. (I must be a 'mug' for buying one—sorry, couldn't resist it!) Watch out also for the delicious German puddings you can sample in the Christmas market.

Luxembourg also hosts its own Christmas market in the Place d'Armes. The whole square is transformed into a winter wonderland of wooden stalls selling all sorts of Christmas goodies. Oh, and don't forget the Luxembourg Glühwein stalls as well.

It's a pity you can't get mugs in Luxembourg. Plastic cups aren't quite the same, are they? Christmas market stalls are also located down by the Gare.

Nearby Metz (see later in this chapter), Köln, Strasbourg and Heidelberg, all have their own Christmas markets. Further afield, Christmas markets in Europe include Prague, Innsbruck, Hamburg and Salzburg.

Liège

Liège is situated to the north of Luxembourg in Belgium and makes another good day out. Famous for its steel industry, it remains an industrial city. These days the steel industry is in rapid decline. But the city is changing and is perhaps more famous now for its old grid-like narrow alleyways and streets, which house a multitude of different bars. Nearby is the city's large well laid out shopping centre.

There is also a prestigious university here, which attracts hundreds of students into the town. At night the bars in the narrow streets in the centre are heaving. The city is famous for it. These are a mecca for the students to drink and dance the night away. The shops are a delight to wander around, and they bristle with shoppers. The bars and restaurants during the lunchtime are always full. The big river that runs though the city is the Meuse. It's nice to view it from one of the bridges and watch the world go by.

If you're coming from Luxembourg by car, there's the direct motorway link via Arlon and up through the Belgium Ardennes. If you're going by train then you will head north through central Luxembourg. It's an hour on the train before you reach the border.

The train passes through some terrific countryside, including the Luxembourg Ardennes before passing over the border. It's an hour from there into Liège. The scenery changes as you head northwest. I note this simply by the way the style of the buildings alter, in this case manifesting a more Belgian style.

The station or Gare at Liège is currently being enlarged and totally rebuilt. It looks quite a job. I expect them to redevelop the whole area soon.

It's quite a stroll to the main centre and shopping area, and I had to ask my way. That long walk is worth the hike but it took me half an hour. It worked up a thirst so I had an excuse to try out some Belgian beer. Of the three hundred plus beers that are brewed, I managed two of them.

Metz

One of the most visited places that people enjoy for a day out across the border is Metz, in France. Why? Well, for the shopping, actually.

The city is easily accessible on the motorway and rail network from Luxembourg and takes about an hour to get there. If you're coming on the train, it's a magnificent station to arrive at. The neo Roman style building is over three hundred metres long and was constructed between 1905 and 1908 by a Berlin architect Krőger during the period of the city's annexation to Germany. The wonderful Place du Général de Gaulle stretches out in front of you as you walk through the station doors.

It's a short walk to the main shopping area, which is to the north east of the station entrance, assuming north is in front of you. It's a delight to wander around the many different shops in the centre. There's also a marvellous indoor and outdoor market, its presentation so French, yet so irresistible. There are also many good restaurants where you can relax and enjoy a good cheap meal, including some local delights from the Lorraine area.

However, there is more to shopping in Metz than just its centre. On its outer edges you'll find many out-of-town shops, including IKEA.

One cold and wet December day in 2003 my French class, together with a mixture of levels, all joined together to have a day out in Metz. We all met on the Glacis car park. Once again our group was of mixed nationality, including two German girls, a Dutchman, a lady from ex-Yugoslavia, a Spaniard man, a Portuguese man, a German Italian, two girls from Finland, an Italian, a lady from Tibet, a couple from Spain, myself the Englishman, the French teacher and finally the return of the two mad Italian Romeos. (The latter two always bring a touch of fun and laughter to the day out starting with "Bonjour Davvveed!" in a very Italian French accent.) Once we were all assembled, we headed in various cars down the motorway to Metz.

Our rendezvous was the tourist information office in the centre of Metz where we all met up at 10am. Here we met our French guide for the morning who naturally spoke to us in French. Our tour started in the blustery rain-swept street outside the Catholic Cathedral Saint-Etienne. Soon we ventured inside where all of us learnt about the different things you see in cathedrals.

One thing I did find interesting during our tour was the stained glass windows where each told a different religious story. How they were built and by whom I also found of interest.

It was bitterly cold inside the large Cathedral—colder than outside! My Dutch friend whispered to me after we had been there a fair while, "Have you ever spent so long in a place like this?" He had a point.

We emerged to head off through the streets, which lead down to the Moselle River where we ended up in the Place de la Comédie. During the summer, the area is a delight to see, but in mid-December it wasn't quite the same! We walked down various streets that looked so charmingly French, our walking tour being interrupted periodically by the rain.

Metz used to be a military city and dotted all around are ex-garrisons that these days have been converted into something else. This includes the *Arsenal*, which today is the *salles de spectacles*. The City also used to be a Roman city. Our group discovered a little more about both these periods. The tour took us to see many of the old military buildings together with some roman buildings that have been carefully preserved.

Afterwards our party enjoyed a fabulous meal in a local restaurant followed by an afternoon round the shops. It was all the more enjoyable as it was Christmas time. The shops were packed and full of Christmas shoppers. The best bit was looking around the Christmas market, which I thought was really good. The *vin-chaud* went down a treat and another mug was added to the collection.

Our trip to Metz had been fun. It had enabled everyone to talk to each other in French and the day had been a real success.

Namur

Another trip I went on was to Namur in Belgium. This time with the Polyglot club. We met up early on a sunny Saturday in May up at the Glacis. From here, we went by car via the motorways to Namur. The journey takes about an hour and a half.

My travelling companions in the car included two Germans of each sex and a Swedish blonde. The journey up to Namur helped me get to know my new friends and provided an opportunity to have a good open discussion on everyone's different lifestyles and situations. We were a real mixed bunch in our party that also included French, Luxembourgers, Belgians, and myself from England, who made up the rest of our small contingent. The club members met at the Novotel Hotel in Namur-Wepion with the other Polyglot clubs from within Belgium. There was one club from Antwerp and two from Brussels.

The difference between the Luxembourg Polyglot club and its Belgium counterparts hit us all when we met. Our club averaged twenty to forty years of age whereas the three Belgium clubs averaged fifty to seventy-five years of age. Nevertheless, it was a good day for European relations.

The events laid on by our hosts included a trip on an old railway line on a rail bike. This was great fun as it involved a very strange bike ride on the rails up the railway line and back. It certainly kept everyone fit! The trip goes through some lovely Belgian countryside. If the weather is good, it's a fun trip. Mine certainly was as I was in the company of three girls.

We had gone uphill for the first stage of the ride passing blossom-covered trees and going over old bridges. We enjoyed the silence and the beauty of the spring countryside, which all around us looked so picturesque. We arrived at an old railway station. The station platform is now transformed into a seating area. Nearby there is a monastery called De Abdij van Maredsous where they make their own beer. For us thirsty cyclists it was a great place to quench our thirst and try out this beer. We wolfed down a round of Belgian cheese and ham sandwiches that had been prepared for us. This was great as it gave us time to recover before the ride back, which was downhill.

A short drive away took us to a Belgian fish farm. Here we spent a few hours seeing how the trout was farmed—an interesting experience since I've never been to a fish farm before. The trip showed us the whole process of fish farming from the beginning where we saw the different ponds where the fish grew, right through to the smoking process. At the end of the tour, we sampled the smoked trout. It was delicious. You could purchase some if you wanted, which I did. The end result simply melted in the mouth.

The trip gave us an opportunity also for a quick visit into Namur. As we entered the city we walked over a small bridge called the Pont de Musee and continued down the street. We found ourselves in what appeared to be the central square. It was called the Place d'Armes and was clearly the heart of the city.

In Namur, there are some lovely shops to nose around, including Belgium chocolate shops. However as we were on a whistle-stop tour the chocolate had to wait.

For centuries and until recently, the city was a military town with its garrisons defending the city, based at the strategic points of where the Rivers Meuse and Sambre meet.

Some of the party wanted to visit The Citadel, the city's most famous landmark. It's a huge fort, located on the hillside that overlooks the city. Only another visit will allow me this pleasure.

One of the girls wanted to visit a huge church called the Saint Loup. "It's more beautiful inside than out," she said to me. The outside looked fine to me.

There's a quaint little hidden square in Namur where we sat outside a bar and had a quick drink. The whole area oozed with that continental style, which is great.

The evening was rounded off with a meal in the hotel restaurant where many stories were told and swapped. I met a Roger Moore look- and sound-alike who was actually English and married to a Belgium lady. Both were members of one of the Belgium Polyglot clubs.

However, the best bit had to be in the car going home. It was full of laughter and fun. It was here I discovered that Germans do actually have a sense of humour—don't they, Wolfgang!

The day in the Ardennes had been enjoyable. I found the area extremely beautiful. All along the wide Meuse River is a delight with its distinct style of architecture, its houses being so different from nearby Luxembourg. It's definitely a place to visit and for me to go back to.

Nancy

Nancy is in the Lorraine region of France. It's a real old French city. You can access the city by car or by train. By car, the journey will take about one and a quarter hours. If you travel by train, there are direct links from Luxembourg with the journey taking around two hours. The station, as you will discover, has been preserved, but was built for a city much smaller than it is today. Its new glass extensions, I think, look daft, but perhaps are better than destroying an architectural wonder.

I've been there twice now—once by train on my own, the second time on a college outing with my French class…

Most of the class turned up on what turned out to be a very hot day. We were a mixed bunch in the college group. There were three Italians (who I must say had a great outlook on life), an Italian German, three Brazilians, and a girl from Portugal. There was also an Irishman, a Spanish guy, a German, an English girl and a girl from Cape Verde. Also, myself the Englishman.

From the station, as you wander down to the main shopping area, there's a large strange looking building like an old factory on your left-hand side. If you go up the escalators, you'll discover a huge open area of Hi-Fi shops, CD shops and bookshops. For a day out in Nancy, the main shopping area, which is a little further down, is a delight to wander around. Whatever your taste you'll find it here, from posh clothes shops to C&A. It's a good opportunity to stock up with some of the best wines from the region. The beer's not bad either.

There's also a lovely market in the centre. It's split into two with an outdoor market for clothes and other non-food items. Next to this is a huge indoor market housed in a purpose-built old market building that could easily be a hundred years old. It's like a very old-fashioned greenhouse with its high roof. It oozes a real traditional market atmosphere and is split into three parts.

Inside is a real farmers' market with all manor of delights. The centre area has vast fresh fruit and vegetable stalls, which are extremely tempting. On the two sides of this and in the adjoining corridors, there are many different butchers' stalls. I like to try out the different sausages they sell. These have ranged from Mediterranean sausages to cheese sausages. I've also tried the Basil sausages, all of which were tasty. Alongside the butcher's stalls are the fresh fish ones, for Nancy might be a long way from the sea but the fish is freshly delivered and looks extremely tempting. I mustn't forget to mention the many cheese stalls that are in all the areas of the farmers' market. If you're a cheese connoisseur you'll love trying out the huge variety they sell here. Naturally, being in the region of Lorraine, you'll be able to buy yourself a real Quiche Lorraine.

The English could take a lesson in the presentation of this type of indoor fresh produce market, called a farmers' market and separate outdoor clothes etc market. In my old home town of Chelmsford, the market compared to this is pathetic.

Nancy's centre must be in the old sixteen-century square, or Place, called the Place Stanislas. Its buildings are wonderfully preserved and are a tribute to the era they were constructed in. In the centre of the square stands a statue of a famous Polish King, Stanislas. His father in law was the French King Louis XV who, in 1736, gave him the duchies of Lorraine and Bar. Stanislas subsequently embellished and developed Nancy into one of the most beautiful cities in France. The square is named after him. All around the square are plated railings, which give the area a bit of class.

Nancy's main Tourist Information office is situated here on one side of this historic square. If you're in a group, as we were, then a tour guide to show you the best sites can be arranged from here and is something I would strongly recommend. Two of the other sides of the Place are lined with restaurants and bars, which in the summer are a pleasure to sit outside at. When we were there, we saw a bride having her pictures taken in Stanislas Square. She was being photographed against the plated railings and fountain that are in one of the corners. Later that day we witnessed a warm-up for a running race that was due to begin shortly after we left.

Our tour took us to some wonderful places that showed us all the different old French architecture. We saw a variety of different places, from the old converted taverns, grand palaces to the back of a row of houses where the stables used to be. Just above this the rich owners used to cross specially constructed iron bridges to sit out on, overlooking the stables and enjoying the view of the park beyond.

A beautiful place to visit next to the Place Stanislas is the Parc de la Pepiniere—a huge park that's square in shape. A large fountain stands in the middle of it and there is an old-fashioned bandstand next to an avenue of trees, which run down one side of the park. Again, the layout is so typically French, and was designed in the same era as the city. There are many museums nearby to visit, including the Museum Lorraine, which is the one we visited. This is a grand historic museum, which captures the region's history. Other museums include the Musee de Beaux-Arts and the Musee de l'ecole de Nancy.

If you're into antiques, then the Grande Rue between the church of St Epvre and the Porte de la Craffe is well worth a visit. The whole rue (street) is stuffed with all sorts of goodies. My French teacher when on our tour of Nancy and in this particular rue came across a very unusual item. It was a very old translated French copy of *Mein Kampf* by someone called Adolf Hitler. (Incidentally, I've never read nor do I particularly wish to read *Mein Kampf*, but some people I know have asked if we actually saw this book. Well, yes, we did, and the French teacher will verify it! Interestingly, at a later date I mentioned this to a Luxembourg friend who told me he was unsurprised about the French translation of the book. Why? Because part of France during the war was occupied by the Nazis. The book, he informed me, had been translated into Bulgarian, Italian and French etc—during the war years. "However," he said, "if the book had been published in 1938 in French, then it would take on real value.")

The weather did a U-turn during the lunchtime period. It was just at the end of the tour. Suddenly the wind blew up in huge gusts. The black rain clouds were rapidly descending. The tour ending was rushed as we all wanted to get to the restaurant before the downpour. As we walked at a very brisk pace towards our restaurant, we walked down the rue where the antiques were. As we hurriedly walked along it the owners of the stalls were rapidly packing everything away. The wind was gushing along the street, sending expensive glass artefacts flying from the stalls. My, there must have been a few unhappy stallholders that day! We made it to our restaurant and a minute later the heavens opened and—talk about a flood! It was incredible. Still, the meal was great.

There are loads of lovely inexpensive French restaurants to try, which serve some delicious food. I personally like the marginally cheaper Brasseries where the food and beer are equally as good. They are a good place to go if you fancy just a steak and chips. Some even do a nice strawberry tart as well.

In April, Nancy hosts its own huge fair. Located in the Cours Leopold, the fair is a mecca for all families to meet up and have some fun.

Our trip to Nancy gave us the opportunity to speak French all day. Amazingly, for me, I managed! Everyone enjoyed the trip, especially after so many hours of studying we had all put our French into good use.

Saarbrücken

If you fancy a day trip to Germany beyond Trier, then why not go to Saarbrücken?

There are various ways to get there and again it makes a change from Luxembourg. The quickest way is by car and in July 2003 the new motorway was opened that after more than thirty years finally links Luxembourg with Saarbrücken. There's also a coach service, which leaves from the Gare in Luxembourg and takes about an hour and twenty minutes. It runs at various times of the day and you should get yourself a timetable from the Gare on this service.

The most scenic way to get to Saarbrücken is on the train. If you're a single traveller then a SaarLorLux ticket costs €18 and is valid on a Saturday or Sunday. Saturday is the better day to go as the shops are shut on a Sunday. The shops in Germany mostly shut at 4pm on a Saturday, so you need to arrive in good time.

The train journey takes you from Luxembourg to Trier. From there you change trains and get one for Saarbrücken. The journey from Trier to Saarbrücken is best done on a fast train. Check your train connections. The train ride is a pleasure to make and takes about forty-five minutes. If you're lucky, you'll get the double-decker train where you can sit upstairs if you want the best views. The seats are comfortable and you can lie back and enjoy the journey.

The route takes you along the Moselle River and continues along by the side of the Saar River. It meanders along the sides of the deep valleys that the river has cut over time. Vineyards climb up the slopes reaching up into the yonder, the forests looking magnificent in whatever season you take the journey in. As you get nearer to Saarbrücken, the countryside transforms into urban and industrial sprawl. You're entering a large German industrial zone, remember. There's a giant steelworks that you pass en route which has seen better days. All around is the old decaying industry of another time period. Its industrial history stares at you through the window of the train as you pass by.

Saarbrücken is in the region of Saarland. This area, I'm told, used to have its own language or dialect called Saarländisch, which is still used by market traders throughout this central European region to this day.

It only became part of the former West Germany in July 1959. Before that it had a mixed history of being either part of France or Germany. Both the French and the Germans in the past have exploited the iron ore deposits in the region of Lorraine, now part of France and Saarland's rich coalfields, which in turn fuelled the iron and steel industry in Saarbrücken.

The fast train should only stop once, at Saarlouis. If you misconnect on your trains, you'll end up getting a slow train to Saarbrücken. The journey time then doubles to one and a half hours, which takes the fun out of the journey especially if you end up sitting in one of DB's new trains. They look nice but the seats are hard and are horribly uncomfortable.

Saarbrücken itself is a large modern German city. The river Saar runs right through its centre. From the station is an open area where there are nearby trams to catch. If you keep walking forward from the train station, you'll reach a large new shopping centre on the right-hand side. The main High Street is located a little further down the gentle slope on the left-hand side. The High Street seems to go on forever and has some wonderful shops in it. The joy is that you can walk traffic-free around the shops. Side roads on either side have other shops enticing you in with some real German bargains.

Saarbrücken does suffer the concrete effect in large places in the High Street. There are some very unglamorous buildings along it. But you have to remember how badly it was bombed during the war, as it was a very industrial area. Nowadays parts of the original old city are still there to enjoy, especially the area at the end of the High Street where there are some great little chic areas to nose around.

Saarbrücken is a shopping town. There's not much else to do. However, I'm sure that someone will soon tell me otherwise.

The Tour

During my first summer in Luxembourg, it rained a lot. On one particular Saturday morning, the heavens opened, emptying themselves over the entire region. I mean, this was mid-July and it was meant to be summer! The rain persisted, as well. I had hired a car for the weekend to show Martin, a friend of mine, around. It seemed like a good idea.

The two of us had been to Arlon in Belgium crossing via the motorway over the border. We had had lunch there. It is a lovely little Belgium town not far from the border. These days it's a frontier town as many people who live there commute into Luxembourg. In the summer they roll out the World War 2 tank that helped liberate the town. It sits in the old cobbled square next to the other cars in the car parking area, taking up the commanding spot.

Us lads had eaten in one of the restaurants that lines one side of the square. It was nice to sample a Belgian beer *in* Belgium. On one side of the square stands the town hall with a plaque to commemorate the liberation of the town in 1944. On this particular day, we sat in the restaurant as the rain clouds were hovering. Earlier both of us had strolled along the high street doing a spot of window-shopping. Arlon must be one of the few places I've visited where there is piped music pumping out at a low level all along the high street. It's unusual and really pleasant, actually.

Luckily for us, it had just started to rain as we left. Driving from Arlon over the border into France, the car headed for Thionville when the worst descended on us. It was terrible. Arriving in Thionville, the weather was so bad we didn't stop to get out and look around. The windscreen wipers were on maximum. We sat in the car outside the Gare (station) wondering when and if it would stop. After a while, we moved onto a public car park across the river. However, as neither of us had any French Francs on us, we couldn't feed the meter, so it was pointless staying. It was raining cats and dogs. We drove round town but as it continued to bucket down, we cut our losses and headed back across the border into the Grand Duchy. A sunny day makes the trip out all the more worthwhile. Unfortunately, it does tend to rain a lot in this region. We didn't let it put us off, however.

We then headed east to Remich where the rain had eased off. After a quick stretch of the legs I drove over the bridge that crossed the Moselle River and passed through the disused border crossing into Germany. "Guten Tag Deutschland."

Turning left, we continued the drive down the beautiful Moselle valley. The river looked magnificent. Luxembourg was on the river's far side. Its vineyards on the rolling hills looked so green in the dullness of the day. Further down at Grevenmacher, we crossed back into the Grand Duchy before meandering back to the city. The weather may have been awful but next time we'd remember to take a brolly. The trip nevertheless had been fun.

Trier

If you take the train from Luxembourg, you'll see a completely different viewpoint than when you go in the car. The scenery by train by the side of the rivers is fascinating. There are vineyards all around the edges. There are houses stretching up from the water's edge, edging their way up the rolling hills. The road signs are different to those in Luxembourg as are the out-of-town shopping centres. It's all very German.

When you arrive at Trier railway station or Bahnhof from Luxembourg, if you are going further into Germany, then this is where you're connected into the German railway system. In German, that's 'Deutsche Bahn'. Look out for the 'DB' signs.

German railways are different. There are double-decker trains and high-speed trains on some lines. The ticket system, however, is complicated and very expensive. It costs you more to travel on a fast train than a slow train. Failure to remember this simple rule will result in a penalty fare on the train you're on. Ticket prices tend to be a bit cheaper here than Luxembourg when booking long distance. However, you have the hassle factor to think about for the sake of saving a few bob.

From the railway station it's a short walk into the centre, which incidentally is not well signposted. The centre is straight on or *immer geradeaus* on the road that runs away from the station entrance. Keep going and when you get to the Roman arch, you've arrived. Welcome to Trier!

Trier itself was an important old Roman city. In fact, at one point it was the Capital of the Roman Empire, and there was me thinking it was just Rome! It was an important defence point for the Romans. They constructed a wall right around the city, parts of which still survive to this day. You can see this wall as you drive into the centre. The most famous building in Trier has to be the huge Roman gateway known as Port Nigra. It was one of four original Roman gateways into the city. Only Port Nigra survives. Its huge arch that you can walk under is breathtaking, its splendour making it Trier's top tourist attraction.

It was once said to me, "If you've not seen the Roman arch in Trier then you've not been to Trier." This is probably very true as it is the site to see. If you've been to Trier then you'll know what I mean. The other site to see is the Roman amphitheatre in the city.

A trip to Trier makes a good day out. It's a large modern German city. It makes a change from Luxembourg and gives you the opportunity to do a bit of shopping in Germany. It gives you the chance to sample the German way of life, to sample a beer, to try some German delicacies. I like to eat in the restaurants and to buy some clothes that I'm told are cheaper than in Luxembourg. Now the euro is here it does make comparisons a lot easier.

When I go to Trier, I head for an old fifteenth-century pub that does some good German food. The name of it is the Stratos Schlabbergass in Glockenstrasse. From the Roman arch head up the high street and take the first left where the pub is located on your left. Right, have you got it? They do a wicked chicken and chips in the pub. Just remember to ask for tomato salad with it or you'll get a bowl of lettuce leaves, which is typical of most restaurants in the region. There are a couple of very good fish and chip shops in Trier as well.

The square in the centre of the city is a delight to wander around. It's a real old typically German square. The fifteenth-century wooden buildings inspire many tourists to take a few snapshots of the square. Sometimes there are flower sellers in the square selling their fresh produce. Mini events are also held here.

A lot of the old city has either survived or been rebuilt after the war. The thing I like most about Trier is that because it survived better than a lot of other German cities it has that certain feel to it, as well as character. Many German cities, I think, lack this feel due to the wartime bombings. As a result of the rebuilding some of them have the modern concrete effect, which, I think, looks ghastly.

There's a huge church just off the main square. It appears to have been built over many centuries. Certainly, it has had new churches built over the previous ones. You can see this if you look at the walls both inside and more so outside. It's well worth a nosey round. I took my Mum and my Aunt Matilda over from Australia here as it was a good place to shelter from the bitter autumn wind that was blowing outside at the time of our visit.

There are historical sites to visit if you wish. There are also museums to go to, including a Roman museum. There are also Roman baths to see. Next door to Port Nigra on the right-hand side is an old Roman courtyard. In the summertime they host live music nights in the courtyard. You can sample a German beer listening to the music. The jazz and classical music nights they put on here transform the Roman courtyard. It gives the place a touch of class. Next door to this is the Trier tourist information office, which is a very handy place to visit for information on the town. There's also a toy town train, which you can take to show you around the historic sites of Trier. It starts from this area. Finally, on the history side, is *the* house to see in Trier—where Karl Marx was born.

But most people simply go to Trier for a wander round the shops, a meal and a drink. The main shopping area is located behind the Roman gateway to the city. The high street stretches out beyond it, entering the main square. The shops then fan outwards beyond the square where you can buy a multitude of goodies.

If you go by car then car parking can be fun. On a Saturday, long queues form, so go early. There are plenty of car parks including multi-story and underground.

As for the nightlife, there are plenty of good German beers to try in the many bars that litter the city. Trier is also a university city, so it gets a fair few students in it, adding to some lively bars. If you've sampled a beer or two then its time to grab a kebab down by the station or nip into Burger King before getting the train back to Luxembourg.

Other

To end this chapter I'll leave you with a thought a friend of mine Matthew once gave to me in The White Rose about going further across the border.

"Why don't you go down to Geneva on the train? The scenery is fantastic as the train goes along the lakes and through the mountains."

You know what...I took his advice...and he was right! But that's another story...

Examples of other cities to visit from Luxembourg include:

By train:

France	Strasbourg (2 hours)
Germany	Frankfurt (5 hours) Koblenz (3 hours)
Belgium	Brussels (3 hours)
Holland	Amsterdam (7 hours)
Italy	Milan (9 ½ hours)
Switzerland	Zurich (6 hours) Geneva (7 hours)

By coach:

Germany	Stuttgart (4 hours) Köln (3 ½ hours) Hamburg (9 hours)
Austria	Vienna (12 hours)
Italy	Venice (12 hours) Florence (12 hours)

19

Across the border—Battlefields & Forts

Fort Fermont

If you fancy doing something different with your weekend, then why not nip over to France and see Fort Fermont, a living example of the Maginot line. What is that, you ask? It's a line of defence built by the French between 1929 and 1940. It ran almost the whole length of France between the Mediterranean and the English Channel. Unfortunately, the project was never completed due to time and budgets running out.

The Project was named after the man who pioneered the idea, a monsieur Maginot. It was built to stop the Germans invading again after the terrible First World War. Unfortunately, for France the portion between Belgium and France was never built and the French thought that infantry and cavalry divisions would be enough to stop any attack from the Nazis. As we all know by now, the Nazis simply bulldozed their way through Holland and Belgium and marched into France, totally bypassing the Maginot line.

The Fort itself is like a small underground city. I didn't realise it was so big. Its entrance is up a long lane. You'll arrive in what was the armourers' entrance where it's hard to imagine what awaits you at this point. The important thing to mention here is that volunteers and friends of the fort have shouldered the fort's whole upkeep. What you see is, in a word, impressive.

After going through a door into the entrance area, you'll immediately feel yourself in a time warp. History is all around you. There are train tracks, lifting gear, and many explanation maps in the current entrance hall. In this area, lorries were unloaded, their armoury carefully transferred onto train wagons. You then go through a massive thick defence door. This leads into some original lifts where, as you enter, the slatted metal framed doors close behind you.

The lift descends, its journey appearing to go on forever. Suddenly you feel transferred back in time. There's the smell of the oil and grease in the lift that gives you that bit of realism. Down under where you arrive in the lift is a large wide tunnel area, lit with dim lighting. You immediately see lots of overhead cables and rail lines. The tour guide then explains the layout of the tunnels and what lies ahead for you.

The tunnel stretches out in front of you. After maybe a hundred metres, it curves sharply to the right. There's a machine gun defence post in a gunroom behind. It points directly down the tunnel at you, defending the tunnel. Next to the gunroom is a massive defence door, which was ready to be shut and sealed at a moment's notice should the enemy invade. It used to be guarded twenty-four hours a day. The reason for a sudden sharp change of direction? Well, it was to shelter the underground fort from any explosion in the tunnel during any attack.

Round the corner, away from the machine gun and defended door, is the armoury area. This is where the arms were carefully unloaded, ready to be transported into the fort for storage. Heavy lifting gear was used. No smoking was allowed and the walls were built in such a way as to minimise any sudden accidental explosion. Behind this nowadays is a small museum, which shows you many examples of the fort in the period of its main occupation by French troops—fascinating to see.

The best bit has to be the train ride. This, you understand, is no ordinary train. It's an electric train that uses the original system. The train is very open air but has a roof over its carriages to protect you from anything falling off the roof. It starts entering a further tunnel. We seemed to go along it for miles, deep into the line of defence. We were heading for the main fort. This journey itself I found terribly exciting. The whole feel of it can let the imagination run wild. You might think of the hundreds of troops who operated this fort twenty-four hours a day, all working different shift systems. The train passed various other tunnels that branched off. Some we would see later, others not, as they were closed off, dangerous, either having fallen into disrepair due to time or due to bombing.

The underground train ride reminded me of the London underground lines. In particular, it reminded me of the old Metropolitan and City line known as The Drain, which runs between Bank and Waterloo stations. In the good old days, the train that was used before modernisation was itself ancient but is the nearest thing I can think of to give you the feel and sound of the train we were on.

The next bit of the tour took us up yet another original lift. This one was even greasier than the last. It did give you the impression of being in another era. You could almost have been in 1940 the way it all felt. Up the lift went. We entered into the Armoury where the massive artillery guns were fitted out. Here there are three massive guns of different sizes. The whole experience is awesome. You can see how the officers lived. Everything is here in its original form. There are double doors to go through to take you outside. These were specially built to be opened one at a time because of attack and for the ventilation system.

Outside the fort, at this point, the huge concrete gun structure hits you in the face. It stands there in all its glory, a living monument to the past. The three artillery guns are now decommissioned, but they continue to point outwards. The massive concrete moat was built to dispel invaders.

Now, I always thought that the Maginot line was one continuous line of defence, i.e. one long tunnel defending France. But it wasn't. It was actually a series of forts built with long underground access tunnels behind them. You would never know they were there, the important point here being the gun defences. Each fort all along the line was built to defend its region. It would also cover its neighbour in case of attack. The guns could be fired to a circular distance of six or more miles. They could unleash huge amounts of firepower every minute.

The forts, whilst covering the three hundred and sixty degree area around, could not, however, see all the terrain. Therefore lookout posts were built in-between them to provide cover. These lookouts would then be able to telephone or send a telegraph back to the forts should the enemy attack. Within seconds, the guns would be able to repel the enemy.

In another part of the fort there is even a real moving gun tower in place. This is also decommissioned but it's thrilling to see. Its awesome wartime reality gives you the feel of what it must have been like. You can see it both underground and on the surface. If you see the surface view, then it's a short walk from the main artillery gun fortress. The gun transposes, rising upwards and then moving freely round three hundred and sixty degrees. It's camouflaged by a small dome of sturdy metal that seals itself into the concrete when not being used. It's an incredible and unique working monument to the era. Regrettably, most have now rusted away.

It was time to go back down in the lift and take the train back along the tunnel. About halfway back, the tour stopped at the barrack area. This is where the men ate, slept and lived. In this barrack area we saw the sleeping areas of the different ranks. The dining area was actually in a tunnel corridor with fold-down tables. The actual dining room was used as a bar area and is daubed with drawings done by the Americans who used the fort during the latter part of World

War 2 when attacking the Nazis in the Ardennes region in Belgium and Luxembourg. Next door to this is even a cave for the wine.

The kitchens were awesome. Huge stoves were in one area along with a very large oven. There was the largest coffee urn I've ever seen. It must have held up to five hundred cups of coffee in it. Massive saucepans littered the kitchen. In the other area was a huge notice board, which listed the number of personnel in the fort. Every soldier had to have his ration. There was no extra food allowed and none to be wasted.

There was a special hot shower room used by the men who may have been in a gas attack. This was the only hot shower in the complex and the only other place with hot water was the kitchen. Everyone including the officers showered and washed using cold water. Bleak! But to some soldiers it was heaven, as they came from poor peasant families who lived in small villages where there was only one water pump in the village to get water from. It's hard to imagine today with hot and cold water on tap everywhere.

The fort was on its own and had to survive as one unit. The men did have time off after every two weeks or so. The fort had to be self-contained. It also had to run on its own. It had its own electricity supply that was powered by huge engines. Again, there is another whole area where you can see this. Some rooms are full of electricity boxes. The fort also had installed huge pipes for ventilation. There are massive filtration pots so the air can be forced around the fort if the fort was cut off. This filtration system was never used, but it still looks impressive today.

There is also a separate area for the washing of clothes. This is situated down one of the tunnels that lead back to the lift where we started. There is running water in the gulley on the opposite side from the narrow basins. It looked distinctly red in colour.

The return to the surface took us back to where we started. However, in a hangar opposite the entrance is a museum of the period. Inside is a multitude of examples of the era. You'll discover everything from cars to trucks, from huge different gun turrets to other smaller memorabilia.

Did the fort work? Well yes, it did, actually. The Nazis did attack once before they bypassed the line and the fort was damaged. The story goes that when the French tried to repel the attack they couldn't find the attackers. They disappeared. Quite why this strange one-off attack was done no one to this day knows. Maybe the Nazis were testing the defences?

The soldiers who were in these forts in the Maginot line defending France were naturally not happy when they had to surrender it to the Nazis. However, all that's another story…

Fort Fermont is a unique place to go. The whole fort is fascinating. It's open mainly for the six-month summer period and tours start at 2pm and 3.30pm only. Visitors should also wrap up well as it's very cold down under. The tour lasts for around two hours.

Its location is not so straightforward to get to. After all, it's all underground and secret. However, from Luxembourg head to Longwy in France. The fort itself is in-between Longwy and Longuyon. It takes no more than about an hour to reach by car. The best thing to do is to check out travel details on the internet. Just type in: Maginot line and Fort Fermont, *et voila*.

Verdun—The Battlefields

Most people will have heard of the First World War. It took place between 1914 and 1918. There were some terrible battles where hundreds of thousands of men lost their lives. One of the worst areas on the front that had been created was at Verdun. The town was destroyed along with about nine villages. The battles that took place there were some of the worst of the war.

You can visit the area where the action took place. It's an historical preserved area where there are thousands and thousands of war graves. These days the only invaders are the tourists who go to pay their respects to the dead. It's a sombre visit because of the nature of what took place there. Most who visit the battlefields will find the emotional impact huge.

The battlefields are best done by touring the area by car. Then you can go on foot when you get to each site. Don't even think of walking there from Verdun town. It's about six kilometres from the town with a huge area to cover once there. The battlefields will take you all day to look round by car and then you could easily spend another day there depending on how much you want to take in. Certainly, you can do the main sights in a day.

The war reduced the area to a barren land. Not a tree stood. It was a mud bath in winter. These days it's hard to imagine. Forests have grown up over the landscape. There are huge areas that are fenced off as they remain too dangerous to enter. Mines litter the place. Even after all this time, they are still very dangerous. These areas or zones are marked with red paint on the trees and must not be entered, or you will endanger your life and the lives of anyone with you. They are littered with live bullets, gas grenades, bombs, shells, boots, canteens and bones.

Time may have passed since the Great War but the remains remain highly dangerous. The Blue areas are safe to go in. These include the footpaths that have the trees, etc, marked with blue paint.

If you're going to Verdun to the Battlefields there are several areas you should visit, and also some areas you ought to see. Time will be the deciding factor.

In the centre of the area is a massive war memorial called the Ossuaire de Douaumont. It really is huge. You can see it for miles around, its white stone standing out. It's indeed a reminder to anyone about the horrors of war. Inside there's a large remembrance area where you can go to pay your respects. Underneath this huge area are the bodies and bones of the soldiers of both sides who perished here. Their bones can be clearly seen through the special windows to demonstrate the horror. They're not a pretty sight. It's from here that the body of the Unknown Soldier was taken to its place of rest in Paris.

Inside the shop area there's a cinema where you can watch a short film of the Battles of Verdun. However, I found the most moving bit was the old photos on some very old slides. These are located on some very old-fashioned devices, located in the shop to the left. Here you'll clearly see what it was all about, since much of the horror has now faded; the passage of time has washed it all away. Outside and on the drive up to the memorial is a massive war cemetery. It's a moving experience to see it.

There are many forts to see and many battlefields to visit. The two largest are Fort de Douaumont and Fort de Vaux.

Fort de Douaumont is a short drive from the memorial. Built around 1870, it was constructed in the period when France's borders with Germany were different. Germany had won in a previous battle the area of Alsace and parts of Lorraine. Forts were then built to defend the new line. Verdun was chosen to be a large military town. That is one reason the Germans attacked it in such force. The fort is huge and is not what you imagine on the outside. Built to withstand shells, it saw many battles. It changed sides several times. Conditions were awful. Life was primitive and was downright hard. The washrooms look dire. There's even a delousing room. The toilets were abysmal and the nauseating smell made many ill.

In this fort is a gunnery that was used to repel the enemy. However, lack of food forced the fort to surrender at one point to the Germans. Certainly, at times it became its own tomb. Thousands and thousands of soldiers passed through this fort as it was one of two large forts in the area. Not many made it back. Outside the fort up on top are the remains of the gun towers. These are large metal domes sealed in by concrete. These days they are totally rusted up. However, you can imagine their power. Their thick solid steel structure was built to defend the guns from attack. One nevertheless ripped apart like a piece of wood being split open. This happened as a result of a direct hit. The gun remains littered around the area to this day.

I must mention at this point a restaurant we visited in this vicinity. It was a most strange experience for all of us. The restaurant is dated but serves its purpose well. The menu was mostly limited to rabbit. The rabbits are shot in the woods and served up. They were tasty and, by heck, it was different!

The other large fort worth seeing is Fort de Vaux, a short drive away. Here it is much the same and well worth a look around. There's a war museum called the Memorial de Verdun which, inside, shows the horrors of the war. If you have the time check it out. Other places on your tour to see include the Trench of the Bayonets. Here, during one of the battles, an entire regiment was buried after an explosion. Only their bayonets were left sticking out above the surface. Sadly, inside the monument built to preserve the tragedy, the war graves have been vandalised. Souvenir hunters have stolen most of the original bayonets.

One of my friends decided to take a walk into the woods on one of the paths that lead away from here. When I pointed out that he was now in a red zone he had to retreat very carefully. There are many, many trenches throughout the area. Many are built of wood. You can walk along some of them, but don't walk too far off track or you could get blown up. It's still dangerous beyond the signposted area. Nine villages simply disappeared off the map because of the battle. You can see where several of them were on the tour round. There's not a lot to see, which, if you think about it, says it all.

There are many more places to visit, but it's better to see them for yourself to get the full picture of the area. It takes about an hour by car on the motorway via Metz to get here.

Verdun—The Town

The town of Verdun is well worth a visit to have a nosey around. These days it's a small, modern French town with a spark of life to it. There are some nice restaurants and bars down on the quay area. In the summer it's a delight. You can sample a beer on the moored riverboats. When we were there, we witnessed a good old-fashioned fight, right in the centre of the restaurant we were in. The whole place cleared out including our group. The parties concerned smashed wine glasses on the counter arming themselves with the broken edged glasses and the action commenced. Did we mind? No, not at all—it remained a talking point for months! Now you don't get that in the tourist guide.

Festivals are held here throughout the summer. The most famous one is 'The story of Verdun.' On the night I was there things were a little more up to date. It was the last night in a series of different live musical acts. Eddie and the Hot Rods were playing. Eddie who? Come on, didn't you ever hear of punk music? They were a one hit wonder in England with 'Do what you wanna do' in 1977, okay! The lead singer looked like a younger Mick Jagger and they now play his music as well. So much for punk.

20

Escape to Luxembourg!

My first trip to Luxembourg was back in 1983. Life was a lot different then. There were no mobile phones and not many computers. Communications were more basic. Lifestyles were a world away to what they are today.

Now most people come to Luxembourg for a holiday or to work. I came here under altogether different circumstances…

Back in 1983, the press reported that there had been a massive 'Jailbreak' from Chelmsford prison in Essex, England. Many prisoners escaped to all over the United Kingdom. Some escapees were recaptured. Some made it to the nearest pub. Others made it up to Manchester. I'm sure that some prisoners crossed the border into Scotland.

There were even some clever prisoners who made it over the channel to Europe. It had been a daring escape and the prison authorities reluctantly had to report a mass breakout of about eighty-three prisoners.

Crikey! This just doesn't happen in the UK. The last time there was a mass breakout of this magnitude was during the Second World War and that became known, as 'The Great Escape'. What made it worse was that some prisoners who had really thought about their escape plan made it as far as New York. Now, that's something. I mean, what is their name—Ronnie Biggs, or what?

Funnily enough, and deviating for a second, I did actually nearly meet the man himself—Ronnie Biggs, that is. He was living in Rio de Janeiro in Brazil up until relatively recently. People talk about him and I did hear when I was over there that he ran visits to his house. He ran hosting parties for generally English tourists who wanted to get the T-shirt 'I've met Ronald Biggs the Great Train Robber.'

Well, I wasn't so much after the T-shirt, more the opportunity of meeting a living legend. Okay, the T-shirt might have been nice but tacky. How English or what? Anyway, I rang him from my hotel and spoke to his son Michael. To cut a long story short he said he would arrange a meeting. However, it never happened due to his fathers' very poor state of health at the time. Ronnie Biggs had just suffered a stroke, the good-time years of wine, women and everything else now long since over. Life was beginning to catch up with him.

Now I'll let you into a little secret. The prisoners who escaped had hatched their meticulously planned routes down to the last detail. They were also dressed, mostly, in what could be described as various forms of prison uniform. Oh, and they unfortunately had to wear a ball and chain attached to their ankle. Now you wouldn't think that prisoners could still wear a ball and chain in this day and age, would you? Well, they do. But let me assure you that these particular persons were not your average bunch of rogues. They were everyday people who had volunteered to be prisoners. I mean, were they mad or what?

Actually, they were people like you and me who were there to raise money for Charity. (Don't forget to pronounce this word *Chaarity*—sorry!) The charity was the Essex Association of Boys Clubs. The 'Jailbreak', you see, was a bit of fun. It was a challenge. It was a day out! The prisoners had one 'goal'. They had to get as far from their captors in twelve hours as they could, without spending any money or at least not their money. The winners would be the ones who had escaped the furthest. After twelve hours, they would telephone from their end destination. As I have said, the winners in the year of 1983 (yes, I am showing my age here) made it to New York.

I think they may have had a little help from the Essex Police and their helicopter, which assisted them in their escape from Chelmsford to Heathrow. The escaped prisoners then took a flight to New York. Now that's pretty good, especially if you're an escaped prisoner.

The teams of prisoners, as it turned out, won various prizes for different categories. One of the other categories was 'Furthest escape into Europe'. The winners were a team that ended up in Switzerland driving Jackie Stewart's sports car. Naturally, I doubt they would have travelled at 30 mph in a vehicle like that. What speed they did is for you to imagine.

The team that came second that year made it to Luxembourg. It was *that* team that I was in. Boy, was it a trip to remember…

At the time, I was in my early twenties and worked in the City of London. One of my hobbies was Hospital Radio where I was a presenter. The hospital radio station had teamed up with the organisers to follow the contestants. It had been a bit of a last-minute decision, but I had decided I would volunteer if I could join one of the teams. After all, it was voluntary and both the organisers and hospital radio were looking for help to cover the event. Little did I know what that would mean!

The team I was assigned to were actually a bunch of real life prison warders. They, as I soon discovered, had a wicked sense of humour but were a bloody good laugh. I joined them a few days before the event and during a quick pint in a local pub we went through the escape plan. I was also told the order of the day was a prison costume, which would be supplied to me.

Now as far as I can remember the other team members were Mike, Shaun and George. The team had originally decided to call themselves 'The Three Arrows'—but with my late inclusion in the team it was renamed 'The Four Arrows'.

The great day arrived. It was a Saturday and all the teams assembled outside the prison where a crowd had developed. It was actually quite a gathering in the forecourt outside the prison. In fact, Springfield Road had never seen anything quite like it.

The HQ was located in an old, wooden, traditional English village hall opposite. Inside the HQ, the place was abuzz with teams and officials who gathered paperwork and studied maps. They were checking prisoners' details, their plans, giving them instructions on what number to phone at the end of the twelve hours etc…The officials were sitting on old wooden chairs, their papers scattered on trestle tables, typical furniture of traditional village halls.

Once the paperwork had been processed, each team made its way over the road to the prison forecourt. After some time the huge prison gate was opened and the different teams were let in! The doors closed behind them.

The whole thing reminded me of that television programme 'Porridge' with Ronnie Barker. I had visions of Norman Stanley Fletcher…and the sound of one hundred and one prison gates closing behind me.

Every team had their own type of prison costume. I soon discovered that ours turned out to be the real thing. Yes, ours were 'real prison pyjamas,' but don't tell anyone, will you! They were light blue in colour and I noticed they had a slight addition on them. They all had the legendary large prison arrows painted on, not in black but a sombre red.

These days, as far as I know, prisoners in the United Kingdom don't actually have uniforms or pyjamas with arrows on them. They probably did years ago, but these pyjamas were special with the arrows hand painted by real prisoners. Well, it was all for a good cause. Now come on! The actual prisoners thought it all hilarious. The arrows were either facing up or they were facing down. I can't remember. However, the point is, as I was informed, they were put on the opposite way to what they used to be officially.

We were also wearing a ball and chain. Every man had to supply his own ball. (No doubt you're now wickedly thinking out one hundred and one ball jokes, but don't!) The ball was a ballcock painted black. A ballcock is something you find in a toilet system, for those of you that don't know. (Even less of the jokes here, please; after all, this is not 'Up Pompeii.')

The chain the lads had bought from a local DIY outfit, being of the plastic fence variety. Needless to say, I was the odd one out. Why? Well, working in the City at the time and joining the team at the last moment meant some quick escape planning. So, I ended up with a metal chain, which could have been the real thing, the way it looked. It most certainly *felt* like the real thing, I can assure you. In fact, it was damn heavy!

In the large courtyard, the clock was ticking away. The gates would open at 9 am. That would give the teams twelve hours for their plans to succeed or not.

At the stroke of nine, the huge gates swung back. We were 'free'! The teams made their escape from the prison, rushing through the entrance of the prison. The TV cameras rolled, the camera flashes went off. We were off, pausing in the forecourt to pose for more photos for the press, friends and family. Moments later, we were away.

The Four Arrows team was heading for Dover. The team travelled in a car provided by a local travel company. One of the girls from the company was driving us lads all the way to Dover. How nice! After that, our next stop would be the ferry that would take us across the English Channel to Calais.

En route many jokes were told. It was a fun trip. Our driver on arriving on the outskirts of the port of Dover then followed the signs for the ferry terminus and Calais. She then drove up to the departures hall for the ferry that we would be taking. The team alighted, picked up their bags and thanked her before making their way inside the building. After 'checking in' with the tickets that had been provided for us the four of us proceeded to the customs hall. When we got there explanations were necessary as to who we were and what exactly we were doing.

The customs guards advised us to remove our balls and chains and to try and cover up before we actually went through customs. We did our best. However, all of us had noticed some guy looking at us from the other side of the customs barrier. This was before we went through ourselves. He looked a little odd but none of us thought anything of it at the time.

The four of us walked outside towards the ferry. Standing next to it, I took some photos of the team before we traversed the gangplank and boarded the ship.

Eventually it set sail and everyone felt happy but hungry. We 'escaped prisoners' decided to treat ourselves to a steak in the restaurant. The lads indulged in a pint, or was it six? One of them then noted again that he had seen that guy again watching us through the window of the restaurant. That guy was wearing a raincoat.

Incidentally, the tickets for this entire escapade had come from a local travel company. They were sponsoring our trip—I mean, all the way to Luxembourg. For free. Brilliant!

We stepped outside to breathe in the sea air. The White Cliffs of Dover were now well and truly behind us. France was beckoning. Calais, here we come! But not before the lads had bought a quantity of supplies of beer to keep them going.

The boat arrived at Calais. It docked and the team made their way off the boat. Having cleared French customs everyone headed outside. At this point we all felt it was safe to put on our gear again and then head off for the station. Before boarding the train, the lads nipped into a local shop and bought yet more beers and cigarettes; if you've ever been to Calais you'll know that the 'booze' is considerably cheaper there than it is in England.

Things get a little hazy here as it's over twenty years ago. However, whilst we were in the shop, which was next to the station platform, an argument developed on the platform between one of the team and one of the train guards. The train was literally about to depart and we had to hurry from the shop. There's a good chance that the argument was between one of the team and the guy in the raincoat. Nevertheless, nothing more was thought of it as the train departed Calais station.

Our destination was Thionville, which was the nearest place to the Luxembourg border we could reach with a French freebie train ticket. Don't ask me why the ticket didn't get us to Luxembourg. Anyway, off we went through the countryside of France on our way to this unheard of place called Thionville. I mean, on the map it looked like some tin pot border town. The beers were cracked open and readily consumed—and here I am talking crates rather than six-packs! It was a lot of beer. Well, we had time; after all, there were six hours to pass.

Somewhere along the way the train was due to stop at a place called Lille for a few minutes. This would enable us to put Plan B into action. What was plan B, you ask? Well, it was this. We had a friend who was working in a police department in Chelmsford. He would arrange with his French equivalents for us escaped prisoners to be met in Thionville and helped over the border for the final part of the journey into Luxembourg. Great! So far, so good.

Time was ticking away. At Lille station, Mike, the team leader got out to make the call, to double-check that we would be met in Thionville. (We had intended to make the call in Calais but ran out of time, what with buying the beer and hurrying to catch the train.) It was dusk and a little foggy. It was late autumn and the leaves were beginning to fall. The station itself, a large old French station or Gare, oozed with nostalgia from the bygone days of stream trains. (Today there's a brand new station at Lille where the Eurostar trains arrive.)

Mike managed to find a call box somewhere in the station and luckily had a few French francs left from the beer money, for the call to Thionville. He made it back just in time, but it was close! The train edged out of the station as he ran up the platform and jumped on board. The journey continued on into the evening, the train heading south and east as we sped onwards, towards our destination of Thionville. The train itself was one of those corridor trains you get on French railways—SNCF. The lads cracked open some more beer and many jokes were told. Things would be okay. We were happy.

The clocks in France are one hour ahead of the UK. Everyone had put their watches forward by one hour. That meant the team had to be in Luxembourg City by 10pm. We had little doubt we would get there.

The beer was going down rapidly. I never thought anyone could drink so much! Let's face it, the four of us were rat arsed. I had brought a tape recorder with me to record the journey and at some point later we played it back. It was a great tape with a good story to tell with live recorded action to replay back home. Actually, it was hilarious—we didn't know it then, but when you listened to it, it was clear everyone was getting more and more incoherent. Let's face it, we were totally pissed—even me! The lads were giving me some education lessons in drink. (Well, that's what I told my mother.) Unfortunately the tape at a later date disappeared. I had lent it to the then programme controller who most regretfully mislaid it. I was not a happy bunny. It could be worth a fortune today.

At some point on this part of the train journey the lads thought they would go on a fund raising mission on the train. After all, it was a corridor train where you could go along and choose your own compartment. So off a few of us went, taking our prison hats with us to use as a receptacle to collect money in. Our French wasn't brilliant. Well, actually, mine was bloody awful. Nevertheless one of the lads could conjure up a few more words than 'Bonjour' and 'Merci' and tried a couple of compartments. The train was not that full; after all, it was early Saturday night. There was a good-looking woman sitting with one or two other people in the next-door compartment but one to ours. She was happy to share the moment with us and eventually put a few francs in the cap. We moved on. The results, after a few more people contributed to the hat, even surprised us when we counted the booty. The rest of the train journey passed by uneventfully.

The train eventually arrived at Thionville at some point just before 9pm local time. That left us about an hour. It slowed as it approached the station. We got up from our seats and went into the corridor to join the rest of the people who were themselves waiting to get off.

Mike the team leader decided to have a cigarette just as the train was stopping. In the hustle and bustle of the moment, we hadn't noticed the good-looking woman bump into him with her luggage. She offered him a light, which he accepted. The smoke drifted in the dull stale air of the corridor. He thanked her, though he noticed something odd, which at that moment he decided to keep to himself.

The four of us walked along the platform looking conspicuous in our prison gear including our balls and chains; mine was beginning to hurt like hell. We were looking out for our contact that our friend in the UK who worked at the police headquarters had arranged for us to meet. Walking down the platform and under the underpass, we walked up the other side. As we did so, strange things began to happen.

It was dark and everyone was tired, probably on account of the drink inside us; but it could also have been because of the sheer distance we had covered.

Suddenly six fully dressed police officers appeared and surrounded us. Then it got worse, for the next thing we knew a further six heavily armed French police officers appeared and surrounded us. This was not exactly the friendly welcome we were expecting! Far from it. These particular police officers looked menacing.

Something told me the situation didn't look right at all. Suddenly, from nowhere, about six other people appeared to join the police officers. We were totally surrounded! At this particular moment the whole team became sober and fully alert.

Amongst the other people standing at the back of them was the man in the raincoat who had been following us since we had noticed him at the customs barrier back in England. Next to him was the good-looking woman from the next but one compartment! What the hell was going on?

We were frogmarched into the police station. Were we under arrest? There was commotion all around us. Bloody hell, it suddenly looked as if our cheap hotel was going to be a night in the local French police cells.

We were conducted into the reception area of the police station that adjoined the train station, where Mike the team leader desperately tried to explain in his better-than-any-of-us-could-muster French. He said, "Actually, we're not real prisoners," and he added, "This is all for charity."

No one seemed to understand the sheer farce this was, and not understanding a word of what was going on around us, things began to look desperate. Mike stood there in front of the reception desk listening and trying his best to explain the situation. He listened carefully to what was being said to him in French by the police officer. Eventually, in all the commotion, he turned around to us, his motley crew, and said, "The good-looking woman in that railway compartment next door but one to us, the one who had chatted to us, the one who had put some French Francs into our hats, is actually an undercover detective." He added: "When the train pulled into the platform the good-looking woman accidentally on purpose bumped into me as we left the compartment. She offered me a light. In a split second I noticed her watch—it was the watch of the French secret service. In fact, it had the crest of the French Secret Service on it. I know this from my own contacts in the prison service."

We all looked at each other.

"Bloody hell," I thought. "This was turning into a James Bond situation."

Having been met by six local French policemen, the four of us now found out we had been followed by another six undercover spies on the train including the guy in the raincoat *and* his sidekick, the good-looking woman. We then found out they had *also* called Paris for backup—*another* six fully armed heavies, these being the ones who had and were still surrounding us.

They were in no mood for our story. As far as they were concerned, Mike, Shaun and George and I were the real thing. We were escaped prisoners.

Somewhere along the line the wires had obviously crossed and something had gone wrong—badly wrong. Now it was time to use the one thing that might save us.

Back in England, before we left, Mike the team leader, the one who spoke more French than the rest of us put together, had hatched the bright idea of preparing a letter to give to our man in England's contact here in Thionville. It was written in English on the top half and was in schoolboy French on the bottom half. He hoped it would serve the purpose should the team ever need it. Right now, we did need it. And fast! Mike dug it out and placed it on the reception desk. The French police officers then read it.

They took it away and in another room discussed its contents. Time was ticking by. Our team had to be in Luxembourg City by 10pm and at this rate we wouldn't make it. This was going to be a disaster. What had caused everything to go so wrong?

The French officers eventually reappeared and stood there looking menacingly at us across the reception desk. Us lads did look a motley crew; in fact, the four of us looked absolutely ridiculous dressed as we were. I mean, our team was dressed in prison pyjamas with arrows on! We were dragging our ball and chains and had our overnight bags with us, not forgetting the bag with my tape recorder in.

I asked myself, would escaping prisoners really dress up as we were, so they stood out from the crowd waving their ball and chain, yelling, "You hoo, hi, I've just escaped from prison and do you like my clothes, don't they go well amongst all you lovely people!"

One of the French police officers began to speak. He wasn't happy. Mike did his best to listen, trying desperately to understand what was being said in French and reply the best he could. The conversation seemed to go on for hours but was in reality only minutes. The other three of us could only look on and hope.

All of a sudden, it was over. Mike, our Four Arrows team leader, then explained to us dimwits standing there like a bunch of lemons that "The French police indeed had wind that there were four escaped prisoners. The tip-off came from the English police themselves; and then, with our call from a phone box at Lille station, their worst fears were realised that there were indeed four prisoners who had escaped from England and who were on their way via Thionville to Luxembourg."

Did they think we were going there to deposit our booty in one of those dodgy Luxembourg bank accounts? This thought struck me at a much later date. After all, we could have had the booty stuffed into our bags ready to deposit into the first bank we got to. Let's face it; anything was possible up until that moment.

Suddenly, the four of us were free—free to leave the police station. The irony of the situation was, of course, that the French police were meant actually to be *assisting* us in our escape! It was *they*, the good French police officers themselves, who were meant to be taking us to the border. That was the arrangement that was supposed to have been organised by our man in England. Oh dear, oh dear, oh dear. Just wait till we all got hold of him! (Incidentally, our man in England wasn't called Johnny English. But it does make you wonder.)

If you remember, in those days, there was no such thing as 'Open borders'. That was a distant dream of some European bureaucrat, to emerge in future years. Right now, there was a border to cross. This was yet another possible obstacle.

The French police were not happy. They did *not* see the funny side of the farcical situation we found ourselves in. They most certainly were *not* going to help us on our final leg of the journey.

"Non, non, non monsieur," the police officer returned when Mike had the cheek to ask him for assistance. (Tell me why Frenchmen appear to be the same! I mean, look at their leader, Jacques Chirac. Now *he* didn't do himself any favours, did he, by saying, "Non, non, non monsieur," to Tony Blair during Gulf War Two in the spring of 2003. I mean, ask George Bush the American President if you don't believe me.)

So the team had reached a sudden dilemma. "What do we do now?"

Well, there was only one thing us lads could do. We had forty-five minutes left. Someone would have to bag a taxi. The four of us walked outside and into the darkness of the French night. A taxi was hailed and a conversation held with the French taxi driver and Mike. After this everyone piled in and the taxi drove away. The Four Arrows were at last on their final leg of their journey. The team was now heading towards the border!

When we got there, everyone had their passports ready. What would happen now? Had the Luxembourgish police been tipped off about our escape? The four of us prayed.

The Luxembourg border guard stepped out. The taxi stopped and the driver wound down his window. Everyone passed their passports to the guard who then examined them. He eyed us up and down and the team held their breath. After all, everyone was dressed so ridiculously. However, I also seem to recall that the four of us did happen to slip on a sweater to cover our disguise in order to help ourselves continue the journey. Us lads in the back of the taxi had tucked our balls under the passenger seat to avoid suspicion. (Now don't ask me where Mike had put his ball as he was in the front seat.)

The customs border guard thankfully waved us on! We had safely crossed the border and were now in Luxembourg.

Yes, the team had made it into The Grand Duchy of Luxembourg, home of the world famous Radio Luxembourg. Now, this was exciting! After all, who of my friends had ever been to Luxembourg? The taxi drove onwards towards the city.

The Four Arrows were almost there. The clock was ticking with minutes to go as the taxi arrived in Luxembourg City. It was so exciting to be actually here at last. The team had finally made it to their end destination. All we had to do now was to arrive in the right place.

Thankfully, it wasn't an overly cold night. Mike had instructed the taxi driver to take us to the central square, as years ago he had visited the country and he had vague recollections of where to go. I suppose if the team had all thought about it at the time, it wouldn't have mattered where it ended up in Luxembourg. After all, our goal was Luxembourg, so anywhere would have been just fine. We could have simply gone straight to a hotel, or whatever. However, Mike wanted to do it properly. After all, why spoil the end of the trip by taking half measures?

The rest of us sitting in the back seat didn't have a clue. We were like a bunch of naughty giggling schoolboys on an excursion out. Let's face it, when you go to a new country and to its capital city and you haven't done a little prep work, then you won't know, will you?

As it turned out, the taxi must have arrived at Place d'Armes, the central square that really is the heart of Luxembourg. On first sight, as we drove up in the taxi, there appeared to be a lot of people about. After all, it was a Saturday night. Maybe the cinema had just ended?

The city seemed to be in full swing, even in late October. As the team got out of the taxi, it was quite a moment. Not only did they step out onto Luxembourg soil, they seemed to step out into the glare of the party. Bright lights hit us as everyone stood there feeling momentary like lemons. The team rapidly gained their composure, waving to the crowd. We were all still dressed in our prison gear including our balls and chains.

The crowd seemed to welcome us with open arms. It was amazing after what the four of us had just been through in France! It was surreal. It was as if we had just stepped out from one world into another.

The taxi was sorted out and the driver drove off into the night. The team started talking to the crowd who by now were gathering around us, their curiosity having got the better of them.

Suddenly we were surrounded again, but this time by friendly Luxembourg faces that appeared happy and eager to hear our story. It felt to all of us as if we were celebrities arriving for a movie premier. The Four Arrows were there in the heart of Luxembourg. God, it felt good!

So there we were, the moment had come and gone. So what next? Well, the four of us knew someone would have to ring in and that somehow the team would then have to find somewhere to stay for the night.

We had all brought some Luxembourg Francs with us. Mike the team leader managed to change some notes into coins. He also thought he remembered the area where he had stayed once before. The four of us set off and somewhere along the way we managed to find a phone box. Mike made the call, using the coins he had just changed. The rest of us huddled outside by the open door, all-eager to hear what was being said.

The telephone boxes in Luxembourg were yellow in colour and were a bit different to your British Telecom red that we were used to in England. The folk at HQ were delighted we had rung in. You have to remember that in those days there were no mobile phones. Communication was severely limited. Mike reported our position and quickly relayed our story to eager officials at the other end, the phone box eating up our cash since it was an international call.

When the call was finished, the four of us walked around the area. Mike was desperately trying to remember where it was he had stayed all those years ago. Searching for the hotel the team must have ended up around the Gare area, but I wouldn't swear on it.

Eventually we found his hotel and went inside and rang the bell. A middle-aged woman came out who looked vaguely as if she came from Portugal. We asked, "Do you have a cheap room available for four persons with four single beds, please?" Luckily for us she replied, "Yes, we do have a room."

To this day, the name Vasco rings a bell. That was it. It was called The Hotel Vasco. However, I could be wrong. To be honest, no one paid much notice. None of us was flush with money, so the four of us ended up in the basement in this grotty old room that had a little window at the top. As it was night time we couldn't see anything through it anyway. The room had four single beds and not a lot else, but in the circumstances it served our purpose. Lets face it, it was cheap. We dumped our bags down, including my tape recorder that had captured everything on tape up to this moment.

Everyone could at last remove the escape gear! I couldn't wait to get that bloody ball and chain off. You have to remember that I'm the one wearing practically the real thing. My right foot suddenly felt a lot lighter. Relief—it was heaven!

Then it was time to head for the local bars to celebrate. The team would have a real Luxembourgish beer, or if I knew this lot, it was going to be one of many. In the words of all good beer drinkers, we were about to get pissed as a fart—again.

21

The long haul home

In downtown 1983 Luxembourg, the night was still young in the lads' eyes when we hit the bars. Many beers were downed. A good time was had by us all. Considering everyone had had one or two during the day I don't know where they put it. I think the lads probably had hollow legs.

Later when the bars closed, which in Luxembourg is well past one in the morning, the four of us moved on to sample the nightlife of Luxembourg City, heading towards the cabaret bars. By now, the fog was swirling in the autumn night air.

Inside one of these cabaret bars we got talking to the girls. By now, everyone was well pissed. At some point the subject got onto sex and some bright spark decided it would be a good idea if I lost my virginity that night. I was not too keen on the idea as I was knackered and exceedingly pissed. Luck was on my side, as fortunately the lads didn't have enough money to pay for me to have the pleasure. Still, everyone had had a good laugh out of it. Later, the team staggered back to the hotel and between us managed to get a few hours sleep.

In the morning we rose and prepared ourselves for the return journey, feeling incidentally like death warmed up. It only now dawned on us that the journey home would be at our own cost. There was just one small problem. No one had given much thought as to how to get back.

As the four of us stepped outside everyone could see it was very foggy. We headed down to the Gare, which was close by and enquired about trains to Calais. The ticket man was very helpful. He said, "Yes, you can get to Calais if you take the train from Luxembourg City to Brussels in Belgium. From there you'll have to take a train over the border into France to Lille and then another train to Calais."

Now you would have thought it would have been easier to simply retrace our steps by going back the way we had come. But the alternative route was an option, which was considerably cheaper.

That autumn Sunday in Luxembourg City was different to the ones back home. After all, we were not doing our regular thing and everything around us was continental; the buildings, the streets, the squares and the people, looked so different, so European: compared to life back home. It was exciting to see a different lifestyle.

The team had time for a quick dash round the city. I do vaguely remember seeing some lovely little squares known as 'Place de…' Mike wanted to show us somewhere he remembered from his visit to Luxembourg City years before. We were making for a bridge, which years later I discovered was the bridge Adolphe. As everyone stood there looking out from the top of the bridge we gazed out into the valley beyond. On this particular autumn's day you couldn't see a lot, as the valley was shrouded in a thick swirling mist. ("The Famous Luxembourg Fog," I called it afterwards.) The view as I see it now is spectacular. It is a pity the lads didn't see it at the time. Disappointed, we headed off and made for a local café where we drank a coffee and had some breakfast.

Now, if it had taken us a day to get here, it was sure as hell going to take at least as long or longer to get home. Everyone collected their gear from the hotel room and before departure said, "Au revoir et merci beaucoup," to the lady on the reception desk. The four of us arrived at the station and got on the train for Brussels. Luxembourg City had been a great experience; more of a whirlwind whistle-stop trip somewhat blurred by the beer. The train departed.

Crossing over into Belgium the train headed northwest, passing through the Ardennes region, which I must say on that autumn day was stunning to see. The scenery of the rolling hills covered by forests of different trees was magnificent. The leaves on the trees turning many shades of red were awesome.

Everyone tried to have a kip, as by now sleep was catching up on all of us and we did have over three hours to kill on this leg of the journey. It was late afternoon when the train arrived at Brussels. We had a little time to spare so the four of us went outside the station and had a quick nosey before locating a typical Belgian café for a coffee and some food. We then hopped onto our next train, which would take us over the border into France. It was an uneventful journey. In-between borders everyone showed their passports to the customs guy on the train and the journey continued towards Lille station. From there another train took us up to Calais and the journey was again relatively unexciting. However, it had taken forever to get there and was much longer than the journey out.

By now it was night time and all we had to do next was get a ferry ticket and find our way home. Now with all that planning you would have thought we would have catered for this! Well, you just thought wrong—most of us hadn't a clue what to do. "How are we going to get back to Chelmsford?" I asked. "We'll get the train," Mike assured me.

Luckily for us and after a slight wait we managed to get the last ferry back to England. In anticipation, everyone adjusted their watches, hoping that once in Dover we would be able to get a late train up to London and one back to Chelmsford. On arrival at the dockside, the four of us departed the ferry, passed through customs and headed out of the ferry terminal. We managed to find our way to the station, where, unfortunately, the last train had just left and the next one was not due before five in the morning. It was now around midnight and none of us fancied a night in the waiting room at Dover station. Everyone was tired, cold and just wanted to get back.

So we decided to get a taxi home! There was just another small problem. Everyone was running low on cash. When George asked a Pakistani taxi driver, "How much do you charge to take four people to Chelmsford in Essex?" he replied, "One hundred pounds, mate."

"How much!" we exclaimed.

All of us nearly dropped down dead in shock. £100 was a huge amount of money in those days for a taxi fare. We checked our wallets and pockets and soon realised that between us we just didn't have anything like this amount of cash on us—and this was in the days when cash machines had not fully entered the dictionary. Yes, they *did* exist, but none of us had any cards on us.

"How much to the Dartford Tunnel, to the far side of it?" George then asked him.

"Fifty quid, cash only and up front."

"That's daylight robbery!" I added.

We all counted how much we had. It was not looking good. "Between us its £51.57p lads," said Mike.

"Oh dear! Looks like this could be a bench job in the waiting room of Dover station after all," replied George.

There was only one thing we could do. We'd have to ring someone at home and get them to pick us up. The only thing was, though, who would that person be? A discussion was held which explored all possibilities. Things were not looking good as no one could think of anyone who would come out at that time of night to rescue us. No one, that is, except me.

I made the call.

"You're having a laugh!" the stern voice at the other end said, adding, "Do you realise what time it is and that you've got me out of bed. I was fast asleep."

At this precise moment it dawned on me that my dad was *not* amused.

"But we're stuck!" I pleaded.

"I am *not* driving down to Dover to pick you and your friends up!" he yelled.

"Can you meet us at the Dartford Tunnel then?" I pleaded.

A rendezvous location at the Dartford Tunnel was arranged and he slammed the phone down.

I explained to the others the precise comments of the phone call.

"Good old dad," I thought. "When our luck had run out, he was there to save the day for all of us." The lads and I were all very grateful. But then they had never met my dad when he's not happy…

Mike then collected everyone's cash before he went back to the taxi driver and said, "We want the journey for £50 to the other side of the Dartford Tunnel."

Naturally, he licked his lips with glee. Everyone got in and Mike handed the cash to the driver. The taxi headed for Dartford. We got there first and waited for my father to arrive. When he eventually showed up, he was not a happy bunny. In fact, he was livid with me.

"Don't you ever do that again," he stated with a glare as we climbed in. "I've got to go to work in the morning."

I didn't have to go to work the next day, but I got the message. He was seething. Most of the journey was in silence. All of us were exhausted. I felt as if I was heading home with my tail between my legs…

So there it was; the jailbreak was over. The team had made it back in one piece and everyone went their separate ways, getting on with their own lives. About a month later, everyone met up again for an awards ceremony that was held at The County Hotel in Chelmsford. The Four Arrows were presented with the second prize in the 'Escaped furthest in Europe' sector for getting to Luxembourg. It was a good moment as we collected our certificates and trophies. Overall, the lads had raised a fair wedge for the Essex Boys Club Charity. Many more beers were drunk that night and the whole event was judged a huge success.

The question on everyone's mind was, "What are you going to do next year?"…

22

208 plus

When I was a kid, I used to listen late at night to the English service of Radio Luxembourg. It was famous. It *was* Luxembourg, putting the Duchy on the map.

I used to listen under my blanket with my mother yelling, "Have you turned that radio off yet?"

And, of course, you'd always say, "Yes mum," and simply turn the volume down to a lower setting.

I didn't want to miss a beat as the music faded in and out. Hence, the famous 'Luxembourg fade' everyone still talks about today.

Someone introduced the transistor radio in the late 60's or early 70's and listening on your 'tranny' was cool.

Radio Luxembourg was fun. When I was older I could be driving late at night down the motorway practically anywhere in the UK and when the BBC shut down at midnight, there was always Luxembourg. The number of lorry drivers who used to listen to the station driving through the night was huge. Let's face it, in those days there wasn't a lot else.

From its beginning in the thirties until the eighties the station was successful for a number of reasons. The station had advertisements that weren't allowed on the BBC, its music was up to date and popular, and it was ahead of the rest in what it played.

The station's transmitter was massive. I've driven past the masts several times up at Junglinster. The masts are also on most maps. Originally they put out an incredible two to three hundred kilowatts, which made it possible to cover most of Europe. I remember they used to say it was the most powerful radio station in Europe, reaching even into the former communist states where fans used to secretly listen in.

I used to hear stories that Radio Luxembourg annoyed the hell out of the BBC with their every move. I know the BBC responded with years of harassment. This was because they wanted to keep their monopoly and didn't want any competition, but Radio Luxembourg being outside the UK there was little the BBC could do. They even got the British press to stop publicizing the station. This situation unbelievably lasted for years and years except for one or two publications that defied the ban. The BBC even got the British Post Office to refuse Luxembourg a landline. This was extremely petty and arrogant and these days it sounds farcical, especially if you think of the way satellite transmissions have changed everything. But in those early days the BBC didn't want anyone being more successful than them—and the people who ran the BBC from the thirties until the sixties didn't rate the format of fun programmes that Luxembourg put out.

The format on Radio Luxembourg up until the sixties was incidentally very different to what I grew up listening to. As with most things in life it was all before my time.

Radio Luxembourg's headquarters were in a building here in Luxembourg City called the Villa Louvigny. The original building was built in the grounds of the municipal park on top of part of the old Fort Louvigny. The original building was greatly expanded into the building that remains on this site today, which is real thirties in its style.

RTL, the owners of Radio Luxembourg's English service, remained in this building until the late nineties when it relocated up to Kirchberg into modern state-of-the-art buildings, ending an era in the Villa Louvigny.

I remember Luxembourg in the 70's when my friends and I all wanted to be DJs. Luxembourg then had all the great names and I think this was when it was probably at its best. They practically bred such names as Stuart Henry, Kid Jenson, The Emperor Rosco, Mark Wesley, Barry Aldis and the legendary Bob Stewart, who actually was at the station from 1969 until 1991. Then there was the equally legendary Tony Prince known as 'your Royal ruler' who reigned until 1983. Mid 70's DJ's included Peter Powell, Steve Wright and Mike Read.

When a new DJ arrived at Luxembourg my friends and I used to wonder how long it would be before they were poached by BBC Radio 1. At least half the DJ's were spirited away and their careers went upwards, thanks to Luxembourg.

They used to have this brilliant build up when the English service commenced transmissions around 7 or 8pm after the German service handed over the microphone in the late 70's.

Another great moment I shall never forget was the night Elvis died. I may have been listening to the Top 20 Countdown that was on a Tuesday night between 9 and 10pm. The *Daily Mirror*-sponsored news service was at the top of the hour followed by Tony Prince. It was during his show, I think, that Tony suddenly announced the news of Elvis's death. At first, the news was sketchy. Tony just couldn't believe it, especially as he himself was a big fan of the King. Communications, you have to understand, were in those days not like they are today. It naturally turned into an Elvis night and the rest you know.

The beginning of the 80's saw the arrival of more commercial stations in the UK. Their broadcasting on FM resulted in a radical fall of listeners to Radio Luxembourg's English service. It went through a brief Disco period before reverting to its normal great format with such wonderful DJ's such as Mark Wesley, Mike Hollis and Benny Brown. Even the Emperor Rosco reappeared on 208.

Luxembourg was again challenged in the mid-1980's, as were the BBC and English local commercial stations, with the arrival of the American-run pop pirate Laser 558. It was moored in the North Sea and its presence was phenomenal. It challenged the establishment and helped change the format of British radio like the pirates had done before in the mid-sixties. Nevertheless, it upset the authorities and the British Government forced its closure by starving them out.

The Radio challenge to Luxembourg was fierce. However, the damage had been done, mainly by the many new FM stations and Radio Luxembourg's reign was over.

It was very sad when RTL, the owners of Radio Luxembourg, decided to close down the English service. They actually closed it twice. I was listening when they turned it off the first time at the beginning of the 90's when they switched onto satellite. Then, when that failed due to insufficient listeners—or was it advertisers? (they should try it again today as times have changed)—the plug was pulled.

I was listening at the end of 1992 when, for one night only, on the 30th December, they reopened on medium wave and satellite, and broadcast their final act before the curtain came down. There was a host of DJ's both past and present broadcasting, together with the music of the different generations for all the anoraks listening in, hoping to hear their favourite DJ again. Listeners were able to feel nostalgic when they played those magical Radio Luxembourg jingles. 'The sound of 208!' or even 'FAB 208'. Yes, 208 metres on the medium wave said it all. It was never the same when they changed it to 1440 kHz.

I have to admit I was a 70's listener, though I must admit the station of the 80's was good and I enjoyed listening in the 90's to Jodie Scott and Wendy Lloyd on the satellite.

When the station did close, it was sad. It was a pity, really. Still, all good things, I suppose, have to come to an end. There was talk about restarting the English service but nothing ever came of it, which is disappointing in view of the number of potential listeners still out there. In the meantime the name of Radio

Luxembourg, for the moment at least, has sunk into oblivion as far as the European Radio market is concerned.

The English service of Radio Luxembourg has a huge history that one could easily write a book on. Sadly, in the time I've been in Luxembourg I've found that most local people here, especially young people, have completely forgotten about the English service as it was, which I think is a tragedy. These days radio stations use letters for the station name, hence RTL, as opposed to Radio Luxembourg. Most foreigners I know only know the name RTL. They have never heard of Radio Luxembourg and the English service, except, that is, for the older Brits.

However, sometimes there *is* life after death. RTL may have killed off the English service of Radio Luxembourg, but I myself have discovered that thanks to the internet there are literally thousands and thousands of websites devoted to the station. Largely the fans themselves have set these up. When I typed in 'Radio Luxembourg' one day in 2003 I was astounded by how many web sites came up.

Nowadays, in the evenings, you can listen to 208 metres or 1440 kHz to China Radio International. Now that doesn't quite have the same feel to it…

These days here in the Grand Duchy there's a variety of listening options. I have my favourites but like to tune around the dial to see what's going on. RTL is the shortened name for Radio Television Luxembourg. RTL remains a very large private company called CLT-UFA S.A. These days RTL have branched out into television but have continued in a big way with their radio interests. Their interests are both in and outside of Luxembourg.

On the radio here, the largest radio stations are still run by RTL that continue to dominate, and which are still financed by advertisements. They are not owned by the state. Today they broadcast in Luxembourgish, French and German. The Luxembourgish station is called RTL Radio Lëtzebuerg and broadcasts on 88.9 FM and 92.5 FM. You can actually watch this station on the TV during part of the day.

The German station broadcasts on 97.00 FM and 93.3 FM. Both of these stations are classed as national stations. RTL also has a huge separate radio station that broadcasts in French and is as famous in France as the English one was in England. The French channel broadcasts on long wave on 234 kHz with a power of two thousand kilowatts. This makes it by far the biggest transmitted station in the country. Its shear power output enables it to broadcast all over France, making it a very popular station to listen to. RTL also broadcasts on various FM frequencies in France and Belgium.

The other national radio station is the state run 'Radio 100.7', which is on FM. Primarily it's a culture and arts station—a highbrow station, which has only been in operation for just over ten years. The station broadcasts in Luxembourgish.

There are four network radio stations. All of them are good to listen to. I find them unique to Luxembourg, as they are mostly multilingual—which is no big deal, considering the country is multilingual.

The system of running them is also unique. In England, a local commercial radio station is paid for by advertisements. Business can put money in and become shareholders. These days the big boys have come in and taken over all the smaller stations as a result of a de-merger of the airwaves. In Luxembourg, a local radio station is run on approximately €12,500 a year. Think about it. The definition of local radio in Luxembourg, and how it is run in Luxembourg, is completely different from the UK. Nevertheless, run well it is. The local stations, whilst in competition with one another, are not really. Each has developed its own market. I think that their success has surprised the Government here and probably worried the giant RTL network.

The stations here generally follow their historic big brother Radio Luxembourg with their eight hours of three languages. This makes a good day's broadcast and varies from French, English and Luxembourgish to French, English and German etc…

One station is Radio ARA. It broadcasts on 103.3 FM to Luxembourg City, in English, Luxembourgish and various other languages including Italian. The English service is on between 6am and 2pm. It's very schoolboy tongue-in-cheek humour that's broadcast. At the time of writing, Jim Kent is the current breakfast DJ. He's currently King of the Breakfast Airwaves. I always imagine him as a Jim Carey look-alike. He certainly sounds like him. He's daft as a brush on air but lots of fun with everyone. He's also a favourite with the French girls. *Ooh la la!*

Then there's serious Nick Scarlet. He's got a very dry sense of humour that's reflected in the 'alternative' music he plays.

The lunchtime show has had a number of people hosting it following the departure of Teddy Knowler. He was a great DJ whose disco music was great. He was also brilliant at taking the piss out of everyone on air with his "*Ooo ahh*, I come from Bristol"—type accent. Teddy now fills in on other shows. Come back, mate, you're listener misses you!

Right now it's Simon 'The Funky' Gibbon in the hot seat, so look out, Luxembourg. The lively Sally Carter fills in for everyone as and when, and she is not to be missed.

On a Thursday evening between 6.30 and 8pm is the weekly 'Corner Café', which is an arts programme in English that's actually well worth a listen.

Another station is the Portuguese language Radio Latina on 101.2 & 103.1 FM. They play some wicked salsa and Latin music. They also play the music of the Fado, which I understand is the music of the ocean—the ocean in question being the Atlantic Ocean off Portugal. Yes, I know the sea off Portugal is called the Straites of Portugal, but let's not get pedantic, eh!

However, there's also some Spanish, Italian and Luxembourgoire spoken on the station. They play mainly Portuguese music, but if someone rings up and asks for Johnny Halliday, the French artist, then he will get played.

There is a large presence of Portuguese people here in Luxembourg City. The station brings the Portuguese community together. A good example is the story I heard about a boy very ill with cancer of the blood. He needed money for a special operation. The station helped organise fêtes and dinners to raise money for him. Young and old all helped out, which in this day and age I think is marvellous.

Yet another radio station is DNR. This broadcasts on 102.9 FM and is a Luxembourg pop music station.

The fourth radio station is Eldoradio that's also a pop music station. It broadcasts in Luxembourgish on 105 FM and is very 'listenable'.

After the network stations come the local stations. There are a few of these.

One definitely worth mentioning is Radio W.A.K.Y. They broadcast in English and French on 107 FM. The name sounds daft, doesn't it? Whoever heard of a name called WAKY? What does W.A.K.Y. mean, I wonder? I bet the jingle makers had a hoot when it came to making their jingles. The name sounds so American as well. I can assure you, though, it's a fine station.

They tend to broadcast pop music in English and French, with French DJ's doing the breakfast, lunchtime and drive time slots. The mid-morning and afternoon slots are filled with American DJ's—cool to listen too, even though they speak American English.

Nightclub-style music hits their transmitters in the evening after 8pm. On Sunday night at 7pm, it's country music which, having been to Nashville, I enjoy.

There is also some American on there called Shadow Stephens. I mean, does he love himself, or what? Again, he's well worth a listen but I do wonder what his real name is. It's probably bog-standard Reginald Clark or something equally boring. How many Reginald's do you hear as DJ's on the radio?

I used to listen to a very popular station in Luxembourg City called Radio Sunshine, or Tango Sunshine, as it tended to call itself, after its main sponsor. They broadcast on 102.2 FM. It was primarily a top forty-type station broadcasting in English and Luxembourgish.

Graham Oldham was the DJ and was then King of the Breakfast airwaves. Jim Kent may dispute this, but it depends on your taste. Anyway, Graham came across as a lovable fat Australian bearded guy, which he probably wasn't.

Radio Sunshine's licence was to broadcast as a local station. It should provide a variety of programmes including culture, sports, and everything else a local station broadcasts, as set out in the terms and conditions of its licence. It should also not exceed twelve thousand three hundred and ninety five euros in advertising profit.

This amount of money in English radio terms is pretty small. It wouldn't even pay for one DJ. Still, this is Luxembourg and the rules are different here.

Well, along came Tango who became the station's main sponsor. They later also set up a TV station here. This is very successful as it gives RTL Television a run for its money.

However, somewhere along the line, somebody allegedly upset someone in the government. At the end of December 2002, something strange happened in the radio world here. They gave the radio station a week or so notice to close and on 31st December 2002 at just after 6pm, the station closed. According to the government website where a communiqué was posted, the station had broken the terms and conditions of its licence. Hence, after an investigation by 'La Commission Indépendante de la Radiodiffusion' it was forced to shut down.

Mind you, the final hour, which I listened to, was a classic. In radio talk, it was great. Graham Oldham presented 'The final hour' of Tango Sunshine, or Radio Sunshine, as it reverted to. He decided to go out in style.

Now if you're a radio person, then closedowns are important. One of the most famous radio closedowns ever was 'The Final Hour' in August 1967, on 'Big L'—that's Radio London, the pirate radio station that broadcast from a ship, a former mine sweeper, in the North Sea off Clacton in the UK back in the 60's. That was listened to by millions.

The final hour on Tango Sunshine I doubt was listened to by too many people as many were still at work. However, to his regular fans, this one-off live show was incredibly good. The 'final hour' went out between 5pm and 6pm.

Graham Oldham started by telling everyone that he was going to be out of a job. Therefore, he decided to do something about it live on air. Well, it was a bit naughty, but it was so entertaining!

First, he rang the unemployment office to advise them that he was losing his job and therefore what should he do? Unfortunately, they couldn't help him as everyone had gone home. Then he rang the Prime minister whose aide answered by saying "Ya" before hanging up.

Finally, he rang The Grand-Duke himself. When he got through, one of his security people said, "Who are you?"

"I'm Graham Oldham from Tango Sunshine," etc…

The confused security guy then swiftly said, "The Duke is *not* available."

"Where is he then?" asked Graham.

"Err, err—he's on holiday," was the reply. Before you could blink, the phone went dead.

It was great radio to listen to. Finally, at the end of the show Graham announced that he would be continuing his breakfast show but on Tango TV. Since then Graham has progressed to Radio W.A.K.Y. doing the mid morning show at the weekends.

However, after this unnecessary forced station closure, I could feel the bonding of the smaller stations.

23

The Struggle to Survive!

If you've ever had the pleasure of being unemployed then you'll know that after the novelty of staying at home for while has lost its shine, it gets a bit boring. One has to live, after all, so if you don't have a job that brings in the money then you may have a problem. They do say that money makes the world go around. Well, it won't if you don't have any.

Now we're all different and we all look at life from a different viewpoint. This different viewpoint is echoed remarkably well when it comes to those in work and those out of work.

As I've discovered, it's a different world out there. Having the extra problem of living abroad and having to speak another language makes it just that little bit more frustrating.

However, the experience gained and what one learns from it, is an invaluable lesson in life. To sum it up I also wouldn't have missed it for the world even though it most certainly has had its moments. I've been quite lucky for a large portion of my life in that I worked for one organisation for twenty-two years. Overall, these days that just doesn't happen anymore. I wanted to do something different and to this day I'm not sure what I'll end up doing. When I came to Luxembourg I was lucky enough to get myself a job with one of the banks here with a six-month contract.

Then times changed in the banking world. Things rapidly changed after a gradual hidden slide. When I arrived, I was advised by lots of people that "Luxembourg is a great place to work. People work six months, maybe even two years, and then change jobs to another bank or whatever. It's the normal thing to do here." I was told this by many of the expats here.

It sounded great and was—especially if you're lucky enough to still have a job. I've no regrets that the contract wasn't renewed. It would have been nice, but a contract is a contract. Whether it is three months, six months or even a year, when your time's up, that's it. It's time to move on and get something else. That's life!

One of my English friends decided to change jobs just before the downturn. He knew he had been lucky. Two months later, I wasn't so lucky. All the contractors in the department were advised that their contracts were not going to be renewed. Those people would be out of a job. In addition, those who had resigned were also not replaced. A bit of people-shuffling came into play. Budgets were being cut.

At the time, everyone blamed Bin Laden. September 11th 2001 did no one any favours. After that everything just got worse. I'm not talking about just my situation or the place I worked in. In reality, this was happening to many people in the banking world. People were suddenly waking up to the fact that things were not quite as they had been. Life was never going to be the same again.

It's quite ironic that since September 11th 2001 people are hanging onto their jobs like there's no tomorrow. Even if they hate them! Suddenly the banks weren't recruiting, and the days of hopping from job to job in Luxembourg City were well and truly over. Ask any expats, they'll tell you the same story. In fact, I've lost count of the number of times I hear the same tale. It's as if a gramophone needle is stuck in a groove, needing just that little bit of assistance to move on with the music, and in our case, with our lives.

I've met so many different people who've lost their jobs through cost cutting. It appears that when the downturn began in 2001, the banks cushioned the economic situation by utilizing their profits from the previous year's profits. When it came to the end of 2001, savage job cuts kicked in and the bloodbath began.

In the spring of 2003 I met a nice French girl at the unemployment office to whom I got talking. She said, "What did you do before you became unemployed?" I told her. She asked my Danish friend Jasper the same thing. He had also worked for a bank and when his contract had finished it was also bye-bye. She didn't look surprised at all. Then she said, "I was fired! Seventy of us actually in one go." It was shocking stuff, made worse by the fact that I heard through the grapevine that they would only get two or three month's money maximum as a redundancy pay off. Two other French girls I know were made redundant from Planistat in October 2003. Neither of them, of course, was happy about it. "Sixty of us got fired," they said.

This batch of layoffs was a knock on effect of the Eurostat scandal in 2003 where financial irregularities were discovered. Planistat was a supply company to Eurostat, which is part of the European Union office network.

Now I don't pretend to understand how redundancy works in Luxembourg. I know how it works in the UK. Nevertheless, I am aware that it's not the same by any means.

In the UK the longer you have worked for a company the better your payoff. But then it also depends on the company you work for. They all have some form of redundancy compensation. If you're very unlucky then you'll get from the state the UK state minimum! It's not good, but it's better than a kick in the teeth. Being an expat generally means it's you who has opted out of UK living and have wanted to try a different lifestyle. Many Brits have done it. They live all over the world, not just in Luxembourg. At the end of the day, they all survive somehow, don't they? So, what do other expats do when they lose their job? The answer is simple. They do the same as everyone else. They look for another job. If that means moving on, then so be it.

The Luxembourg Government, I think, does well on this point, because all those people who move on have still had to pay their taxes, etc…therefore the state wins and allegedly gets still richer. Luxembourg is one of the richest countries in Europe. But it's not cheap to rent a flat here.

Being on the other side of the fence does show you the other side of life. I myself have written one hell of a lot of letters, over two hundred and twenty to date. One of my Italian friends said to me that he had written over two hundred and fifty but to no avail. If you've got a wife and two kids to support, then it's not funny.

Suddenly, if you don't speak three languages, the door's slammed in your face. If you don't speak French, Luxembourgish and German, you're stuck. English is a poor man's fourth now. When I arrived you were welcome if you spoke English. Then it was important. Firms were falling over themselves to recruit people who spoke the business language of the world. Not anymore.

Now it's all so very different. For every job there are over fifty applicants. If you don't have the three languages for starters, then forget it. If you're over forty, then generally forget it.

I've noticed something creeping in here, which is not allowed as far as I am aware of back in the UK. Here some companies stipulate that you have to send in a photo of yourself. Now this is very sexist as it allows the employer to pick and choose—and to make the point here, I'll add that a young female with blonde hair, big tits and blue eyes may have an advantage!

No, I'm not joking. I'm over forty, have a small beer gut and am balding. I don't have blue eyes either. Pity! But having recruited people myself, I know that one's suitability for a job should be judged on the C.V. and the ability to do the job. Sex and looks shouldn't come into it. But regretfully, it does.

I've spoken to all the various places foreigners have to go to. They all say the same thing. "Yes, the government is aware of the issue," or, "Aah, the Financial Crisis!" And, "The Economic Crisis." They all know about it. There appears to be one giant cover-up.

In reality, I'm not sure that even the Government knows the answer. Certainly, there's massive development up at Kirchberg. But is it too little too late? If the economy turns around, which is anybody's guess, then everyone will be happy. Jobs create jobs if the environment is right. Right now, anything is possible and in a year's time we might all be wondering what all the fuss has been about. I certainly hope things improve here. For the moment, if you're unemployed, the situation is not good.

Most people who have been on contract, simply uproot and leave the country when their job finishes. The way that the government benefits is by way of the taxes it has taken. More importantly, the pension money and sickness benefit scheme that everyone has had to pay into is kept by the state.

In December 2002 unemployment registered at 2.6% nationally. When it hit 3.8% just before Easter, it wasn't good. I did hear unofficially it did hit around 4%. In December 2003 I heard on the radio the unemployment figure had climbed to 4% officially and that this figure had doubled in two years. That means unofficially it was actually higher than this. Why? Remember these unemployment figures conveniently do not include the contractors who have left the country. I'm not just referring to British expats here—far from it. I mean, it includes every nationality of person who has been here on a contract. Add that up and you can see why, suddenly, there's a problem. No government likes to admit it has a problem. Still, the figure is not as bad as France or Germany—yet.

One day I jokingly said to one of the unemployment centres officials, "You've currently got the only growth industry in town."

"Yes," he replied, adding, "We've just taken on another twenty-three staff to cope with the situation."

Life goes on.

Still, from an expat perspective, you have to survive. Every individual has to learn the ropes of the country he or she is in. One way to help you do this is to talk to different people, to hear what they have to say and to listen to any advice they can give you. It is in fact invaluable because when you're suddenly unemployed, you suddenly realise just who your friends are.

It's amazing the people who suddenly disappear out of your life. Once you have crossed that line it's bloody hard work re-crossing it. But don't give up. Life's a bitch and I know a few. One day something good will happen.

There is an old English saying, "Nothing ventured, nothing gained." With that in mind and with my contract having finished on the Friday, first thing on the Monday morning I was straight down to the Bierger-Center. This building is situated next to the bus station also known as the Centre E. Hamilius. Their address is actually 51 Boulevard Royal in the main town.

I was there to sort my papers out. I had to update them on my new address etc…Somewhere in the conversation I was advised I needed to have a Blue Card from this other department, which as I soon discovered was on the other side of town.

It was actually the unemployment building, known as the 'Administration de l'emploi.' It's also known as 'ADEM' for short. I do vaguely remember traipsing backwards and forwards between the offices, wondering why they weren't in the same place.

When you go down to the Bierger-Center, it would be worth asking them for a Certificat-Bescheinigung, which is a resident's certificate. At least it proves where you live should anyone ask you.

There appeared to be no communication between the two buildings. So, when I arrived I ended up explaining my situation to a very helpful man. I said, "I haven't come in for a cent, euro or a penny. But I've come for a Blue Card. That would do nicely, please." He asked me, "What was the length of time of your contract?" and I told him. At the end of the short interview, he leaned over his desk and said, "I see that you have worked over one hundred and eighty-two days, plus you worked some of your holiday. You will be pleased to know that you qualify for eighty per cent of your salary for six months."

I looked at him in disbelief. I was gob-smacked. After all, I only went in for this Blue Card—and there I was walking out with eighty per cent of my salary! This I could never have imagined in a million years. It sounded too good to be true.

An Australian friend had vaguely mentioned he had heard something about the unemployment system here, but he didn't think I would be eligible for it. It took me a week or so before that conversation connected with what had just happened.

So it was back to the Bierger-Center to give them the Blue Card. That appeared to keep them happy. I then had to go back to the unemployment office in order to see someone about an appointment to see someone else. You get the idea now. You seem to go from pillar to post. It's not made easy for you. It's almost as if they want to discourage you. I can only imagine that it's the same in every country.

I went back to the unemployment centre to seek some further advice. I was told in French that "You will have to book an appointment for a week on Friday as that is the earliest we can do." Unemployment in French is 'Chômage'. The term 'Chômage' is actually used here in Luxembourg, rather than the word 'Unemployment'. However, to de-confuse you, I have used the English word 'unemployment'.

So at the due date I turned up and this time went up to the second floor with all my paperwork and showed them everything. As it turned out I was advised I would now have to fill in all the documents they gave me and return it to them as soon as possible. It was also in my interests to return the paperwork as soon as possible, since the unemployment benefits payment date would determine whether I should have my money sooner rather than later. In non-bureaucratic terms, this meant next month rather than the following one.

I took the paperwork home and read it. It was all in French—business French, at that. I could understand the gist of it with a little help from my dictionary. But I decided to seek out advice from some friends. They suggested I go and see someone who could check the documents from a professional point of view and with a lawyer's viewpoint of Luxembourgish law.

One thing you'll soon discover is that Luxembourg laws are Napoleonic. They're based on this period of history. If the rule says, 'You do it like this', then you do. Deviations are not allowed.

When my friend Tom was in Germany, he came back saying, "The bureaucracy is a left over of Nazi Germany. They stamp it here, they stamp it there. They love their stamps. Nothings changed since then. I always thought British bureaucracy was bad. It's worse living abroad!"

I had taken the trouble before this interview at ADEM to find somewhere where you could get photocopies done cheaply. (Don't office photocopiers come in handy!) I then got copies of all the documents I would need. Fellow expats had also recommended me two firms in the city for advice and information that would help me in my situation. These were Horsburgh and Co, and Fibetrust. The first one I was advised would be more expensive than the second. So, I went to see Fibetrust. However, I highly recommend both companies.

The chap I saw was extremely helpful. I explained my full position and worries. It was, after all, all new to me. He reassured me and I walked out feeling a little more confident.

I now had everything prepared and was ready to hand it in. You'll have to believe me when I say this whole process had taken an unbelievable three weeks. It was practically a full-time job sorting it all out! But I persevered and went back down to the job centre to hand it in, joining yet another queue in the process

The result was worth its weight in gold in that I did indeed get my money for not just six months but for one whole year. It was great!

But don't be fooled. It was *not* one big holiday for a year. Strict conditions are attached. The most important one being is that you have to be genuinely seeking work. You also have to sign on every two weeks. Failure to turn up on the day or within the time period is harsh. Just how harsh I later found out to my cost.

After six months you have to go and see a lady psychiatrist who basically asked me to prove I had been seeking work and why I hadn't yet got a job. Now, if you're genuine, then you'll have nothing to be concerned about. But if you're dossing, then she'll know instantly. I showed her all my letters I had written for jobs. I mentioned all my phone calls to the various job agencies, not to mention my visits to them all; and after half an hour or so I must have passed the test. I must admit to having been a little nervous before the interview, for who wouldn't be? But I had no worries since I was a genuine case.

Let me state at this point that being unemployed is not funny. The novelty wears off fast. Yes, I enjoy the day, but I miss the office.

So my life, along with everyone else who's unemployed, is made up of signing on every two weeks. If you've ever seen the film 'The Full Monty' you'll instantly picture the scene in the Sheffield unemployment office! Well, I always think of it each time I sign on, the only difference being, here it is Luxembourgish in style. (Incidentally, as I've already mentioned, there's a bar here called The Full Monty up at Kirchberg.)

The unemployment system in Luxembourg is one of the best in the world. In fact, if you get a three-month job contract then your unemployment money will kick in again afterwards if you're back on the dole, up to a period of two years after you started. If you can manage to get a job in a bar or anything that's full time, then once again it's good. Nevertheless, you have to be lucky on this one. The government will pay you the difference of ninety per cent between your original salary and what you're now actually getting. This lasts for up to four years. After that, you're on your own.

I've heard there may be a sting in this, though. Should you lose the job before the four years is up, then you may lose the ninety per cent as well. Perhaps you should double check. Certainly try to get it in writing if you're lucky enough to get a job on this scheme. This should come from both the government and the employer.

I had been advised not to diversify out of my specialised field (of Agents reconciliation's in international stocks & shares) too much for the first eleven months, in case a suitable job came up. Due to the economic situation, in my case the job didn't turn up. Anyway, don't fully listen to the advice given, but do bear it in mind, because you will need to take what's going.

The eleven months not diversifying could also be a cunning plan by the government; so by the time you realise this, it's too late to do anything about it and your benefits will therefore cease after your year, thereby saving the government in handouts.

After your full year, though, you're still with ADEM as you have to sign on every two weeks, but you'll not be receiving any state aid at all. Nothing, not a euro, let alone a cent. So you'll be on your own.

If you miss signing on, then, without a doctor's certificate, you're stuffed. If you fail to sign on in the morning sign on, which is between 8.30 and 10am, then prepare yourself for the worst. By missing it, you'll loose one day's money. Forget to sign on for two days and you loose a week's money. Anymore and it's a catastrophe. You even end up having a thirty-seven day month being deducted. Ouch! It's a giant wake up call that hits you hard in the pocket. I had this unfortunate experience of missing two days at the end of my year. I did have my reasons which were communicated to them.

Being unemployed does stress one out as it's worrying. The number of people who have admitted to me that they also forgot to sign on surprises me. I suppose the result of being unemployed becomes one of life's experiences.

However, there's a safety net if you can prove you have a genuine reason as to why you forgot to sign on. Me? I lost my case.

The system in Luxembourg is also one of the most brutal. It's designed on the assumption that you will get yourself a job within a year. In normal times, this is good. It's not designed for the current situation. It's a very clever system. The officials must realise this, but so far there have been no changes to the system. After a year life rapidly becomes hard.

I myself have been living on my savings as many people do. This only lasts for so long so you need strong back up. A lot of people do leave the country. However, the country doesn't die or anything daft like that. Life goes on. New people arrive, be it in different professions, and the whole cycle revolves once again. I know of a lot of people who have left Luxembourg and gone back home. Each situation has been different. I know of a lot of Irish who have gone back to Ireland. A lot lost their contracts and were hanging on. Some who worked in the banks took bar work on. When that dried up, as it did for some, they left.

The big problem the Irish and the English have is the language. Most only speak English. Some Irish do speak Gaelic but that's not going to help them over here. Speaking only English has normally been no problem. However, currently the employers now have the upper hand and can be a lot choosier than before. In the old days, it was: "You speak English? Welcome aboard!" Okay, maybe not in those exact words, but you get the picture. No one wants to leave Luxembourg as it is such a nice country to live in. Most will try to come back for that reason alone.

The one thing you have to realise is that here in Luxembourg it's quite natural for people to come and go. By that, I mean new people arrive in the country daily, the other side of the coin being that when your contract finishes or you want to move on in your life to another country, you normally leave the country. People accept it. When it's time to go, then go they do.

I'll end this chapter by saying, "I hope things will improve in 2004. I have heard some new banks are coming to Luxembourg. That's good news."

One has to be positive!

24

Looking for a job?

If you're unemployed here, you need to look for a job. There are several avenues open to you—the first one being word of mouth. I was advised, "Try The Tube bar," as that was where the bankers go after work.

The advice was invaluable as a few chosen words in the right ear could be decisive. After all, a personal meeting in a place like this can do wonders and could be a great back door into a company.

I met a large, jolly Scottish guy in The Tube who encouraged me to give it a go. Some two weeks after I first met him and on my return, I was able to give him the good news that I had indeed got a job here. He was delighted that I had succeeded so quickly. He hadn't got me the job but had given me the encouragement to go out and look. For that, I thank him. The other places to try are all the other expats bars—The White Rose being one of them, the Arizona Bar another.

Then there are the newspapers. The *Luxemburger Wort* is well worth a look. The Saturday edition has a selection of jobs in. "The old traditional employers use it," was a comment I was once told by one of the agencies here.

There are others, like *Le Jeudi*, *Le Quotidien* or *La Voix*, the jobs advertised being in the language the employer has put it in.

Up until spring, 2003 there was a newspaper for jobs only. It was called *Jobs.lu*. It also featured news about the state of the market, the economy and had various statistics in it. If you were looking for a job, it was a good place to start. As you know, this is where I started. But alas, the paper has gone under along with a few other titles. This brought another ten people into the unemployment statistics. The titles that went under included *Luxembourg Business* and the one that everyone claimed to read, which was the weekly *Luxembourg News*. In its day, it was good. However, there were other reasons why it went under, which I won't comment on here.

There was no English language newspaper in print for more than six months until some of the old staff together with some fresh blood launched in September

2003 a new expats newspaper called '352'—the name of the title coming from the international telephone dialling code to Luxembourg, which is 00 352. This magazine does have jobs in as well. Their web page incidentally, is www.352.lu.

Then there are the job agencies. There's about half a dozen of them. In the time that I have been here, a few have merged as the downturn kicked in. Others have just shut up shop and consolidated into smaller units. A good example of this is in the Avenue de la Liberté. Here I know of at least two job agencies that have closed their huge offices, the two being Adecco and Staff.

Whenever you walked past one of the Adecco offices, it always looked empty. This huge former office was then its banking and finance recruitment office, situated on the corner of the Rue Goethe.

The other agency, Staff—a French agency, I believe—was the opposite, ironically. Whenever I walked past, it always seemed to have loads of people calling in. It was however just outside a busy and well-used bus stop near the Place de Paris. (Location, location, location, as they say.) They said to me, "We have no jobs or very few of them and we are getting inundated with people calling in." They relocated back down to Esch-sur-Alzette. After all, the rents in the Avenue de la Liberté must be huge. And now? Well, now the office is a wine and delicatessens shop.

Adecco do have a busy office down by the Gare. They also have yet another office that's about half way down the Avenue de la Liberté.

Fast is another agency that is located up at Limpertsberg. You can get to it on the number 4 bus route. For expats, they are quite helpful.

Badenoch & Clark on the Rue Eugene Ruppert are a relatively new arrival in temping agencies. This firm is American. So far, I reserve judgement on them.

One thing you soon realise is that all these agencies have their patch of clients. So it is well worth going round and seeing them all. Be prepared to do a lot of walking.

Agencies do come and go. Generally, the bigger ones survive the downturn and the smaller ones go under. It's sad when this happens as some of the smaller ones give better service than the big boys do. Still, if there are no jobs, then the agency doesn't get their fees and no income means they shut up shop. Again, it is cyclical.

There are also the agencies which are abroad that specialize in the European job market. Gillow Purdie's in London were very good. Alas, in this current downturn they, too, have gone under with twenty jobs lost. I got my job through them.

'Change' is another job agency. "Where are you," I asked the guy I spoke to on the phone. "In Edinburgh," he replied.

These agencies themselves find a niche in the market and good luck to them.

A lot of employers just don't want to have the bother of marketing a job. They prefer to use the agencies as it takes the aggravation out of finding a suitable candidate.

Other current job agencies here include Vendior and Randstad—but don't hold your breath with some of these. In a classic example of one that is no more, I sent them my C.V. and got an interview a week later. I bumped into a friend on the way there. He later gave them his C.V. and an incredible three weeks lapsed before they took the trouble to contact him.

Another great example of bad agencies arises from a visit to another defunct agency. Within a week of my interview with them I received a letter that said, "Thank you for coming in to see us. Unfortunately we don't think you are suitable for our books." What a load of rubbish! What they failed to say was that they just didn't have any jobs, or had very few on offer. They were covering their own backs and soon after went under.

Incidentally, some people become quite excited when they get an interview with an agency. Don't be. They're only finding out about you, so they have a feel as to the type of person you are. Then, when a job crops up, they'll hopefully remember your name and, if they can be bothered, they may put your name forward. Nevertheless, the interview with them will not get you a job. It's merely yet another stage in the quest.

Some can be downright rude. The French-speaking agencies are notorious for that, especially if you're a Brit. However, to be fair, there are some that *are* very good. You'll have to find out which are the good and bad agencies for yourself. Good luck.

The other way to look for a job is on the internet. In fact, this is the most important way to search for a job these days. Certainly, if you go on-line you'll be astounded as to just how many jobs there are worldwide.

Here in Luxembourg there are various websites that cater to the local job market, the most famous being www.monster.lu. Then there is www.stepstone.lu and www.jobsearch.lu. All are well worth a try.

Since Christmas 2002 and up to the summer of 2003, the total number of jobs in Luxembourg on offer on the monster.lu site has varied between about four hundred and nineteen and six hundred and fifty jobs. Generally, all jobs remain on these sites for two months before being deleted and a lot just sit there, even when the job has gone. The best advice I can give is check all these sites at least twice a week for any new offers that have been displayed. Employers generally load a lot of them in on a Monday. I understand there were over one thousand jobs listed on the monster.lu site in December 2001. However, remember there are other sites with other jobs offered.

On the jobs listed on the Luxembourg Monster internet site there are three main types, available, which stand out more than others. These are Fund Accounting, Accountants and IT jobs. If you can do any of them then you'll stand more chance than the rest of us. The other thing you'll notice is that most jobs on the site are written up in the four main languages of: Luxembourgish, French, English and German.

One also sees jobs advertised in other languages; possibly in Dutch, the Scandinavian languages and those pertaining to Mediterranean countries are all there. If nothing more, they are worth a read.

There are various internet cafés around town, which are great to use. They are all so different and so are their prices. So be careful on that point. In town, there is Sparkies right near the Place d'Armes. You'll get a real friendly expats flavour in here. Then there's the internet café in the Grund. This is more of a local community café. It's in an old Luxembourg building that has lots of character. It is well worth a visit. The National Library next to the Cathedral has free internet access on its ground floor on the left as you go in. Another place to try is the 'Surfin' Fox' in the Rue Michel Rodange. It's on the corner towards the bottom of the street on the right if you are going from the Place des Martyrs. There are others, but these are some of the main ones that are in town and useful.

If you're unemployed, then there's further free assistance from the state. I'm referring to the Job Club set up. Lots of countries now do this. There is one at ADEM on the fourth floor—though they don't tell you that on the first floor! They don't appear to communicate even with the second floor. Until you've had this marvellous experience, it's hard to believe. This facility is only open to people who are registered unemployed with ADEM in Luxembourg.

I was originally briefly advised about the job club over a drink with my Danish friend Jasper. I had forgotten all about it when a week later I happened to be going to see 'The Temporary Guy' on the fourth floor to get the latest when I discovered it.

I like to help people where I can, too. I have accepted help myself whilst in the process of looking for a job. I took an Italian girl who is also unemployed and registered up to the fourth floor to show her the job club. She was a little scared of using the computer after a while away from it, and she too hadn't heard about the club. I bumped into her outside a job fair at one of the agencies. Would I help her? Why not. It was nice to be able to do this.

The club is very good, though there are strict conditions for using it. But providing you don't abuse the system, it's a very useful and free tool. I cannot recommend it enough. The job club is a good idea. It's part of the continual change in the ADEM building since I have been going there. When you walk in the door, on either side of you are what appear to be giant touch-button computer games machines. They're not, though—they're what you might call 'find yourself a job' machines. You touch the screen, playing around with its various options until you find something that suits you. If you want, you can then print it out and take it upstairs so that your assigned clerk can look at it further.

Another good idea is the addition of ticket machines. With the increase in volume of the numbers of unemployed, these machines are great. They are now on each floor and when you arrive you go to where directed and simply take a ticket and when 'that' number flashes, it's your turn. Now this sounds easy, and it is, compared to the way it was before, that is. In the good old days, queuing was random, confusion reigned supreme and was frustrating; leading to bad tempers and harsh words. Queue jumpers used to make up the greatest story to get ahead of you, or they simply jumped in. Now, in the past, having queued for god knows how many hours, waiting my turn, this ticket idea is great! It takes the stress out of waiting. Don't laugh at this—it's true. Now, at least, everyone can sit down!

In the hot summer of 2003, signs indicating a multi choice drinks machine on the ground floor were put up. With so many people through the doors, this was good for people waiting. But, strangely, they were soon removed as it must have proved too popular. Now there are cold-water water bottles located for your consumption on every floor. The multi choice drinks machine incidentally, is on the ground floor on the left of the lifts.

The ADEM office is only open in the morning between 8.30 and 11.30. Mind you, when it's time to close they shut up shop abruptly. This bit does depend on who you are lucky enough to be seeing.

On one occasion I queued for over an hour and a half. This was on top of the first queue of twenty minutes I had encountered on my arrival on a different floor. In this second queue, which was on the second floor, I was at the front of the queue; it would be my turn next when, suddenly, the red light flashed on and illuminated the word for 'closed' in Luxembourgish! The guy didn't even both to come out and say "You're the last one" to the person in front of me. It would have been good manners to do so, wouldn't it? But no, nothing! I eventually left along with the other people who were behind me in the queue. What I had just encountered was sheer bad manners, or what? They might only be burocrats doing their jobs but it only takes the odd one or two to let the side down for all the others who are doing a sterling job.

Two years after I went through this unforgettable experience I can tell you, one of my French girl friends had exactly the same thing happen to her. Incredible!

I did hear a news story on the radio in the summer of 2003, which said, "Luxembourgers who worked in government offices are some of the most racist people in Europe." I'll let you form your own opinion on this matter.

A lesson in manners could do these odd one or two burocrats wonders. To be fair, though, they're probably stressed out themselves, what with the increase in unemployed people visiting. You are expected to communicate in Luxembourgish and French. Some burocrats do speak English. Watch out! The older ones don't, the trick is to be patient, smile and build up a good rapport.

I went to enquire about 'shelf filling' in a supermarket. Why not? After all, it's a job. I spoke to a couple of departments in the ADEM building, which I was advised to do by themselves on this very subject. I was shocked when I got the reply, "The women do that," and, "The men dig the roads and sweep the streets. You need the office further along." That really was said to me—and by a woman. It wouldn't happen in the UK.

Incidentally, if you look in the shops you will see that most are indeed staffed by women. Interesting! This was only half the story. Later on, I learnt that the main stocking up of shelves is a night job when men are in pre-eminence.

One very good scheme that ADEM runs in conjunction with the Centre de Langues is the subsidised language lessons. Normally the lessons are €150 a term. However if you're lucky enough to qualify for these, you'll only have to pay €5. That's quite a difference!

However, the rules for this scheme have changed. I think this is because of the sheer volume of people from all the different nationalities who are taking up the offer. The scheme was so overbooked last year that I heard there was a waiting list of over two hundred.

About four hundred people are allowed to participate. However, under the new rules the scheme can only be for people who are on ADEM's unemployment list. By that, I mean those unemployed people who currently qualify, are the people who are actually receiving paid benefits during their first full year of unemployment. Anyone else who has done their three hundred and sixty-five full days, and whose unemployment (chômage) money has stopped, is stuffed.

Should you be unemployed it is best to ask the ADEM people if you qualify for language lessons. Be careful if the Centre de Langues college term starts within the two months after you join ADEM, then you're stuffed. If you are registered as unemployed for the start of the enrolment relating to the next term, then you will qualify.

Bearing in mind that Luxembourg is a multilingual country, these language lessons are worth their weight in gold. If one is unemployed, it is foolish to miss them.

Beware, if you are absent from your class for twenty-five per cent of the course, not only are you kicked out of the language school, but you will also have to pay back to ADEM the difference of the course, which is €145. It is surprising the number of idiots that end up doing precisely this. I know of several people daft enough to complain when they get kicked out or have to repay the money. Everyone knows the rules. After all, the teachers want to teach a full class. That way the momentum is kept up, without unnecessary explanation on those who have missed classes and are trying to catch up.

My accountant advised me to buy a computer and a printer. "It'll save you a lot of money," she said.

She was right, as among other things it's very useful for sending off letters and C.V.'s. Before, I was sending handwritten letters on various friends' pc's and printers along with those in the internet cafés. Since the job club opened around February 2003, I find it most useful; if you want to, you can prepare your C.V. and letters etc…and send them on-line instantly. Employers these days much prefer this as it saves them work.

So at the end of the day it's up to you. There's help available from a variety of sources. Make use of them if you have the opportunity. Good Luck!

25

On your own

Being unemployed is one thing, surviving is another. Here in Luxembourg it's not easy. Now I must admit I have little knowledge of how the social security system works back in the UK as, fortunately, I was working for all the time I was there.

The ironic thing is that I paid all my contributions for everything over the years and I got almost zilch in return. Wait, I *did* get something, but what I'm referring to here is the unemployment system. Still, that's my decision along with all the expats who try their luck abroad.

However, I do know of various friends who have been or are unemployed here in Luxembourg or back in the UK. Each has an alternative story to tell. Here in the Grand Duchy the system for unemployment is similar, yet completely different. That is not as daft as it might sound. The difference of welfare systems is huge.

The Health service in the United Kingdom is run by the state. You generally get it for next too nothing. It's called the 'NHS'—that's the National Health Service. However, you do pay your national insurance contributions, for this very reason among others. These days you pay a minimum fee when you go to the dentist and when you get your eyes tested, but you do get any accident or operation for free. Then there's the private sector, which you will obviously pay for. This includes dentists, doctors and the private hospitals where you pay for any operations that you undergo.

Here in Luxembourg, when you go to the dentist, doctor, or to the hospital, etc, you pay the money when they give you the bill. This is either straightaway or when it arrives in the post soon after. If it's a big bill then you'll need a big balance in your bank account to pay for it. Over here in Europe—well, it's not cheap.

In Continental Europe it's run differently. Here in Luxembourg the health service is state run, but there are also the private hospitals. These tend to be run by the Catholic Church. (This being a very Catholic Country). One difference is how you pay for it and, more importantly, the ability of claiming some of it back. If you have been in work then you'll automatically be signed up for the social security system. If you're not working and you're a new arrival—tough, you'll get nothing. In other words, you cannot claim a euro back. Nevertheless, do double-check here, as I am merely outlining the way it is for most people.

The good news is that if you are signed up, then you can claim back about ninety per cent. This is done by you keeping all your bills. Don't loose them, for God's sake! Then you submit them to the social security office in the Route d'Esch. A good idea is to make out an invoice detailing what the bills are. You then give them all of these and once you have spoken to the official, if your paperwork is in order, you'll be reimbursed through your bank account about three weeks later—the motto here being that you will have to lay out before you can (or should) get most of it back. However, it's not always the case. I'm merely giving you a simplified version here.

Another very useful thing you should do is photocopy every document you submit. This will then give you backup and proof. It's better to be safe than sorry. This, incidentally, applies to any document you encounter. After all, you never know when you may need it.

If you've been working, then you'll have been paying into the state social security. It appears that for every day you work your fund builds up a little beyond the end date of your contract.

When you're on your own here in Luxembourg you're literally on your own. However, as I discovered by accident, one can interpret this from different angles. Being on your own depends on who you are and more importantly how much money you've got in your savings. It also depends on where you live and—wait for it—who you live with. I'll explain.

There are various help places to visit when your social security money reaches its end point. Before it does end, you should listen very carefully to what advice the people at the social security ADEM offices can give you. They are, after all, human, and whilst doing their jobs, most can be helpful. To begin with, there's the prolongation. This means you might be able to prolong your unemployment money by three months. You can appeal by seeing the person on the second floor of the ADEM building, who, once you've explained your situation, they will create a file and put your case forward. It will be reviewed and you'll soon hear on a return trip whether you've been successful.

The way one can prolong your money is, for example, by considering doing a full-time course to become a dustman. Don't laugh, because it's called learning a new trade. That's what it's all about. If your case is rejected, as mine was, then there's another office with another scheme you might like to try.

This is the RMG scheme. RMG is the Revenue Minimum Guarantee scheme. The *Ministere de la famille de la Solidarite Sociale et de la Jeunesse* is where you go to ask about the *Fonds National de Solidarite*. This office used to be at Boulevard de la Pétrusse 138. I discovered that since April 2003 it has moved to 8-10 Rue de la Fonderie in Luxembourg City, just off the Rue de Hollerich. However, my experiences relate to when they were in the Boulevard de la Pétrusse. When it was there you probably went past it every day without realising it was there, but it was.

I found it quite demeaning, finding out whether I could claim anything. However, it was a fascinating experience nonetheless. Standing at the counter makes you feel a lesser person as opposed to when you sit at a desk and communicate in most other cases. Still, never let that put you off. In fact, the ladies there were again most helpful. I explained my situation, they filled in one form, and they gave me another to fill in which was bright orange in colour. We were looking at two different schemes at the same time. A lot of questions were asked.

One of the forms to fill in allows you to claim for your heating bills. It's called the 'Service de l'allocation de chauffage'. That's very thoughtful, especially in Luxembourg's cold winters, which are colder than the UK. The other form is the RMG allowance. This is another very good scheme if you can get it. The RMG is designed for people who have nothing. Basically, it's a minimum state allowance that the state pays you. The current amount is around €1369 a month, if you are single, which you will receive. It does go up if there are two of you or even three of you, etc...but let's not get too technical.

Anyway, if you receive any form of income from within or outside Luxembourg, you will have to declare it. This does include interest on money in the bank. Do you own a house in your own country? Are you getting income on it? What is it worth? How big is it? How many bedrooms? How many rooms? And so forth. They will investigate you, as they won't just accept anyone. They will want to know how much your rent is. You will have to get your landlord to fill in a form and sign it to prove how much you pay. Other questions they will ask include, "Are you living with anyone?"

Now, if you *are* living with anyone, you're stuffed, as you won't be eligible. Also, if your rent is more than the minimum, then you won't get any more.

Most people who do get this state benefit, however, don't live in palaces and are generally the sort of person who lives in a room in a shared house or lodgings above bars, etc...This benefit will naturally finish once you get a job.

There are lots of hidden catches as well, one of them being, do you have full residency? If the answer to that is 'No' they will then send you up to the Bierger-Center to find out more information. This applies to all 'Temporary Residents' who hold the 'Blue' card.

Now this is a bit naughty because when you get there the people at the Bierger-Center will say, "Why have they sent you here?" adding, "They know that if you don't have 'full residency' then you won't get the RMG. They just don't want to tell you themselves."

That is what was said to me.

It was suggested, then, that I go over to the Ministere de la Justice opposite number 16 Boulevard Royal. So, off I went, and seeing the length of the queue, I decided to return bright and early the next morning.

The next day I was third in the queue, which soon rapidly expanded. I didn't fancy the long wait some of them had ahead of them. I spoke to a lady who called over her male colleague. They went into another office to discuss my situation. Eventually, after what seemed like an eternity, they returned. The man came over to me and said, "You want residency? Get a job!"

That was it. Back to square one. Therefore, it was back to the RMG people who, when I explained what I have just described, said this wasn't the case. Nevertheless, after that, everything fizzled out with these people. With no full residency, or even if you are on temporary residency, you're stuffed for RMG. But before I departed the RMG office, I must credit them for giving me another address to visit.

This time I was sent to the Social Office or Office Social. This office is on the Rue Côte d'Eich at number 24. You have to hunt for it. It's actually the last house on the right just before the tunnel. The house itself is most impressive. You can imagine some old rich Luxembourg family living there in days gone by. These days it has been converted into offices, like so many places have. I went in and found somewhere to sit.

Around me were what looked like a real rough lot of people. The place was probably the lowest of the low as far as handouts are concerned, but as I had been sent there I thought I'd at least ask. I was ushered into an office where the lady spoke only Luxembourgish or French. I chose the French, as after all, this was good practice. Again, she was most helpful. She did explain to me that "If you have anything worth more than €12,500 then you will have to sell it, spend it and be right down to this level, before we will even consider you for any welfare."

In my case, they couldn't help me. To be fair, this office is for people who have absolutely nothing. It's for the real needy. I thanked her and went on my way.

All of this I found a real eye opener. It was all new to me. It was a different world to the one I was used to. If nothing more, I would say it teaches you about a few things in life. I have no regrets about what I did find out, and I would advise anyone who finds themselves in this boat to do just the same.

And so, at the end of the day I was really on my own. Nevertheless, there was more to find out.

My first visit to the social security office at 125 Route d'Esch involved a quick hop on a number 1 bus from the centre of town. The bus stop is opposite their bright, large and modern yellow building, the design of which I quite like. I had headed down there because I wanted to ask them "when my state payments for my sickness insurance would finish?" I went because I was still receiving physiotherapy on my foot and I wanted to know "when or if I would have to take on the whole bill?" I was advised that "I was covered on the 'Caisse de maladie des employés prives' or 'CMEP' scheme I had been on, until the end of April." The scheme I had been on, which incidentally was called the 'employé prive auprès de l'employeur', covered me originally for the CMEP sickness scheme and my pension scheme. That information in itself eased the pain. It would enable me to continue the physiotherapy without needing to take any short cuts i.e. reducing the sessions. I obtained a printout to confirm these dates. This printout I was advised from a friend could be of further use to me in my residency papers. However, as it turned out it wasn't.

When I got home that day, I discovered a letter from the social security people on the Route d'Esch—the very people I had been to visit that morning telling me much the same information. Now, was that coincidental or what!

The difference appeared to be this: the letter advised me in writing that I would be covered on the CMEP sickness scheme and I would get ninety days from the last day of my unemployment time finishing, which was mid January, whereas I had been told verbally on two occasions that I would be covered until the end of April. Whatever! At least in the meantime I would be covered if I fell down and broke my leg.

My second visit to the social security office was several weeks later. I had become a bit concerned over what would happen to my social security fund and my pension. Again, I chose to seek out advice from friends, once again over a pint in The White Rose. You'd be amazed what people tell you, which at times is worth buying that pint.

I went to the social security office knowing that by now my unemployment money had run out, but that my social security payments would last a few more months. You enter via a large revolving door and walk into a large, user-friendly, open office with lots of seating in the open area that's well laid out with TV's to watch while-you-wait. After taking my ticket, I had a short wait before speaking to the guy there. Again, he was most helpful.

My unemployment benefit, although now finished, automatically covered me for another ninety days for the sickness scheme, which is the CMEP.

What I did learn was that, yes, I was still covered in the CMEP for the three months after my money had stopped. The chap then suggested I see someone else there, to look at me changing from the scheme I was on to one where it was me who was paying—in the form of a voluntary contribution.

Again, I took a ticket and waited. When my turn came the lady to whom I spoke was extremely helpful. She also spoke English, which most of them do down there. However, it's polite to try to speak some Luxembourgish, even if it's just 'Moien', followed by a short conversation in French. It makes all the difference and shows you can at least make the effort.

This lady then advised me that the other scheme is also called the *Caisse de pension des employees prives, CMEP*, the difference being that whereas before it was being paid for by your employer, now it would be me who would be paying in. So that meant I would be paying in on my behalf. It was open to me provided I signed up soon. I signed up straightaway.

From what I could deduce, I understood that under Luxembourgish law I as a foreigner do have various rights, and that there are time limits that are very important to observe in order not to lose my rights to things. I don't attempt to understand all the ins and outs, but after three months, you lose something and after six, you lose the right to join the scheme.

The payments would follow two months after I joined, and I could either pay cash every month to them via the bank or they could do a direct debit payment. In addition I was asked, "Would you like to pay once a month or would you like to pay three months payments at once when commencing?" I chose the monthly, it being easier on the budget.

This scheme would run from the day after I had finished my last day of my year being unemployed on the ADEM scheme. Therefore, I was now in two schemes running side by side for three months. I wasn't arguing. Your health isn't worth arguing over, is it? The cost of paying my own way is €83 a month.

Whilst there, I happened to mention my Pension payments…

Now Pensions are a very important subject. So many people do not understand the ins and outs of pension schemes. Back in the UK, in 2003, the newspaper headlines were full of stories about private pension schemes folding. Since the UK Government under Labour introduced some accounting rule called the Financial Reporting Standard 17 (FRS17), and following Gordon Brown the Chancellor of the Exchequer's one-off stealth tax on the dividends in these pension funds about six years ago, many, many private pension funds are suffering.

Now it could be either because of this accounting rule change, or the stealth tax, or because of a totally separate event (though I think they are linked), that the four-year stock market collapse was triggered off, leading to huge black holes in thousands of private pension schemes.

Many schemes have had to sell their shares to pay the current pensioners, resulting in share prices being pushed further downwards. (Some good news, however, is that there was a recovery of sorts since the end of Gulf War Two, in the spring of 2003.) What people thought of as a safe private pension scheme for their retirement, which they could look forward to, is now regrettably turning into a nightmare for many. Many schemes are collapsing and going under. That leaves many with just the UK State pension, which is peanuts—barely enough to feed the cat on. Nevertheless lots of people do indeed survive on it and the future remains bleak for many in the UK.

Here in Luxembourg it's a different way of thinking. It's a clever system here and again I don't pretend to understand it all. But in simple terms, when you are working, you pay monthly into the Scheme 8% of your earnings. The employer pays 8%. The state pays 8%. That is 24% a month into your fund. Now that's a lot, isn't it? It's far more than in the UK. The benefits therefore pay out more, thus making it one of the best pension schemes in the world. The more you pay in, the more you'll get out.

The pension scheme your employer will pay into (if you are working) on your behalf is called the 'employé prive auprès de l'employeur'. However, like most things in life there are catches to it. The government doesn't want to pay out more than it has to, does it? There are rules, as with everything—a very important one being that if you stop paying into the fund you will loose the right to continue paying into it and *all* those payments made of 24% will be lost. However, do double-check this yourself. The government gains it all. I did hear that there is a mountain of extra money in the fund, probably because of this factor. The government was wondering what to do with the money. Maybe they'll increase the pensions for the retired folk here in Luxembourg. Who knows what will become of it.

The lady with whom I had just been discussing my change of sickness scheme then explained to me that I could continue with the pension scheme. The difference would again be that it would be me paying in rather than the employer. It's called the 'l'assurance pension' or 'CPEP', which stands for the 'Caisse de pension des employés privés'. However, there are strict entry requirements, including at least twelve continuous payments into the scheme from your previous employer.

I had various choices. I could either pay the state minimum of around €219 per month. This is made up of the minimum wage of €1368 x 16% to give the €219 figure. This amount would be paid for a minimum of four straight monthly payments, which would cover me for a year, after which I would continue again, etc. I could also pay into the fund every month with the minimum amount, thus accumulating a much larger amount.

Either way, for every payment I paid would in real terms mean that I would be paying 8% myself and a further 8% of the employer's earnings, making a payment by me of 16%. This figure, the minimum of which I mentioned above, is topped up by the state by another 8%.

I wasn't sure what to do, as I hadn't gone in there knowing what I now know. I needed a bit of time to sleep on the idea before committing myself. The lady did advise me of a further place I could seek out for advice on my pension. I thanked her for being so helpful and headed home for lunch. I had certainly come out with more than I went in for.

In the afternoon, I did indeed check out this office whose address I had been given. It turned out to be in the Boulevard Prince Henri and is number 1A. It is also next door to the red-painted steel-framed American Express office that is on the corner next to it. The office I visited was called the 'Caisse de pension des employés privés' or 'CPEP'. I went in and took another ticket. The queue was short, but I still had to wait more than and hour and a half. In fact, I thought I would have to return as I thought the time would go past closing time. A similar experience had told me they simply shut up shop without saying anything to you. As it turned out my thoughts on this were wrong, and the guy who assisted me was a real Luxembourg gentleman.

He was also extremely helpful. (As I mentioned earlier, some aren't. So when you meet a burocrat who's helpful, make the most of it!) He also spoke English, which I know is lazy on my part but I just don't know all the technical words yet in French. Nevertheless, I did give it a go. Anyway, the point is, this office is well worth a visit.

I explained my position and I was again told that I would have to contribute the minimum state payments that the lady at the social security office had earlier informed me. That was a first—two offices working together! Anyway, the chap also did strongly recommend that I pay in every month. I can see his reason as anything paid in gets 8% paid in by the government.

However, you've got to live, haven't you, especially if it's your money supporting you when you're seeking work. Again, he also advised me about the four minimum payments rule. After all, I could always pay in more months after that. I could also have a job, which would be great.

I discovered that in my own situation, provided I had worked in another EU country for twenty years and could prove it, the time period would count and make me eligible for the Luxembourg pension that I had contributed to. However, if I have made one hundred and twenty payments (ten years times twelve months) here, then I will get a proportion of it when I hit sixty-five. But, in my case, it will be on the basis that if I do two years here I will get two years' worth (I think). However, I have to advise them of my twenty-two plus years working in the UK, i.e. contributing to the UK state pension through my National Insurance payments.

Now if I had been working here for forty years then I would get the full state pension. At the time, this would be based on four hundred and eighty payments (forty years times twelve months). A nice little earner if you're lucky enough to get it—the bonus being that the more you put into it, the more you will gain from it when you retire. (This of course is assuming that you don't drop down dead before you retire! It does happen, you know, which makes you ask yourself, "Is it all worthwhile?" Well, that's for you to decide.)

There are different scenarios for each person. Of course, if the rules change between now and then, then I could get nothing or more.

If you leave Luxembourg, the country has various agreements with various countries regarding pension payments. If the country you go to is a European Union country, then there's no issue. Any others, then you'll have to ask for clarification. If Luxembourg has signed an agreement with this non-EU country, it could benefit you or not. It's vital that you should seek further advice on this most important topic. This payment of your pension scheme here is similar to the UK, but with different countries signed up.

If you do leave the country, you could be stuffed. Therefore, my advice, for what it's worth, is double check at the social security office in the Route d'Esch and at the CPEP in the Boulevard Prince Henri.

Therefore, the motto of this story is to tell you, "Your pension is worth its weight in gold, so do, do check it out." Also, to remember that old English saying, "If you don't ask, you don't get."

Good luck.

Another useful place to visit regarding legal information is the Service d'Accueil et d'Information Juridique. This office is situated at number 12 Côte d'Eich, which, you will discover, is in the old town. Here you want the 'Parquet General', which translated literally means, the 'Public Prosecutor's Department'. I mention it because, if you need to see a lawyer for legal advice, then this is a good place to go. It's operated by the Luxembourg Court. A few expats do go here and the advice they get is very good. Even better is that it's free. But again, be prepared to join the queue or get there early. When you are here, I strongly advise you to try to speak the language, either Luxembourgish or French. It will make all the difference. Again, if you're lucky—and polite—you'll be rewarded handsomely.

There are other lawyers in town whom I have met during my time here. Again, I've been lucky. I've had some free advice, for which I thank them. Almost all of them were also very helpful.

If you need legal advice or want to find a solicitor or a lawyer in town, look out for the words 'Avocat à la Cour' on the doorways. Fees are not predetermined by law and you should inquire about the approximate amount you will have to disburse at the end. There is also the difference between a lawyer and a 'Notaire' i.e. notary public who generally does not give any detailed legal assistance; he should only record or authenticate the deeds prepared by the lawyers of the respective parties.

If you want to buy real estate, it is also very useful to be assisted by your lawyer, especially considering the amounts involved.

26

Mini Baghdad

Luxembourg is one of the safest countries in the world. You hardly ever see a police officer here on the streets. It really is weird after seeing bobby's on the beat back in the UK.

I remember the police doing the patrols in their panda cars in the 60s and 70s. I grew up with Dixon of Dock Green, Softly Softly, and Z Cars on the T.V.

When we moved into a village from town in the mid 1970s we kids had a visit from the local bobby. One day he drove up by the side of the village green where we were playing football and read us kids the riot act about misbehaving. His car was a Morris Minor. It was the sort of car village bobbies used to have. Nowadays you only see them in Heartbeat on English TV. The policeman used to live in the village police house and appeared to know everything that went on. He was the respected figure in the village. It seemed he was constantly on the beat.

These days the local bobby doesn't exist anymore; the local authority has flogged his house and the nearest police station is in the town, miles away. If one is lucky they might be open on a Tuesday morning.

So I can walk the streets here in Luxembourg and feel safe. That's pretty good these days. In other European cities, this is not the case. It does signify how society as a whole has deteriorated in the last twenty years.

It also begs the question, "If Luxembourg is the safest country in Europe, how does it manage it?"

Well, lets just say that in this country law and order is effective and efficient, especially in the way it keeps foreigners under control!

One spring morning towards the end of April 2003, I went down to get the post. I happened to look up and got quite a shock when, as I glanced up the hill, there was what appeared to be staring down at me a whole of line of army vehicles. They were on the upper stretch of the Rue de Prague.

"Oh my god," I thought. "What the hell is going on?"

It was an awesome sight, the like of which I had never seen in Luxembourg. I went in and briefly continued my business. My mind was buzzing. I needed an answer. Suddenly the quietness of the morning was shattered by the sudden sound of explosions coming from what seemed like quite close by. These explosions were loud—very loud.

Now the thing was, at that moment across the world there was a *real* war going on. The war I'm referring to was in the Middle East. It was in Baghdad, in Iraq. Now I know they're hunting Al Queda and all the Iraqi leaders, but hey, this is Luxembourg. After all, nothing happens here. I decided I needed to find out what the hell was going on.

I grabbed my camera and headed up the hill. As I rounded the huge hairpin bend I could see the line of vehicles in close up. At the front of the line, at the top of the hill was some form of huge tank-like vehicle. On first appearances it appeared to have a gun turret sticking out from the front . However as I was about to see for myself, this gun turret turned out to be a water cannon. Behind that was a vehicle I can only describe as some form of military shunter, and lined up behind that were several armoured personnel carriers. Their personnel at that moment were relaxing next to these vehicles in the hot morning sun.

I walked up and headed towards The White Rose. I immediately noticed that the Boulevard de la Pétrusse towards the Arcelor building was blocked off. The Rue Dicks was also blocked off to traffic as I entered the street. I walked further up past The White Rose and towards the end of the street. I was now on the corner of the Rue Dicks and the Avenue de la Liberté. There, right in front of me, I could see some form of huge demonstration. At first sight there appeared to be many demonstrators wearing various green garments. Some had hats, some also with green scarves. More demonstrators were wearing red hats, red jackets and red scarves. Some were waving red flags with some sort of emblem on. There was lots of shouting, chanting and yelling, mostly in French. But I couldn't be sure. There were other languages as well. In the noise of the moment, it didn't matter. Suddenly, I was there watching from the side of all these demonstrators.

Now you might just be wondering, why this demonstration was taking place? Well, the explanation is simple. Here in Luxembourg one of the biggest industries if not the biggest, is the steel industry. The plants are situated in the south west of the country in the town of Esch-sur-Alzette. The town borders onto France. The steel works provides massive employment and originally employed many Italian and Portuguese workers who migrated from their own countries many years ago. At its height, Esch-sur-Alzette had three giant steel works. The iron ore originally came directly from the nearby local mines at Rumelange in Luxembourg. It was a boom area with fast growth.

Esch-sur-Alzette is Luxembourg's second city. These days it is still growing and is diversifying from its original industries. It has to in order to survive. Steel does still remain the backbone of the area. However, the industry is in steep decline. One of the smelters closed a while back. The mine has also closed. The remaining plants re process scrap steel.

The steel industry used to employ, maybe twenty years ago, some thirty thousand people in Luxembourg alone. These days that figure is down to around six thousand. Many workers have had to go into completely new professions. They now work in government offices or as postal workers, etc. Industry in Esch-sur-Alzette now includes the new technologies and science parks. The new Luxembourg University will be built there which will certainly transform the social scene in the city.

The present owners of the steel in Luxembourg are a company called Arcelor. They have a fantastic building in the centre of Luxembourg City that's called the Arbed building. This name is set in the stonework. Built in 1922, its architectural beauty makes it one of the finest buildings in the City. It just so happens that this grand building which lies in front of the memorial gardens happens to be their administrative headquarters. Years ago, the building was the administrative seat of the Aciéries Réunies de Burbach-Eich-Dudelange or Arbed for short. This, translated, means the United Steelworks of Burbach, Eich and Dudelange. Arcelor also happens to be one of the richest employers in the country. The company also owns many steel works under a different name in the countries around Luxembourg, namely Belgium and France. The French company Usinor had taken over the Cockerill-Sambre steelworks in Liège and in Charleroi, Belgium. Whilst using the group name Arcelor, the local steelworks are still known by their old names. Usinor had promised investment and guaranteed to keep seven thousand eight hundred jobs up until 2003.

In 2001 Usinor then merged with the Spanish Aceralia and Arbed, the Luxembourg company to form Arcelor, the world's largest steel company. The priorities in 2003 then changed and they announced a cutback in jobs in Liège totalling one thousand seven hundred jobs. The demonstration that was the centre of police attention was mainly the protesting Belgian workers coming down to Luxembourg.

With the downturn in the economy and the competition from the third world countries, the steel industry in Western Europe is suffering badly. As a result, jobs throughout Europe are being lost to the cheap labour employed in the Far East.

As a result, the company plans in the next few years to make around three thousand people redundant locally—and there's worse to come. There will be a further six thousand jobs going over the next few years in the steel works that the company owns outside the Luxembourg border. This will particularly hit towns like Liège in Belgium and Thionville in France. It's a catastrophe for the region—which is why the workers are outraged. They are scared for their future. They are concerned for their families. There are mouths to feed and clothes to buy…

The demonstration was set to commence at 12.30pm. The demonstrators had arrived. The police were waiting. The battle was about to begin. It reminded me of all those war films one watch's where past armies meet at the appointed hour, greeting each other at first in that gentlemanly way, only then commencing the bloodbath.

The sound of firecrackers was rampant around us. There were huge explosions coming from further down the Avenue de la Liberté where a massive barbed wire barrier had been erected to form a line of defence. Its height reached to over eight foot. Its width stretched right across from the Sushi bar to the Books and Beans coffee shop. The barrier totally blocked off the avenue. It formed a line of steel and was made up of razor wire across its top and stainless steel. Standing behind the barrier was a line of police officers all dressed in riot gear and white helmets. They also carried riot shields that acted as protection from the missiles being thrown at them.

I walked down to the front line to take a picture of the action. I was standing on the right-hand side. In the distance I could see further barriers that had been erected around the Arcelor building. One stretched again across the Avenue de la Liberté, this time from the Immosol agency immobilière office to the building opposite. Another stretched out across the Memorial Gardens. It was here that the worst of the action took place. Beside me were the demonstrators hurling abuse at the police. The police stood there, motionless, defending the line.

"Bloody Hell," I thought, "this is a battle and I'm right in the middle of it!"

For a moment, it felt like I was in Baghdad. The action was happening to my left. The explosions from both sides were deafening. In fact, right now it felt like a mini Baghdad.

I decided to retreat fast. Trouble was brewing; I was right! A human line of defence had been brought up. The police formed it across the Rue Dicks. The interior of The White Rose would be a safe bet. I tried to get through this line of defence but I was blocked.

One of the police officers in the line then said to me, "Luxembourgeois?" Meaning, "Was I a Luxembourger and in the demonstration?"

"Ay?" I replied in my Essex accent, a touch surprised. "No, I'm English," I quickly added. Much assured and realising I wasn't a demonstrator, the police officer let me through. My accent said it all.

Inside the WR it was quiet. It felt surreal as the action unfolded. Outside strange things were happening, things such as I'd never seen during all the time I had lived here. I decided to head round to the Place de Paris and view events from there. Taking the long way I watched the events from the corner of this square, joining the lunchtime workers who also were watching from a safe distance.

The action developed with the arrival of the water cannons. One was pointed down the avenue and it was facing us. The other targeted the Memorial Gardens. Both began blasting the demonstrators when things became too hot. Each time it erupted, a warning siren sounded seconds before the water shot out all over the demonstrators, giving each of them an early bath. Obviously, these measures are designed to cool off the demonstrators. It had the desired effect. The next wave then surged forward and the whole process began again.

Pepper sprays were used on the most persistent of the demonstrators. Was it tear gas or merely smoke bombs that the police used on the crowd? The explosions were used a lot. These were 'frighteners' to a certain degree, deterrents, if you like, for the benefit of the crowd around. The Arcelor building was defended at all times.

The scene was both eerie and bizarre. Two hundred metres in front of me it felt like a war was going on, whilst right behind me people were sitting out at the tables in the Place de Paris having lunch. After all, it could only happen in Luxembourg! People were not bothered. There was a lull in the action and I got bored and headed home. And so I missed what happened next—probably just as well. What followed I was able to piece together later.

Things 'hotted up' between the two sides. The main action was centred in the Memorial Gardens; missiles were thrown, bricks were torn up from the paving, and plants were uprooted from their holders and lobbed at the barriers. Graffiti was daubed on the plinths of the modern art sculptures that normally stand there; 'strangely', they had been removed before the event.

"US IN OR," and, "Arcelor," had been sprayed on the sides, along with a Nazi slogan on each. Round the corner in the Avenue de la Liberté on the frontline, on a boarded up shop next door to the newsagent was another slogan that read, "Arcelor SS."

The pink blossoms on the trees that line the avenue looked magnificent in the midst of the mayhem. The police eventually moved in and began the push forward. The demonstrators, who had numbered over two thousand at the peak of the action, were pushed back towards the Gare. The glass bus shelter on the Place de Paris was destroyed, all its glass smashed, leaving only the shell. Some phone boxes suffered the same fate and the phones had been ripped out. The police continued moving forward, using the water cannon and the shunter to shift everyone back towards the Gare.

Various shop windows were shattered by a few of the angry demonstrators. Signs were uprooted and concrete blocks used by the restaurants for segregation of their areas were left strewn across the avenue, leaving a trail of destruction and rubble everywhere. I don't know what happened to the people at the tables. Maybe someone yelled, "Take Cover!"

The demonstration faded out. The battle was over for the day, however, as I discovered in The White Rose later, the real battle was about to begin.

A week and a day later the next encounter was to take place—"Next Friday," as I was advised by my Luxembourg friend who added, "If you thought that was bad, the next one will be a lot worse." He went on to explain, "This time the demonstrators will be coming from France, Belgium and even Spain. There will be over ten thousand."

A week later, I was coming back from the pub. The evening had been a success; I had been to see the Harlem Globetrotters who had been appearing for one night only at the Coque, which is the new national sports stadium up at Kirchberg. It had been a great night and the stadium had been packed. There were over six thousand, seven hundred people watching the antics of the players who make up the world famous Harlem Globetrotters. They played against another New York team. Was it the New York Yankees? To the crowd watching it didn't matter. It was the fun on the court that made the game. Naturally, the Globetrotters won the game. The crowd cheered. The American commentator yelled with delight and we all went home happy.

On the way back from the basketball match I realised something was happening when the bus took the scenic route to the bus station. I didn't actually go home. I needed some food and therefore went down to my favourite cheap pizza place, Creole, down at the Gare. This was followed later by a trip to the WR.

"We're closing at twelve tonight," the barmaid said.

For once, I wasn't surprised.

Outside the preparations for the next demonstration had already begun in earnest. The barbed wire blockades had already been set up. Streets were being blocked off. As I sat in the pub and looked out through its open door a forklift truck went past, loaded with road signs that had obviously been removed from around the area.

It was ominously quiet. In the pub, I quickly finished my drink and left at the witching hour. The place was dead. Most people were in any case away, as it was the end of the Easter week. So many expats of all nationalities were back in their own countries, seeing their friends and families. The only thing that was going on was a Frenchman in heated discussion with three beefy looking bouncers outside a cabaret bar. I think he had just got his bill. He appeared to be on the verge of being frogmarched off to a cash machine with his new friends in tow.

As I walked along the street at the midnight hour, I passed the church that stands on the corner on the right-hand side. I stood there and looked around, noticing that all along the Boulevard de la Pétrusse there were barriers, certainly more than the week before—a lot more. Suddenly, from where I was walking, I saw a foot patrol of two police officers heading up towards the Place de Paris. This was very unusual. I passed yet another patrol as I crossed the street at the zebra crossing. Even more unusual was yet another foot patrol on the large hairpin bend, a quarter of the way down the Rue de Prague. They were searching the bushes and had radioed for backup. It promptly arrived. I didn't hang around to see the result.

The purpose of this frenzied activity was the steel workers' demonstration the following day. There had been a similar one, a week ago which had been the warm up. This time there would be a lot more workers coming up to the Arcelor building to demonstrate against the steel works making workers redundant.

So the police were preparing themselves for the day ahead. They were forming another ring of steel around the building in order to protect it from the elements, the foot patrols I saw being part of the preparation. They were taking no chances. Certainly, by the amount of work that apparently had been going on that night, it meant the events of the following day were going to be big.

The demonstration would again take place around 12.30pm outside the Arcelor building. In reality, the area was ready and fortified by the police for what looked like a much larger battle. This time there would be workers coming into Luxembourg from France, Spain, Germany, Belgium, and I did hear Italy; the police would be ready for them. Even more so than they had been the week before. It would be a mini Baghdad, Luxembourg style. There would be no winners. It was war set for lunchtime and I wasn't going to miss it for the world.

Not that I am a participant in these happenings. I certainly don't encourage anyone to go round ripping branches off trees and lobbing them at the police. Nor do I encourage tins of red and yellow paint to be chucked everywhere to leave their mark afterwards. Vandalising statues with anti-war slogans is another thing I deplore. Plants were also thrown, grabbed from buckets outside restaurants. Plants were also dug up from the memorial gardens. Windows were smashed in surrounding streets. Some bank workers were even advised to stay inside for their own safety. Shops had closed. Some had their shutters down. Others were ready to close at a moment's notice. It was a war zone.

I had never given any of this demonstration business much thought until I saw what had actually been lobbed at the riot police, or the 'B23' squad, as they have emblazoned on their backs. These guys were dressed for the kill. They marched down the street in unison. Dressed in black, they were carrying their protective shields. Each wore a white protective helmet. Each was ready to repel the attackers. They stood behind the barbed wire barriers defending the Arcelor building.

What did amaze me were the objects that were thrown at the riot police. There were giant steel nuts, six inches in diameter—that's about ten centimetres. (I'm sorry I still work in imperial, it must be my age.) Also, there were ball bearings made of solid steel the size of a tennis ball. They looked as if they weighed a ton. They certainly could have been fired from a cannon, but we are beyond that age now, or so I thought. It was incredible to see. A police inspector was showing these to the local crowd of lunchtime workers who were standing on the corner of the Rue Dicks and the Boulevard de la Pétrusse. They had come out to view from a distance the events unfolding before our eyes. Mind you, the demonstrators were also throwing bricks and I did see a catapult being used when I watched it on television later.

This time I was standing on the other side of the line. The area of defence had been enlarged so that the Arcelor building had even greater protection. The police were taking no chances in their preparation for the battle taking place. The line had also been moved forward towards the Place de Paris. It ran across the Avenue de la Liberté at an angle of forty-five degrees, starting from Chez Nous, the cabaret bar and crossed the avenue to Jacques Dessange the hairdressers on the corner. Huge metal containers had been positioned across the Avenue de la Liberté with the barbed wire interconnecting everything. The line of defence reached about eight foot high. This angle of defence was to allow the protesters to march around the area from the Place de Paris to The Lord Nelson bar, continuing up the Rue Dicks to where the police line was. There were further barriers in the road past the Lord Nelson.

The White Rose had never been so close to the action. The red and yellow tins of paint I mentioned earlier were lobbed everywhere. They were spread like muck all over the Avenue de la Liberté, including outside Chez Nous. The paint even reached outside The White Rose. No wonder the police were stopping anyone of the locals who got too close to the front line. It was for their own protection.

The water cannon arrived and sprayed the chanting crowd. There were smoke bombs, probably lobbed by the police. It was difficult to see from the position I was standing in. Each time the water cannon was used the siren would sound, to warn the crowd that it was about to be activated. It certainly would have cooled them down, which is probably why they use it. The workers responded with bangers. The B23s continued to send in reinforcements. All in all, it was quite a scene. All the restaurants had been ordered to remove their tables and chairs from the Place de Paris. Even the post box had gone. I understand that one of the banks had been boarded up.

The demonstration was being covered on the national television channel RTL. What I found amazing was that on the TV that night, RTL showed the riot going on outside The Lord Nelson bar, filmed while RTL were inside the bar. Then they proceeded to film inside the bar interviewing the demonstrators. The rioters were wearing their red and green scarves, T-shirts to match and waving their flags whilst having a beer. Outside others continued rioting, and the police were in the middle of a battle. At this moment they were pushing the demonstrators back towards the Gare. It was almost as ironic as the previous demonstration a week earlier when the rioters were fifty feet from the people having lunch on the Place de Paris. It was unreal and could only happen in Luxembourg.

The shunter arrived along with many minibuses. The police loaded up and dashed off somewhere. Later they would move to the end of the Avenue de la Gare and form another blockade across the street. A pincer movement had then been formed which was pushing the demonstrators back down the Avenue de la Liberté. They were being forced away from the steel building. The demonstrators continued to wave their banners on the way back to the Gare (station). One French woman was giving it everything she had. There was a lot of 'merde' coming out of her mouth, about what I could not fully understand. But, it didn't take a lot to work out. (Basically, in English, that means a lot of shit was coming out. You're learning a bit of French now!)

A total of three thousand workers had turned up for the demonstration. This was actually far fewer than had been expected. I heard ten thousand were due. So, although it was a riot, it ended up a damp squib, if that's the right way to describe it. It could have been a lot worse.

27

Going Underground

Sitting in The White Rose one night, someone mentioned something about secret tunnels in Luxembourg. Naturally, this sounded interesting as it conjured up all sorts of images. The conversation changed course and didn't come up until a few weeks later when the subject was raised again. Something about 'casemates'.

"Have I been down them?"

"No," I replied, as I hadn't a clue where they were. I mean if you walk round town they don't exactly stare you in the face, do they?

There was talk of Nazi gold being hidden in the tunnels. Well, any Nazi story to a Brit is interesting if you are my generation or older. I began to think, 'What are these tunnels like?' and, 'Do they really exist?'

I had twice taken the toy town train known as the Pétrusse express, which is one of the tourist trips you can go on. The train had taken us up to the old army barracks on the Rham plateau, which these days are a hospice. The view from there looked out over Luxembourg. One of the sights to view was of a huge rock that stretched right across the other side of the Alzette valley. The road from the old town ran along the top of it down towards Clausen. Underneath the road I had briefly noticed, lower down the rock, small openings like a window that were dotted along the rock face.

I found the journey on the toy train most interesting as I learnt at lot about Luxembourg's history. But you do feel a prat wearing those stupid headphones that hang down. The train jogs and jolts along the valley, but it makes a very interesting excursion. You sit there amongst the Japanese and Korean tourists and, as you're generally with someone, you don't feel quite so stupid. Get the picture? Anyway, I digress.

Some months went by before I thought about searching for the tunnels. I started by heading down past The Tube and Art Scène bars in the old town. From there I walked down the road past the church of St Michel on the right, heading downwards towards the railway bridge. Now, I didn't know it at the time but the street or rue I was walking on is called the Rue Sigefroi—Sigefroi being the famous Count who bought the rock back in AD963, which I was about to stand on. As a result, he also put Luxembourg on the map, so to speak, as the deed recorded its name. Rue Sigefroi leads onto the Rue Montée de Clausen, which is where I was heading for.

Anyway, I had been advised the tunnels were in this area. Great! After all, I had seen some openings in the rock face, so I knew I was warm in my search. However, it was a very hot day and not the best time to be hunting tunnels, with the sun shining down at over thirty-five degrees on one of the hottest days of the year. The road itself has lots of old castle wall remnants on both sides. This I gather used to be part of the city fortifications at one point. The stonework was typical of any old falling down castle. Well, I searched. Could I find a sign that said tunnel entrance? Like hell I could. In the heat of the moment, I gave up. It could wait for another time.

Some time later a friend of mine called Brian came to visit me here in Luxembourg and whilst sightseeing on his own he had seen the delights of the city centre, and he did all the things tourists do here. When we met up later in The White Rose he mentioned that he had visited some tunnels. It turned out he had done some research on Luxembourg on the internet before coming out here. He had found the tourist information site—"Which was useful," he said.

Right now he was telling me more about the place than from someone who lived there. Why didn't I think of that? But then you don't, do you? Especially when you actually live in the place. It sounds funny but you just don't. Or is it me?

A week later, having thought about it, I went back to the Rue de Montée de Clausen where I had first gone to search for these tunnels. In the meantime, I had taken note that tunnels in Luxembourg are called 'casemates'. Anyway, I located the 'Casemates' sign, descended the path and found a ticket office at the bottom. I paid my Luf's (these days it is Euros!) to the lady on the gate and went through the barrier into the tunnels.

Casemates actually mean rampart vault, which cannot be seen from the outside. So, in practice, all these casemates are not really casemates. They are mining galleries. However, if I'm going to get technical, the word originates from the Greek *khàsma*. *Khàsmata* signifies a pit.

I discovered that these tunnels run directly under the road where I had walked over God knows how many times. I just didn't realise exactly what was underneath. When you stand on top it looks as if the road is simply paved over the top of a broken-down castle wall and maybe there was a road there once before. The tunnels stretch out all along under the road. What transpires is that this rock was one of the big natural lines of defence that made Luxembourg the Gibraltar of the North many years ago.

There's a small history area in the tunnels in the archaeological crypt. Here are also more carefully preserved remnants. The road above is artificial, specially constructed over the ruins, would be a better way to describe it. A sort of elevated road in places, but you wouldn't know it when on top.

Another thing I didn't know was that this whole complex is called the Bock. It housed hundreds of soldiers and over fifty canons at one point. Men created all of these tunnels. They spent many thousands of hours mining and digging the tunnel network out of the solid rock. This was achieved more than four hundred years ago in the sole cause of defending the city from its attackers. It's an incredible feat of human labour.

The tunnels are on various levels. There are steps carved out to take you down to the next levels. One set of stairs you can take twists its way down a very narrow vertical shaft. The stone spiral seems to go down forever. You then go along the low-roofed tunnel and then up a similar shaft, up another identical set of stone spiral narrow stairs which have the same amount of stairs. (Before you ask, I didn't count them.) It turns out that when you look from the outside, you have just gone under the road and back up into the line of defence.

To think of the thousands of soldiers who lived in these tunnels years ago defending the city against the many invaders gets the imagination working. They were protecting the population who lived behind the fortifications. Living there must have been rough.

There are many sub passages and more hidden alleys that end up going nowhere. Some of these are larger than others. Daylight beams in through the cracks. When the city was under bombardment, the population used to take regular shelter in the casemates. It was their way of protecting themselves. What you have to imagine is, what the conditions must have been like when the city was under siege.

Field Marshal Bender lived here during the siege of 1794-95. He had a bedroom, a study and an anteroom. The Bock also gave shelter to the soldiers' horses and their equipment. It housed workshops for arms and artillery. There were also slaughterhouses, kitchens and bakeries.

Some of the smaller alleyways have gun loops. On the defence side is where they would have fired their cannons to stop the invaders getting any further. Indeed, there are a few dummy cannons on display. On the inner side of the rock, from the gun loops inside the tunnel, you can look out and see some terrific views of the old town and other fortifications. Incidentally, these gun loops I had originally thought of as windows.

When the Bock was dismantled, the buildings on the surface were razed to the ground. Nevertheless, they couldn't blow up the rock without demolishing parts of the city. Many of the entrances were plugged, together with other key connecting galleries. Behind this natural wall of defence lie the river and the outer living area of the city of Luxembourg. This is known as The Grund and stretches out in the Alzette valley behind.

One can just imagine the women doing their washing on the edges of the river in the middle ages, just upstream from the water that cascades over the small waterfall. The sluice gates nearby in the river blocked entry to any invaders. The soldiers walked the ramparts, guarding the city walls. The carts and wagons being driven by horses into the city, they would have been laden with goods to sell in the market by the peasant farmers. The soldiers would have been marching in the streets and when off duty would have headed to the city's bars for an evening of debauchery.

The other fortifications and outer city area are clearly visible from the views looking out from the gun loops inside the tunnels. I was fascinated by my visit and thought the trip well worthwhile. I felt that at last I was beginning to learn the history of the great city, slowly but surely. At that moment little did I realise how little I knew.

Several months and many beers later I was one night again sitting in a smoke filled White Rose enjoying a pint of Boddingtons. Now, I normally drink the local Mousel, but one too many of those gives me a corker of a headache the next day. Anyway, it was Boddingtons and the conversation steered round to a Luxembourgish friend Ernie, who had spoken to my friend Simon about a special trip down a secret tunnel. It would be on Saturday at 2.30pm, departing from the car park area known as St Esprit. This is where the top of the elevator to the Grund is situated.

It was a coldish day typical for Luxembourg in early spring. Simon and I met by the lift. Unfortunately, our Luxembourgish friend Ernie didn't show. Both of us had brought warm clothes and, more importantly, each had brought a torch. Mine was bigger than his was, but we wont argue over the size of the torch—please! We headed over to where there was a group of people gathered. When it was approaching 2.30pm, we decided to check that this was the right place and that it was the right group for the casemate trip.

Simon approached the leader and asked him in French, "Is this the casemates tour?" The man replied by saying to Simon in French, "What tour? There is no tour." He then swiftly told us, "If you want to go down to the casemates you should head over the road and the place you want is on your left." He said this as he pointed it out to us.

Wait a minute, what was he talking about? I mean, there we were, along with everyone else, waiting for the tour to start. Simon then mentioned this special tour and brought out a piece of paper that transformed the moment.

The paper turned out to be from 'The Friends of the Luxembourg Fortress Association'. This is called in Luxembourgish Frënn vun der Festungsgeschicht Lëtzebuerg. Ernie had given it to him and it was this and some words in Luxembourgish that saved our bacon. I mean, this guy wanted us to go to the tourist casemates up the road on the Boulevard F.D. Roosevelt.

Suddenly, as if nothing had happened, the tour leader said in French, "Yes, there is a tour and you can go on it."

How very strange. We got the impression that the guy was a tad racist and that he didn't want any foreigners there. Maybe he wanted to keep the tour secret? After all, we were about to go down a secret tunnel.

"The tour will be in Luxembourgish and a little French," the tour leader added. That was okay with us. After this strange start, the group was split into two and, thankfully for us, we went off with another guide. This other guide is the one who we have stuck with on future tours.

We were all taken through some barriers and, staying in the vicinity of the elevator lift, found ourselves in a large open courtyard area that at that time was being excavated. You could clearly see where the surface level had been. As I found out later, they used to have fêtes and celebrate special occasions in this whole area until relatively recently. All around, the huge city walls stretched up on two sides of the triangular area we were now standing in.

In the sixteenth century the Spanish developed the plateau of Saint-Esprit into military barracks. After the siege of 1684, when the French took over the rule of Luxembourg, Vauban the French military engineer built the Citadelle du Saint-Esprit on the plateau. He also reinforced the ramparts and the bastions and expanded the garrison of the citadelle.

After The Treaty of London that Luxembourg signed in 1867 all the garrisons were torn down along with most of the fortifications.

In the former courtyard we were in, the archaeologists had found some skeletons of humans in the excavations. Talk of the Black Death and of disease went round. Whether these bodies were of soldiers or women and children, I don't know. Anyway, we ended up in a barn, known as the Reitbahn. Just at that moment, outside, the heavens opened. Another downpour.

Inside this barn, which was built in 1828, were all manner of broken stones that had been carefully laid out, and each looked numbered. We discovered that this building used to be a riding hall. On one of the walls were daubed some original and genuine small Nazi slogans. There was an original small Nazi poster of some event, a leftover from the war, its faded images there for all to see.

Our tour guide explained in Luxembourgish to everyone about the barn. Simon could get the gist of it as he understands and speaks considerably more words than I do. It was a great pity Ernie, our Luxembourgish friend, had failed to show. (His wife had made him go clothes shopping with her, we found out later. Poor sod.)

Soon it was time to go down the tunnel. It was a very exciting moment as this trip was a one off. Yes, for one day only that year and for one day only ever, you could view this particular tunnel.

It was rumoured that the government was going to build a law centre on the whole site. This would destroy the tunnel and over six hundred years of history. What a tragedy. There was a petition to sign later, should you wish to do so. Surely they could build over the tunnel?

As it turned out the barn has since been demolished and the law centre is to be built. What happens to the tunnel remains to be seen. Another part of the city's heritage will be destroyed and some concrete and glass modern monstrosity will go up in its place. All in the name of progress. I have since been advised that what Simon and I possibly saw in the barn may not have been Nazi posters etc…But as the barn has now been demolished I can't prove it!

Now, the name of this particular tunnel is The Casemates of the Holy Spirit, and where we were standing was the Heilig Geist Plateau or Holy Spirit Plateau. The entrance to the tunnel was through a green door in the side of the rock. We were now right behind the eternal flame of the National Monument of Luxembourg Solidarity. This commemorates the dead of the Second World War and those who fought against the Nazis during their occupation of Luxembourg. We were right by a wall under the trees, which overlooked us. The green door was unlocked and we made our way into the tunnel, down the steps with our torches on. It was cold as we descended.

There was a railing of sorts in place for some of the way. It was damp and a bit wet. Strange designs confronted us in the torch light, their formation being a result of the water drip-drip-dripping over the course of time. You ducked to avoid banging your head on the tunnel roof. This was a real tunnel. None of your tourist tunnels here. Those are enlarged for your convenience. The tour group continued downwards.

We found out that people used to shelter here in wartime. The British Embassy even came here during the original Gulf War back in 1992. That was a surprise. Civilians used many of the tunnel networks during the Second World War. Up to 35,000 people sheltered in them from the bombing raids. Four hundred years before, when the Austrians and Spanish had invaded, the occupying soldiers at the time lived in the tunnels, over six hundred of them. With them in the tunnels to keep them happy were four hundred whores. That is what I was told. Whether it's true, I don't know!

At the bottom, the main tunnel splits into two. One tunnel heads left along the bottom of the rock face. It heads out in the rock, curving left by ninety degrees and goes a further maybe hundred metres beyond that. If you take the main passage to the right, you will follow the rock face along until just before the viaduct.

All along the route were lots of small passages that go nowhere. There are small natural openings in the rock for ventilation. There are also carved out very small openings for gun embrasures. One such gun embrasure looks out directly at the fountain on the other side of the viaduct in the park area of the Grund. Not many people will have seen that view like I did.

The whole trip in this tunnel was fascinating. We retraced our steps and headed towards the surface. It was like being on a school trip, as you just wanted to dash off and explore all those passages, your torch shining out in the dark. There was no light here for your convenience. If you got left behind and your torch battery went, you'd be stuffed! So you had to keep up with the others in order to maximise the light factor from all the torches that lit and reflected off the tunnel walls.

On hitting daylight, we continued with our tour. This time we headed to a building on the edge of the Holy Spirit plateau. It used to be an ancient military hospital. The basement of the building was used as a jail. We all had a look at the jail part. The building was built during the Prussian occupation and was constructed between 1857 and 1860. Since 1967, it houses the national archives.

The tour continued, down some stairs to the Grund area. We walked down the steep slope, taking a left, which took us over the bridge past Scotts bar on the right-hand corner, up the old narrow cobbled street on the right until we got to another green door, which was situated on the left.

"Another secret tunnel entrance. Wow," I said.

The locked door was opened by our guide and we started to enter the dark passageway in front of us. It was like entering a void. Suddenly in the darkness of the moment and hitting you as you entered was a giant caked spider's web.

It was incredible, as it seemed to spread out right across the top of the ceiling directly behind the entrance, forming a natural barrier across the doorway. It gleamed in the light as it hung from the roof of the passage. It was like a giant pillow. It also appeared to move. The girls in front screamed. Yes, it was most definitely moving. There, hanging from it and most definitely moving, were millions and millions of very tiny spiders! It was a very scary moment. The whole giant spider's web must have been more than nine inches wide. It was caked in moving baby spiders.

Terrified, we entered the short passage leading to a room beyond, which must have been some seven metres square. We shone our torches. Suddenly, something large glistened at us from a position just above us to our front left. Wait, there it was again, this time fractionally to the right. My God! It was a second wave of spiders that at first sight appeared to be attacking us. They were dotted all around us in the darkened room. This time these spiders were not the tiny ones we had just encountered. This time, staring us in the face, was an army of giant spiders.

Every giant spider was just hanging there, not moving. Each one appeared to mark out its own territory, which covered maybe eighty centimetres in diameter. These huge spiders were literally the size of your hand, their bodies being practically the size of a golf ball. Each giant spider appeared to be hairless and shiny. Their rear body stretched back, their curved body developing into a point at the very back. It was almost as if at this point they had a sting that they were waiting to unleash on us. They were enormous. The giant spiders looked gruesome as they hung there, glistening in our torchlight. They seemed to stare back at us, as though guarding the entrance. They were horrible. As you walked beneath them, you were expecting them to fall on you and give a nasty bite that would kill you.

Suddenly some of the girls in the party turned back. They were having none of it. These evil looking spiders scared them stiff. I mean, what harm had they done us? After all, it was us who had invaded *their* space. As it turned out, they were quite harmless. Well, I didn't hang around to find out. (Get it! Hang around—wasted!) We quickly walked further up the passage. What we had just encountered had to be seen to believe. It was creepy. It made the hairs on the back of your neck stand up. As Simon later put it, "Even us non-arachnophobia people were terrified."

We moved on and continued our tour, heading up yet more steep steps following the passages round, careful not to bump our heads on the tunnel roof that sometimes gave you a nasty shock when it lowered suddenly. We surfaced onto the top of the plateau in an area that looked out right across the Alzette valley. It was a magnificent view of the city. One could just imagine the Spanish commanders standing here all those years ago.

The girls who had U-turned met us all at the top, having taken the road round and up to where we now were. They were relieved that there had been an alternative route up to the top.

Now there's an old English saying that says, "What goes up must come down." Right now that meant a return trip down the stairs and past those giant spiders. We all shuddered at the thought of this but we all, minus the girls, managed the return trip and afterwards many tales of these were swapped over a pint. We all felt mighty brave with the thought of us making it through those huge webs lined with those giant spiders. UUh!

The trip had come to an end and before we left our guide gave us some literature on some tunnels including the next rendezvous. It was now time to head off for a beer into some bars in the Grund, where, in one of them, we met some very nice Ukrainian barmaids…

The motto of the story is that if you see a green door that goes into a rock or wall you'll know it's probably the entrance to a secret tunnel. Just don't knock on it and do a Shakin Stevens[1] or you might have some old lady run out and do a Nora Batty on you.[2]

---

1.   Shakin Stevens was a pop singer who in the early 1980s in the UK had a hit with Green Door. He, like Elvis, used to shake his hips when he sang

2.   Nora Batty is a female character in the English comedy television programme 'Last of the Summer Wine,' set in Holmfirth in Yorkshire, UK. The programme has run for over thirty years. Nora Batty is one of the old ladies who had a tendency to run out of her front door with a mop and chase her neighbour down the street.

28

Shine that Torch

The torch I purchased for the first special tunnel trip lasted well. I had visions of it fading at the end of some tunnel and me getting stuck down there. As it was, all was well, but I did get some new batteries just in case. Certainly, the success of the trip was discussed at length in The White Rose with all our friends.

"When's the next trip?" was the question most asked.

Well, as it turned out, none of us had too long to wait and about two to three weeks later it was time for another tunnelling expedition. This time, however, there would be more people. This time we had an idea of what to expect.

The rendezvous was at 2pm at The White Rose. One or two were late, but it didn't matter. As long as we could get the 2.15pm number 18 bus, then that was all that mattered. This time there were six of us, including a Spanish and Finnish girl together with four Brits. We hopped on the bus, paid our one euro ten cents and sat at the back. It was one of those bendy buses where you have to negotiate the swivel bit half way down. They are nice to go on, each one being a little different from another. The bus headed over the bridge Adolphe and up to the bus station. It headed through the town and over the red bridge. The weather was cloudy and hopefully it would not rain. Our destination was Kirchberg.

We got off the bus outside the Novotel Hotel at Kirchberg and walked back along Rue du Fort Niedergrünewald, passing under the bridge. A little further on we took a left fork and went up the lane into some woods. The wooded area around here is popular with cyclists who like to practice their mountain biking skills. We arrived at the edge of the woods to see a fort of some sort in front of us. It looked huge.

In the literature we had with us was the picture of a fort, the name of which was Fort Thüngen. Our rendezvous for our tunnels trip was 3pm in front of this fort. We were early, which gave us a little time to nosey around the area.

Fort Thüngen is impressive on the outside, especially at its rear. As we soon discovered, it was built by the Austrians, but it was the Prussians who in later years transformed it into its present form. Its commanding position gives it a bird's eye view of the city.

Our party found itself at the rear of the fort. Here we discovered a huge open lawn area that stretched out towards the city. It looked as though it had been carved out of the surrounding forest.

From the city, you can see its splendour staring at you. It looks like two mini towers that rise up menacingly. There is also a third smaller tower between them in the centre, which is built above the grand entrance.

At the bottom of these towers is the main entrance, which is slightly to the left of centre. Before you enter, you have to cross an arched stone bridge that crosses an empty ditch in order to gain access to the main entrance. There was no water in the ditch.

The shape of the fort is deceptive from the sides. Only when you view the fort from above will its true shape stand out. The *réduit* is shaped like a giant arrow. The three towers at the rear of the fort are, when viewed from above, like the back end of an actual arrow. At the rear of the fort on each of the rounded towers just below the level of the ditch are slits in the walls. Originally, we thought these were there to allow the soldiers in the fort to pour hot boiling oil into the water in the ditch to help repel the invaders. However, as we later discovered, there was no water in the ditch and, what is more, those slits were actually the outlet of the drains! How disappointing!

Fort Thüngen was built because of all the previous attacks the city had encountered in that area. However, the fort was never actually used in battle. It was used, however, for military training purposes.

The fort then stretches forward quite a long way. At its front, which is the 'envelope', is a new development designed by a famous Chinese-American architect. Here the twenty-first century has arrived with the construction of some monstrosity of a building that can only be described as a giant greenhouse. The new building looks hideous. It has obviously been designed to reflect its modern architectural features against the impressive Austrian Fortification behind it. This concrete greenhouse, the roof of which is mostly glass, slopes downwards, giving it its predominantly greenhouse effect, which to me and many others appear to be totally out of place.

This giant greenhouse, as we found out later, was built over the part of the fort that was the envelope area of the fort. That's the bit that faced the attackers. It has been carefully built over the original foundations, which were left after the fort was demolished at the time when all the other Luxembourg forts were also being dismantled. This greenhouse, which none of us liked, apparently was part-funded with foreign money, and, I gather, has been a controversy from the very beginning. I can clearly see why. The architect who designed it should head for the back of the class—his creation is the mother of all modern monstrosities!

French, Austrian and Prussian troops occupied Fort Thüngen up to 1867. It has had a colourful history. It was actually started in 1688 by the French military engineer Vauban. He was responsible for the building that is known as the *redoute de la hauteur du parc*. It was later, when the Austrians were occupying the fort in 1732, that Sigismund Freiherr von Thüngen was a governor ad interim of the fortress.

The fort was made up of a large *réduit*, a vast envelope with the small *redoute* and two lunettes at the beginning. The Prussians in 1836 added the three towers of the main fort or *réduit*, putting the crested acorn designs on these roofs. They also enlarged the casemates to nine hundred and fifty three square metres. Fort Thüngen was one of the largest forts of its kind in the old Fortress of Luxembourg.

The tour guide arrived, greeted us and recognised both Simon and myself from before. He suggested we might like to join the club and pay a subscription fee. We paid our money and were now in the Friends of Luxembourg Fortress Club. I call it 'The Tunnels club' as we spend more time underground in tunnels rather than above ground. Did that mean we now got a discount? No such luck. However, we would get to know more information about the Luxembourg tunnels, which all of us found fascinating. By now, those people who had wanted to take this tour had turned up. The tour was again in Luxembourgish and some French and was now ready to commence.

The tour started in the entrance hall of Fort Thüngen where there were some maps and pictures of the forts. These showed me the answer to what I had been searching for and had never dreamt of finding so easily. Staring me in the face was a map showing every secret tunnel under every fort; in fact, it showed the entire Luxembourg secret tunnel system! It was great. Now it all made sense.

We learnt a bit of history of the forts from our guide who, among other things, mentioned the Prussian arrogance.

The tour continued, this time to the rooms on the ground floor that's in the round of the fort as you look at it from its rear. The rooms are, believe it or not, round inside as well. The first room that we went in is the one on the left. It has been restored and is now a giant round kitchen. An interesting feature here is that if you stand just in the right place in the room and you talk, the sound of your voice will change. The whole room will echo with this change creating a unique experience. In the other room is a giant replica of the fort in days gone by. It stands in the centre of the large stone round room.

A similar, much larger, design of old Luxembourg showing every fort around the city and other features can be found in the National museum opposite the Tube bar in the old town. Other well laid out wooden boards showing Luxembourg City in miniature during different time-periods can be seen in the Luxembourg City museum in the Rue de St-Esprit.

It was time to go into our first tunnel. There was an air of excitement. From inside the reception area there is a set of stairs that descend. We descended the stone-built winding staircase, passing various tunnels that ran off from the stairway. We continued down and were now in our first tunnel of the day. This one was actually lit and was quite high. This led us into what felt like a maze of passages. It was actually a passageway, which on a map is a bit like a large letter S. The passageway was relatively straight and this tunnel turned out to be one hundred and sixty nine metres long. It felt longer, but at the time it was hard to tell. We came out into the bright daylight. This time the door that had been at the end of the tunnel was disappointingly not a green door but a slatted grey one. It didn't matter. We were now outside and stood in the sunshine.

We had arrived at another fort; this one was the Fort Ober-Grünewald. Vauban (see later chapters) also built this fort. We wandered amongst the ruins and through an archway. All around us were signs of renovation. In fact, here they were actively rebuilding the fort walls.

The project to restore the walls and other features is being paid for by the state. It's interesting to see how they're doing it. Most of the original brickwork was used in the construction of the new city, in the time after the defortification of the city. Many forts were literally levelled and most were covered over.

This fort had had mixed luck. However, the project to rebuild was being done by using both old traditional skills and modern building methods, the most noticeable being the front stone masonry that looks old but is actually recreated. Right behind the masonry and supporting it is a layer of modern breezeblock that I can safely say was not being used four hundred years ago. Nevertheless, you won't notice the breezeblock when it's finished.

The tour took a deviation to the left. We had reached a small steel walkway that overlooked the city. Here was a magnificent view of the railway viaduct. A sentry box was also in view.

The group backtracked and the tour continued, taking us on a little scenic tour that went through the woods to the right and north eastwards or so from Fort Thüngen and to the right of Fort Ober-Grünewald.

One of the places we visited was a very strange building that sits in a valley. Behind it lies the forest, beyond which was the Kirchberg Plateau. There is a stream that runs down the centre of the valley. On either side are mud track ways, which must have been there for hundreds of years. At the edge of the forest the mud tracks turn into roads, which converge at this odd building.

Now I have to admit at this point to a big misunderstanding of what this building was due to the language barrier and the fact that I wasn't concentrating on what was being said. However, I can now tell you that where we were standing apparently used to be a gateway into Luxembourg City, the name of which was *La Porte du Grünewald ou de la 'Hiel'*. My misunderstanding was partly caused because we only saw one side of this building (on both this visit and a later one) from the forest side. Had we ventured down a little further, all would have become obvious. If you go there you'll see what I mean. What I had missed was this. Years ago, the building was a gateway into the city. The gate is clearly evident on the inner side. However, on the outer defence side the area has been filled in with a path, a tree, and lots of mud. This now forms a garden area so you can barely see the gate without looking really closely. This is a great pity as a drawing I saw there on a much later trip showed that once upon a time on the outer entrance was a drawbridge. Above it was a gap in the brickwork enabling soldiers to drop things on top of invaders. Nice!

I also discovered a fortification wall ran right across where the road now passes through, which soldiers used to patrol. You can just imagine it as you stand there.

The gatehouse was built by the French between 1684 and 1688. When the Austrians arrived, they added a whole floor to it, which practically doubled its height. These days the gatehouse is a flat, but I think the building deserves a bit of restoration to help transform its gateway on both sides into something like it used to be.

Meanwhile, back on the tour, the long building close by we discovered used to be a flour store. It was built by the Austrians in 1733. The flour was stored in kegs to protect it and was used by the military.

A hike through the woods brought the tour out at the *réduit* Niedergrünewald. Here a project was well under way, which was the rebuilding of it to how it used to be. Originally, a canon would fire shots from this position across and into the valley to help repel the enemy.

We continued the walk. The group followed a stone wall that was on our left. We ended up a little further up the path where we found ourselves in a spot that now overlooked the valley right over Pfaffenthal. It's yet another fascinating point. The suburb below is spread out behind one of the oldest entrances to Luxembourg.

In the old days, before bridges were what they are today, roads ran along the valleys. One of the main entrances to Luxembourg was along the Alzette valley, through the two giant gated towers. Situated on either side of the Alzette River, these towers are called The Vauban Towers. They were named after Marshall de Vauban, the French military engineer who designed them. He was responsible for strengthening the defences of the Pfaffenthal valley. A massive defensive city wall used to cross this entire valley between forts Niedergrünewald and Berlaimont. The Vauban towers were part of this. Soldiers would probably have patrolled its walls looking out for any invaders.

Over the last few years up to 2003 the whole area underwent massive restoration. The results are impressive. The crenellated wall that crosses the Alzette valley has been restored. You can see this as the wall crosses down to the railway gate just below.

Above this point to our right was the red bridge, which is actually called the Grand Duchess Charlotte Bridge, but I've never heard anyone call it that. It's generally known as the red bridge because of its distinct colour, red. It is seventy-four metres high, is three hundred and fifty-five metres long, and is twenty-five metres wide.

The tour leader then took us all on a short hike up into the woods. At this point we were certainly feeling fit with all the walking we'd been doing. Here in the middle of the woods we discovered some stairs and yet another secret tunnel entrance. The door, which wasn't green, was opened. We descended into the tunnel below and found ourselves in yet another fort. This fort was known as Fort Nieder-Grünewald.

When the forts were dismantled, like many others, this one had been stripped of everything, leaving only its tunnels intact. However, this fort was different from the rest because, since it was dismantled and covered over one hundred and fifty odd years ago, it has been completely overgrown with forest, keeping the fort a hidden secret.

In one particular tunnel we walked along the wall and ceiling was covered with what looked like salt. The water had dripped through forming lime deposits, creating a white effect. If you brushed against it, it would result in you getting white on your clothes. Some side tunnels appeared immensely long and when you turned around the tunnel looked completely different. Our tour guide said, "Don't shine your torch on the floor, shine it on the ceiling." A cracked head is very painful.

Now one tunnel can look like another and it's fascinating to see where they go and where they end up. Some tunnels link one fort with another. One such tunnel we were in gave us all a surprise as the underground tour continued. We found ourselves without realising it going from the tunnel system of Fort Nieder-grünewald into the tunnels of Fort Olizy. It was here where we ended up ascending into daylight. There were steps that led us up and out by the side of the main road to Kirchberg. We were about one hundred metres before the red bridge.

The opening where we had surfaced is on the left-hand side, if you're coming from the bridge side. There, if you look carefully, you will see some bricks with a cover round them. This 'secret tunnel entrance' is the exit of the gallery on the ground of the former Fort Olizy. It's hard to believe there are hidden forts below. We stood there like lemons for a while, resting, before descending again.

The tunnel network map we had showed the dual carriageway Kirchberg road slice right through one of the forts, but I don't remember seeing this. However, the modern road has had to be cut through part of the ceiling of one tunnel and it's interesting to see how they have built the road from down under, giving it a most unusual perspective. It was well worth seeing.

We found ourselves taking a right, then a left and then another left. This led us into more tunnels of Fort Olizy. Our journey between the two forts had taken us some three hundred and thirty metres. Fort Olizy was named after supreme Commander Olizy in 1737. The only remains today are underground, buried by today's future of roads, grass and trees.

Whilst at Fort Olizy we followed the tunnel round and round and round. Well, it felt like that. In fact, we had actually been right round the fort. En route we saw gun loops behind which was soil. The soil would have been put there when the forts were filled in and levelled. We ended up where we had started from.

The group headed off up the same tunnel we had come down and at the end of which I believe we did a left turn. This led us all to more tunnels that were also part of the Fort Nieder-Grünewald complex. Some tunnels, especially the dead-end ones, literally got lower and lower and lower.

"Shine that torch!" someone yelled as we made our way forward into the dark and damp passageway.

Occasionally someone cursed as the roof descended and the person hit his or her head on the roof. After that, the word, 'Attention' with a French accent could be heard echoing along the tunnel. This was in one of the runner tunnels that spurred off from the main tunnel that we were in, but the 'attention!' had actually been said on quite a few times that afternoon, and each time it was echoed gave the rest of us time to lower our heads. We retraced out steps, and made our way back to where we had started.

The whole experience was great fun and exciting. The group then surfaced and the tunnel was made secure. You could easily get lost down there. For health and safety reasons, probably because the tunnels are so low in places, is why they are maybe not open to the public. Let's face it, there's also no light down there and it's pitch black. Let me emphasize this again. The blackness is one hundred per cent where you can't see a thing. You just wouldn't want to be left behind down there.

The group headed back to Fort Thüngen where our guide took us inside. I must admit I thought we were simply going back just into the entrance hall, but I was wrong. We were led into the vast area beyond it into an area that forms the main part of Fort Thüngen. I have to admit the whole place at the time we were there resembled a building site. The reason for this was that the fort inside was being turned into a museum called the Museum of the Fortress with the entire inside being renovated.

Our tour group was led over new concrete floors, past new arched-ceiling open rooms and into a vast open area. We crossed the area on quite a few planks of wood. Everyone went up some new stairs to the level above.

"This would all be part of the exhibition area," our guide advised us.

Everyone continued right up to the area above the entrance hall, where we climbed some more stairs that took us onto the roof of the fort. Boy, what a view! The city was in the distance at its rear and the monstrosity of the greenhouse to the front.

This greenhouse is going to be a modern art gallery, its official name being the Musée d'Art Moderne Grand-Duc Jean. What a waste of money. Well, let's hope they start by planting a few tomato seeds in some grow bags! Then we can see some real modern art that will grow right before our eyes. At least the tomatoes will get plenty of sun.

We were incredibly lucky, as members of the public were not normally allowed to see any of what we had seen. I felt quite fortunate to have taken this trip. The group returned to the hallway and the tour was over. My friends all thought it had been great fun.

Everyone who goes down these special tunnels enjoys the experience, each remembering his or her favourite bit of the tour. The chances are that once anyone has been on one trip, he or she will want to go on another.

Our small contingent of six headed off to the city, walking from the rear of Fort Thüngen across the open grassed area and back down to Fort Ober-Grünewald. It was here that we decided to descend some stairs that would take us down into the valley below.

At this point we met an American lady who was lost. "Could you help me get back into town?" she asked. Of course, we could. Apparently, her husband was working and he wasn't interested in going out. So rather than go round the shops she had decided to have a look around town. Good for her. She had been to the Luxembourg City Tourist Office in Place d'Armes who had assisted her. They had suggested some walks and they had given her some route maps including the route she had taken, which had directed her to where she now was. I gather she had become a bit disorientated, which is why she had asked us for help.

The Luxembourg City Tourist Office has several guides and themed walks that you can trek. These include the circuit Vauban, which is the one our American friend was taking. There is also the Mansfeld, the Circuit Goethe, the circuit Schuman. There is also the City Promenade, the City Detective and the circuit Wenzel.

Together we descended the stairs until we came out at an entrance near the Brazilian bar called Birimbau, which is right by the railway bridge, on the road called the Allée Pierre de Mansfeld. Here, we all turned left and followed the river round, which was on our right. We walked along chatting with our new friend. Our destination was The Britannia Pub, which was on the corner further round. It was at this point that one of the girls in our group departed with the lady as both were heading into town.

"Have a nice day," the American lady said.

We did, and sat in The Britannia downing a few beers.

I must add here that there is an alternative walking route down to the Britannia. This route is very different and is equally impressive. So, if you're feeling fit, take the road to the left from outside Fort Thüngen, from its entrance as you come out across the bridge. You should be heading down the Rue Milliounewée, which is a very old road. Further down is a junction. You can't miss it, as there's a modern triangular building that sticks out over the road.

The road at the junction that goes to your right is the Rue Jules Wilhelm. Just beyond this is another road, which is also on your right that's unmarked on any roadmap. You should continue down on this very old steeply descending road, which is in the ravine. In distant days past, it would have been one of the few access roads that you took from the Plateau of Kirchberg down towards Clausen. The road is not used now except for access to a very old Jewish graveyard, which must be somewhat creepy on a moonlit night.

The bottom end these days is sealed off to cars. The road will give you an idea of how streets were constructed many years ago. I had walked down there and come to another famous Luxembourg landmark called the Tour (Tower) Malakoff. It was built as the 'Judenturm', which means Jews Tower, by the Prussians around the year 1860. It looks as if it was used as a tollhouse where you paid to pass through. Beyond the tower the road forks. You can either go to the left or to the right. I chose the left, which was the Rue Malakoff. I passed by some very old traditional farmhouses. The road comes out on the Rue de Clausen, which, if you turn right, will take you directly down to The Britannia, where it's nice to rest and have a pint…

29

Bits & pieces of the Forts

Luxembourg's secret tunnels were indeed secret for longer than you might think. After the Second World War, no one knew exactly where they all were. Tunnels were always being uncovered. This was generally when road works or building excavations dug them up. Each tunnel was then explored to see where it went. A good example was when one day a large hole appeared in the Boulevard Royal. Apparently, a hidden tunnel wall had collapsed. This resulted in the road above falling in. Naturally, both the road and the tunnel wall were repaired.

Nevertheless, it wasn't until after the fall of the Berlin wall that the Luxembourg Government got a call from someone in the former East Germany saying, "We've got your plans for all your tunnels. Do you want to see them?" I think you can guess the answer to that.

Apparently the Nazis who had invaded Luxembourg in 1940 had taken the plans to Potsdam in Germany. After the Nazi defeat in 1945 the Russians created the state of East Germany. The plans therefore remained hidden and untouched in Merseburg in the former communist state of East Germany for nearly fifty years. Since then the Luxembourg Government has been able to uncover and restore more of the country's past for its future generations to see.

I have seen one of the actual maps that was pinned up during my second tour of Fort Thüngen. It was explained to me that when the Prussians were the occupiers of Luxembourg they continued to use the French plans they found in the fortress in 1814. The spoken language was Luxembourgish and German. The written language was German. For military terms the language was French.

Luxembourg at all times was surrounded by a huge fortification system which, if you look today, simply isn't there. The forts were all dismantled in the years after the signing of the Treaty of London, which took place in London on the 11th May 1867. Here it was decided that 'The fortress' would be abandoned. It was here also that the Declaration of Neutrality for Luxembourg was established. After this date, Luxembourg became a neutral and independent country. Luxembourg City became the country's capital. The same year the Prussians, who were occupying Luxembourg at the time, departed—on the 9th September. The twenty-three forts and sixteen other powerful defence works were closed, and the dismantling began. The first fortifications to be dismantled were the city walls. It took sixteen years. Of the original twenty-three kilometres of casemates, twelve to fifteen kilometres remained that ran all round the city. Some parts of the fortress could not be dismantled without the demolition of parts of the city. Thankfully these bits survive to this day.

In 1870/71, when Luxembourg was a neutral country and the dismantling had begun, the Franco-Prussian war took place beyond its borders. Luxembourg took no part in this war where France lost territory to the Prussians.

Fort Thüngen's dismantling still had to be done. The Luxembourg government of the time was clearly worried about the nearby war so they decided to speed up the dismantling process. Breaches were made to the fortress walls to make the fort unusable. This was done by the Luxembourgers themselves who wanted to render them definitely useless.

Fort Thüngen's dismantling was completed in September 1877. The area around the former forts Thüngen, Niedergrünewald, Ober-Grünewald and Olizy then became ornamental gardens and over time, mostly forest.

Most of the walls and masonry from the forts were used to construct the new Luxembourg, which you see today. This new Luxembourg, having been designed in the late eighteen hundreds, was mainly constructed in the period 1905 to 1920. I say this because if you walk round the city and look carefully at the buildings you can see the date of the construction of the buildings. Usually the date is inserted in stone at the top in a strategic place. Each building is slightly different but stands gracefully, its structure totally of the period.

Sadly, they are now tearing down many of these buildings in the name of progress. Modern six-story flats are replacing them. Only a few are modernised. These few manage to keep their fronts but are now very modern inside. As a German friend commented later, the city must have been built using only one or two architects, as the buildings are much the same in their style. He thought they were boring compared to the German architecture of the same period. I would certainly argue the point. After all, they have undoubtedly the elegance that makes them so Luxembourgish—for those buildings that remain constitute the Luxembourg we all know and love today.

There are many stories to be told about the tunnels here in Luxembourg. As to whether they are true or not I don't know…

There's the story about the children who went in the tunnels on one of these tours. These included both girls and boys. The boys pretended they were big macho men who were brave and courageous when the girls were around. When the tour went into the tunnels, the boys rushed down the tunnels ahead of the girls and well ahead of everyone else. Some time later they returned scared to death and suggested the girls went first with their larger torches. The reason? Well, it was just that bit too black even for them. The girls were, however, delighted with the opportunity of going first. It was also very easy to get lost, especially if they took a few too many turnings without remembering their route. They were not so brave after all—but the girls were actually braver.

There's another story about the nuns, the soldiers and the whores. Well, as you know, all good Catholic nuns are pure and celibate. Still, the soldiers had an arrangement with the nuns as a result of which the nuns seemed all prim and proper on the surface while things were somewhat different below. This is where the secret tunnels came in handy for both parties. The nuns used to visit the soldiers and the soldiers used to visit the nuns. The nuns also used to assist the actual whores by giving them assistance to entertain the soldiers. The tunnels were used as cover to get each from the barracks to the nunnery and vice versa. Each party came away happy and no more was said.

The railway was built after the forts were constructed. The British built it. The line from Luxembourg to Ettelbruck was built in 1859. There were huge valleys to cross, so high viaducts had to be built. The railway also goes through some of the forts. This can be clearly seen in Luxembourg City.

The railway viaducts were built generally with a slight curve on them. This was to assist with the gradient of the slope, the curvature acting a bit like a river does as it meanders its way downstream. They were prepared for two tracks though in the beginning just one single track was needed.

The Viaduct that crosses the Pétrusse valley was built between 1859 and 1861. Its other name is La Passerelle. Its twenty-four huge arches stretch right across the valley, the arches varying in width between eight and fifteen metres. This road viaduct has a height of forty-five metres above the Pétrusse valley and is two hundred and ninety metres in length. It was the original bridge of the two that stretches across to the old town from the station. It used to be half its current width before it was modernised and widened some years ago. In days gone by it used to have a tram that ran across it.

The viaduct was designed in such a way that if the city came under attack, its curved design would create a few obstacles. The cannons used to attack the city would each have had to be lined up and aligned separately in order to fire on their target accurately. This would take time and allow the defenders to attack them.

The majority of the forts above ground were pentagonal in shape and design, one of the exceptions being Fort Thüngen, which is shaped like an arrow.

Each fort, though, had its own tunnel system and in the forts that were pentagon shaped, the main tunnel ran right around the inner edges of the whole fort. In some of the larger forts avenues of tunnels ran interconnecting with each other. Some tunnels were higher than others were, while others ended up going nowhere.

At the front of the fort, which was at least two sides of the pentagon, there were separate runner tunnels that branched outwards from this main tunnel. There were, say, six or more runner tunnels in a fort, which each ran forward under the main defence wall. Some of these tunnels stretched more than twenty metres in length and then split into much smaller sub-tunnels, again heading away from the fort's outer defence wall. On each side of these sub-tunnels were about half a dozen very small tunnels that spurred out, each measuring no more than about two metres in length.

Now, as it turned out, the idea was that when the fort was under attack, the attackers outside the fort would get an unexpected surprise as they tried to scale the fort walls. Explosives would have been planted in the tunnel that was right under their feet. Bang! They would be blown up from below. The invaders would then try to access the fort through the hole in the ground made by the explosion. This would give them access to the tunnel system. The defenders, knowing this, simply blew up the tunnel further down which then totally blocked off any form of entry. After all, they could always dig another tunnel at another time.

Luxembourg City used to have many sentry boxes. These boxes were positioned at strategically placed points on the outer edges of the Fortress, each one having a bird's eye view of everything that moved in the valley below. The correct name in English for these boxes is echauguettes. Some people know them as Spanish turrets. This name is a literal translation of the Luxembourgish term *Spueneschen Tiermchen*. In French it's *guérite*. In German, it's *Postenerker*.

All the echauguettes are circular in shape. However, there's one that isn't. It's hexagonal and located close to the Pulvermuhl railway bridge. They were used to take pot shots at undesirables but were to be dismantled before a siege, which is contrary to what I thought. These sentry boxes are still dotted around the city defences—originally over thirty-seven, but I did hear over fifty (it depends on who you talk to); there are now only nine remaining.

The Rham plateau was once one of the strategic points used in the outer defence of the city. Various forts were built up on it. Near the top is the former Fort Dumoulin that was built in 1836 by the Prussians on the site of a former temporary field fortification, Fort Fetschenhof, itself built during the blockade of 1794/95. In 1843, after the retirement of the first Prussian Commander of the fortress, Jakob Dumoulin, it was renamed Fort Dumoulin. The fort was dismantled in later years after the treaty of London in 1867.

Other forts were also once on this plateau. These were Fort Rumigny, which began in 1688 as a tower known as the *redoute de la bombarde* and Fort Rubamprez, which the Austrians transformed and respectively built, both in 1735.

At the tip of the plateau was the tower or *redoute du Rahm*. The Spanish constructed this in 1674. When Luxembourg the fortress was dismantled, part of *redoute du Rahm* was dismantled in 1874/75. The French built the *ravelin du Rahm* in front of the medieval Wenzel wall in 1684/85, which was situated between the Wenzel wall and Fort Rubamprez.

The French, between 1684 and 1688, built some of the large magnificent former barracks that you can still view on the Rham plateau. The Austrians, and in 1860 the Prussians, greatly expanded them. They were used to house batteries of troops. After the de-fortification of the fortress and some years later, around 1890, the barracks were turned into a Hospice, which they have remained to this day.

My, how times change!

30

Luxembourg the Fortress

It started with a chat with a taxi driver friend of mine who is Luxembourgish. "Can you help me to get in touch with the guy from the tunnels club?" I asked him.

Somehow, our membership had lapsed and the telephone number we had didn't exist anymore.

He replied, "I will see what I can do."

In the meantime, I had written the club a letter in my best French to ask the same thing. This had gone to a P.O. Box number so might not be read for ages.

Well, as it turned out, I didn't see the taxi driver for a couple of days, after which I learned from him that he had been trying to get hold of me. Yes, indeed, he had managed to get in touch with the guy via a call to the National Museum to get the number. He had also been trying to get hold of me in particular, as there had been a tour that day—which by now I had missed. Oh well, you can't have everything.

The next evening I made the call in broken French to our tour guide. He knew exactly who I was—one of the two crazy Englishmen from last year. I managed to say enough in French to ascertain from him that there would be another tour a week on Sunday. Three days later I received in the post some literature from the Friends of the Fortress Association. Therefore, either the phone call had done the trick or the letter had. Anyway, I now had what I wanted, which was the date of the next trip and some information about it.

As it was, I couldn't go on the next trip that was a week on Sunday. However, I could go on the one after, which was a week on Thursday. This was actually a religious holiday, Ascension Day. So, it would be an ideal day for trooping round a couple of Casemates.

The Thursday arrived and word had been spread that there was another tunnels trip. As it was a national holiday, some people were doing other things. Still, four of us made it, including an English chap who had come over with his wife visiting a friend of mine.

This trip would take us to the forts of Fort Bourbon, Fort Wallis and the Bastion Beck. The forts are all in town. They were within walking distance from the town centre and, more importantly, they were within walking distance of The White Rose that naturally was our meeting point. Everyone met up at 2.30pm, armed with torches and dressed in our thick sweatshirts, coats and jeans. The group headed off at a leisurely pace towards Place de la Constitution, where in the middle stands the statue of the Golden Lady or Gëlle Fra, as she is known in Luxembourgish. This was where the main tour started at 3pm. For us regulars, we wouldn't have missed it for the world.

It was a sweltering day. The sun was shining and it was the sort of day where you wear just a T-shirt and shorts. The tourists were out en mass in the car park area in the Place de la Constitution. Our small group waited next to the statue of the Golden Lady. Here some people were also dressed up in sweaters and coats carrying a torch. The tour leader arrived. We exchanged greetings and the tour commenced.

Our first stop would be to Bastion Beck above which everyone in our group was actually standing. Bastion Beck was named after Governor Baron Johann von Beck who was a native of the city. It's probably the most visited Casemate in town and has been open to the public since 1933. Our group would also be visiting it. However, we would be going to many places where the tourists didn't go, which is one reason why the association is so special.

Bastion Beck goes back to medieval times when there were fortifications on the site. The fortress became Spanish in 1556 after the abdication of the Emperor Charles V, who divided his possessions between the Spanish and the Austrian Habsburgers.

The Spanish reinforced the fortifications. The work was undertaken by the Swiss fortress builder Isaac von Treybach who built Bastion Beck.

After the siege of 1684, when the French took over Luxembourg, Louis XIV commissioned Marshall Sébastien Le Prestre de Vauban to reconstruct the fortifications. He was responsible for the building of many of the forts here in Luxembourg. He was an accomplished military engineer and was an expert of sieges. His work turned Luxembourg into the future 'Gibraltar of the North'.

The walls of Bastion Beck in the Place de la Constitution rise twenty-seven metres above the Pétrusse River. Back in 1685, Vauban raised the height of the fortress walls to an even higher level than they are today.

We descended the steps where a WC was signposted. (That's a toilet, if you didn't know better.) On one side of the steps at the bottom is a WC. On the other side is the entrance to the Casemates. The group took this entrance. We found ourselves following more steps, going down and round, until the tour guide stopped right under the statue of the golden Lady.

Now I discovered that the Luxembourgers built the statue. It was erected to commemorate the dead who gave their lives in the Great War of 1914 to 1918. The state couldn't afford the statue but somehow the money came together and it was built. The statue was inaugurated in 1923.

When the Nazis invaded Luxembourg in 1940, they wanted the statue removed. The locals refused, as to them it was a statue to commemorate the dead. The Nazis could find no locals to remove it. Nevertheless, removed it was on the 20th October 1940, and it remained removed for more than forty years. The Nazis had had the statue towed away to a place where it was forgotten. In the early 1980s the statue was discovered. It was found in some disused land on the edge of a quarry area. After all these years it could be returned to its original site. It was only in 1984 that the statue began a period of restoration to return it to its original form. And so the statue today represents more than the dead it was built to remember after the Great War. It symbolizes freedom for the Luxembourg people.

Some months before this visit I remember sitting in the waiting room of my physiotherapist. I was bored, so I picked up one of those magazines you find in these types of places. This particular one featured an article on the Nazis in Luxembourg. The magazine was called *Telecran*, which is the local TV listing paper with an overview of that week's news in Luxembourg in the front of it. Anyway, in this particular issue was a feature of The Nazis in Luxembourg. It showed the plans the Nazis had for their future vision of the city. Much of it would have been transformed into some Nazi wonder. One of the plans they had was to build a large theatre in what is now the car park area on the Plateau of the Holy Spirit. Luckily, their vision was never realised, but the plans I found fascinating.

You'll discover that the older generation of Luxembourgers can't stand the Germans because of this occupation. This, however, applies to many of the older generation in all countries the Nazis fought in and fought against. In the UK and France the older generation can't abide the Germans. There is hatred, even today. However, I'm told that the hatred is far worse here. In Luxembourg, some twenty thousand Luxembourgers were sent to the concentration camps in the Ukraine. Most never returned.

What you have to understand is that a percentage of every family and village suffered as a result of the Nazis. Imagine one of your family being taken away and being either shot or sent to a concentration camp. It's not a pleasant thought.

Almost a whole generation of Luxembourgers were forced to learn only German, as Luxembourgish and French were banned during the occupation. This over the years has caused them to struggle in their own country compared to their fellow citizens who speak several languages. After the war, no reparations ('no dédommagements') were paid to Luxembourg from Germany, nor have they been paid to date. This remains a bone of contention between the two countries.

Although I haven't seen it myself I have heard that for years if a German stepped over the border he or she would be ignored by the older generation. For example, a German visitor would be ignored if he or she entered a shop; if the Luxembourger felt they had no choice but to serve them, they would give that person the brush-off. The older generation Luxembourgers to this day have never forgiven the Germans. That's one reason why not many older generation Germans come across the border. These days the younger generation thankfully have a different perspective on life. Time has moved on and people get on with their lives, in peace.

The tour continued and the group headed downwards, descending many steps. We passed through a roof area of modern concrete where the roof had been made safe and rebuilt. Continuing down the steps and passageways, the group then reached a wide area where the fort looked out on the valley through large gun loops that are clearly visible from the outside. This is where the cannons would have been fired at the enemy when defending the town. At the end of this area was a green door that was opened by the tour guide for us. This took us out onto a small area about half way up the cliff face where there was a little patio area and some steps that descended on the outside down into the Pétrusse valley.

After sampling the sunlight, the group retreated inside where we found ourselves doing a small horizontal loop round some tunnels. This brought us out at the other end of the cannon area, which we had visited minutes before, after which we did a little backtracking before everyone took a right fork into another tunnel, heading downwards again. The tunnel was adequately lit and had a high ceiling probably for the benefits of the tourists. Eventually we came to a wide section and it looked that within twenty metres the tunnel ended. On further inspection, we found a locked door in the rock face. Now, if you're a tourist, it's here that one would turn around and head back to the surface. However, if you're in the fortress club, there's more!

The door was unlocked and opened. Yes, it was another green door! The group passed through to find itself at the bottom of the Pétrusse valley. Everyone rested for a few moments to get their breath back. The Adolphe bridge towered over us, looking magnificent in the afternoon sunlight. The tour group then headed off to the next destination. As it turned out, that would be Fort Bourbon. We crossed over the small bridge across the Pétrusse River. The group was aiming for a door that was on the opposite side of the valley to where they had emerged. There were also some steps to climb which took us up about twenty metres. The green door stood there sombre in the afternoon sunlight.

From the literature that everyone had been given by our guide, it looked as though there was originally more than just the small bridge that crossed here. One of the pamphlets showed a barrier built across the Pétrusse valley at this point. It looked fairly high, maybe thirty feet, and reinforced behind. In fact, the tunnel that the group had come out of and the one everyone was about to go into were once linked across the valley by a flat level passage. This gave us an idea of the height. Below this passage at one point was where the river crossed. It passed underneath two arches. As I discovered later, this was actually a key defence position. The barrier was called the 'Bourbon Sluice'. The Austrians built it between 1728 and 1729.

The Pétrusse River was controlled with this. The water would have probably built up behind the lock to a height of some twenty feet. It would have been used for drinking water. However, its main purpose was that when the city was being attacked lower down the valley, the sluice gates could be unleashed and the water would gush down and flood the plain below. Due to the small amount of water that generally flows on this river, I doubt this lock was fully used. Otherwise, there wouldn't have been any water downstream for ages.

We were about to enter the tunnel that would take us to the lower tunnels of the former Fort Bourbon, which was named after the French house of Bourbon. (The French King's family.) Once the door was unlocked and opened, the group found itself climbing many stairs. From here on everyone needed their torches as there was no other light. At the top of these steps the tour group rested. About another fifty metres further we encountered something interesting.

What we encountered were hundreds of very small stalactites hanging above us. They were white in colour and overall were between a foot to a foot and a half in length. They were extremely unusual—it was the first time I had ever seen anything like this in all my tunnel trips. All along the passageway were the gun loops of the former Fort Bourbon. There were also small runner tunnels, which ran off on both sides of the main tunnel that we were in.

At one point there was clearly some building work that had gone on in one of these tunnels to our right. As it turned out, this was where the bridge called Pont Adolphe was constructed.

In the old days there was no bridge. The bridge was only constructed after the forts were dismantled and the new Luxembourg was built. It was built between 1900 and 1903. At the time it was the biggest arch stone bridge in the world. It has a span of eighty-five metres and is one hundred and fifty-three metres long. The bridge is forty-two metres above the Pétrusse valley.

Suddenly there was a sharp turn to the right. The way ahead was heavily blocked off. This was because beyond it was a bank. (In Luxembourgish the bank is called Spuerkees. In German it's called Staatssparkasse.) A sealed door was unlocked and the group found itself climbing the steps and surfacing onto the street above. We found ourselves standing in front of the bank in the Place de Metz, on the left-hand side that faces the bridge Adolphe. A woman walking past with her dog did a double take as she saw people surfacing from nowhere. (It reminded me of when the cybermen first came out of the tunnels in the London underground years before in the UK television programme 'Dr Who', back in the 60s.)

The tunnels where we had surfaced were in the old days part of a building called the Lunette IV fortification that stood next to Fort Bourbon. The group then crossed over the road and headed down some stairs that led from the street level of the Boulevard de la Pétrusse, down onto a path that ran along the side of the valley about three quarters of the way up.

The group stopped outside a newly renovated fort front that faces a wide-open stretch of sloping grass. The name of this fort was Fort Elizabeth. It was named after Arch Duchess Marie Elizabeth who was the general governor of the Netherlands and of the Duchy of Luxembourg in the eighteenth century.

The fort is very Austrian in its style. It has a long gallery in which are Austrian-style gun loops. You can see them on any day should you be passing and look in. The visible parts of the fort have only recently been renovated. The details of Fort Elizabeth were only found when the plans of the tunnels had surfaced in Merseburg, Germany, after the Berlin wall had come down.

The tour continued, heading for Fort Wallis. "You'll be able to make everyone a cup of tea!" I was jokingly informed as the tour party headed perilously close to my flat. (At the time, I only had a little milk in the fridge!)

Now, I have walked past the entrance to this fort on God knows how many times. I have done so as I have walked down the Montée de la Pétrusse. This is where Fort Wallis's entrance is. The actual street runs at forty-five degrees to the right of the Viaduct. The road commences at the junction where the Avenue de la Gare ends and the Viaduct begins. To the right is the Boulevard d'Avranches. To the left is the Boulevard de la Pétrusse. I mention this corner in particular as in days gone by the road layout was very different. If you look carefully, the clues stare you in the face. The Rue de Prague once linked directly with the Montée de la Pétrusse.

The Avenue de la Gare road at this end by the viaduct did a strange wobble to the left if you were looking from the Gare end. This is because the road went around the walls of the former Fort Wallis and the edge of another walled defence called *Avancée Thionville*. In-between these two fortifications was another tiny building called Lunette 1. The road curved around these fortifications. When the forts were dismantled and the new Luxembourg emerged, the Avenue de la Gare was straightened into the road you see today. The other road layouts were also amended and many new roads created.

Today, if you are driving a car, then you don't drive into the Montée de la Pétrusse in a hurry. If you do, you'll know about it—or your passenger will. If the car is driven too fast, it's likely to take off. This is because the angle is very steep down this particular street. Anyway, about fifty metres down the street on the right-hand side and set back a little is yet another green door. The tour guide unlocked it and we found ourselves entering the tunnels of the former Fort Wallis.

Fort Wallis is named after Franz Paul von Wallis who was a Commander of the Fortress of Luxembourg. There were no lights here, as the public doesn't normally have access to this fort. We continued our journey heading downwards. There were some tunnels that had been cut off, presumably when the fort was dismantled. The road of the Boulevard d'Avranches passes right overhead. Most people would be oblivious to the fact that a huge fort once existed here and that a huge tunnel system still exists right beneath their feet.

There were many steep steps to go down. In fact, as they continued down in the flicker of the torchlight, they were a bit tricky to negotiate. There was no handrail so you had to watch your step. It was also cold. The ceiling in the early part of the downward descent is high and it is quite remarkable to see the way the rocks stare back at you in the light of your torch as you head downwards. Somewhere along the line, we must have passed under the houses that are on the Montée de la Pétrusse. The tunnel was long and went on and on. Suddenly there was daylight ahead. As it turned out, we were by another green door. However, it was what was before this door that proved to be another hair-raising experience.

There, staring us in the face, were cocoons of giant spiders. There were spread out on the roof of the tunnel in the last few metres of the tunnel. They were all clearly in hibernation, as they hung there wrapped up in their cocoon-shaped balls, which must have been about an inch in diameter, each one in its own area. I wouldn't like to be there when they 'hatched'. Everyone moved swiftly on and headed out into the daylight.

Where the group surfaced was also a surprise—in someone's garden next to the viaduct. This was well down the Pétrusse valley near its bottom. The family of the garden we were now in were themselves somewhat bemused by our sudden appearance. Still, that's the joy of having a tunnel entrance in your garden where very occasionally tours will surface. At least they can say to their friends that they have a secret tunnel in their back garden. A public footway runs down the side of this garden. Our tour group took this and headed down onto the road below. It crossed over a small bridge that took us over the Pétrusse River once again. We walked about a hundred metres along the Rue St Quirin, then re-crossed the river and headed towards a small church built into the rock face.

This church is actually called the Chapelle Saint-Quirin. It's a tiny, donkey's year old church that these days is only occasionally used for services. However, it suffers from the damp badly and the inside is sparse. There are basic long wooden seats to sit on. The church dates back to 1355. It was named after Saint-Quirin who was consecrated in the eleventh century. The steeple wasn't added until the nineteen century. There's also an altar area, part of which was very occasionally used as an old jail. Some prisoners were kept here in days gone by. The entrance door of the church is made of steel bars. However, it's locked to keep the tramps out, though one is allowed in to nosey around. The church has clearly seen better days. Still, it makes a great photo when looking at the place from a distance.

The group then headed towards the Grund where, in the Rue St Ulric, the tour was wound up and most people went their separate ways. Our English friend who had left his wife in the hotel hastily retreated together with one of my friends. As it turned out, she was furious with him for being away for so long. Well, she did have the choice and it was her loss.

We continued walking along the street. The tour guide had invited anyone that wanted to, to join him for a drink in Bonaparte's. This is a very plush bar in the Grund. On the way, he drew our attention to the flood level markings in the Rue St Ulric. These are about a hundred metres down on the left as you enter the street from the Rue de Prague. There are two markings on a house, which show the two highest levels reached by the floodwaters. The lower marker was reached on the 4th March 1806. It reached some fifteen feet above the current road level.

The second was reached on the 9th February 1756. This was about twenty foot from the current road level.

A few of us dedicated tunnel folks arrived at the pub where Simon and I were greeted by one of the Ukrainian girls we knew from before. The tour guide wanted to show us upstairs to a room that we might like to see—a special room built into the rock face, and where you can have your own private party; people do have private parties here, but you'll need a bob or two, for the room is very posh. Another very interesting feature in the room is a huge map that stretches out across most of the wall. It's a map of Europe in 1807. I found it fascinating to study. It shows Luxembourg as part of France. France's borders at the time stretched all along the Rhine River. These borders were recognised at the Treaty of Lunéville in 1801. Belgium didn't exist and Holland was smaller. The rest of Europe looks on this map a lot different to how it is now, or how it was in-between. If you can, check this room out. As I say, its somewhat special.

Simon and I had our drink of orange juice and lemonade sitting in the patio area of Bonaparte's. Here one could unwind in the late afternoon sun and relax after the long tour of the afternoon. We thanked our guide and already I was looking forward to the next trip, which, as it turned out, was in just over two weeks. A taxi was called and the two of us headed off to Tainos, our favourite Latin and Caribbean café and restaurant that's in Pfaffenthal. Here a few Mexican beers were downed followed by a delicious Brazilian national dish called Sancochio, which I can only describe as a bit like a chilli and a stew together.

The tour had been a success and to round off the night it was a taxi back to The White Rose. Where else!

31

Fort fever

One year after I had first visited Fort Thüngen, I decided to make a return visit. This time the tour was meant to be going to a few new places I had not been to before. It would also be taking everyone to some old places. As it turned out it was just Simon and myself on this trip, as for one reason or another I hadn't organised it properly. We met at The White Rose and headed up on the number 18 bus, paying our one euro twenty cents fare. Out destination was once again Kirchberg.

We arrived back at Fort Thüngen and were amazed to see the rear of it, which used to be a lovely open grass area, now resembled a huge pile of bulldozed stones. We discovered these had been dug out in the last year from the area around Fort Ober-Grünewald.

Simon pointed out that Fort Thüngen was also known as Dräi Eechelen in Luxembourgish, Trois Glands in French, or Drei Eicheln in German. In English, the fort is known as The Three Acorns.

Why is it called The Three Acorns, you ask? Well, this is because of the three acorns that are on the roof of the fort on each of the rear towers. When the fort was dismantled the acorns remained. Each has now been renovated.

The name originated because oak trees are regarded as a symbol of strength—the 'heart of oak' and all that. Oak trees actually grow nearby and are to be found to this day in front of Fort Ober-Grünewald and are alongside where the steps go down to the valley below. I'm told that not many oak trees grow in Luxembourg, whereas other varieties of tree grow in abundance, such as fir trees and the trees that look to me like Silver Birch.

I had bought a book in English on a previous tour, called *Luxembourg as a Federal Fortress 1815-1866*. André Bruns, the President of the Friends of Luxembourg Fortress Association, wrote it a while ago. I found it fascinating. On the cover was a photo of Fort Thüngen taken about ten years ago. It showed, apart from the three towers, the rest of the fort lying dismantled. It was fascinating to see the fort like this and it's amazing to see what they've done to it since. It has more or less been practically rebuilt apart from the towers that have been renovated.

Fort Thüngen had progressed a lot in the year since I was last there. Inside the rebuilding continues, with many new features. You can see how they've preserved the old and carefully built on top of it, so that you get the feel that you're in the original fort. This time, compared to when I had been there a year ago, there's a tiled floor laid on a raised level. The whole structure has been added to. It now begins to look like a new fort even though it will eventually become a museum.

On the ground floor there are new trendy lights in the ceilings ready for the displays that will go in the area. Fireplaces have been restored, except that now there's no chimneys, so the fireplaces are really only ornamental features. How do I know this? Well, I peeked upwards to check. This is a pity, as you can't beat the old open fire. Still, these days you have air con to keep the place warm. There were still a few planks to walk on but nothing like what was here a year ago. The rooms were taking shape and the wiring was now in. Up on the first floor in the tip of the arrow, if looking from above, they had also created a triangular seating area with as yet no seats. They will probably host talks on the fort from here in the future. There's still a long way to go but the end result will put Fort Thüngen on the tourist map.

For the moment, I was ahead of any tourists and can look back in the years to come and say, "I remember when this ancient fort was still a building site."

The actual trip was much the same as the previous year but it filled in a few gaps that I had forgotten about and it showed us some new excavations. I did notice there had been a lot of rubble and mud that had been excavated from Fort Ober-Grünewald. The stonework was now looking a lot more complete. Nevertheless, there's still a lot to be done. The breezeblocks continue to be used behind the main stonework. As it turned out what we saw used to be the Réduit Ober-Grünewald.

Nearby, on the way to the Granary, there has been some form of excavation. This has revealed from the mud and forest that has been removed yet another old building. This is the remains of a large powder store. It does make you wonder what else is in this whole area, which right now is covered over with forest.

A further hike in the woods brought us out at the Réduit Niedergrünewald that overlooks the valley below. I had seen it a year ago when it was being renovated. Now a year later it was fully restored. It looked magnificent. A cannon used to be stored inside the building. When the city was under attack the cannon was hauled up and used to help repel the enemy.

The tour continued and the group walked through the forest towards our next fort. It was at this point that the tour developed a bit of a bite to it. On entering the tunnel at Fort Nieder-Grünewald, we ventured down the stairs and into the tunnel. This time the group was met with thousands of mosquitoes that were resting on the ceiling! After about ten metres the ceiling was clear. Nevertheless, even though I was wearing jeans, I still got a nasty bite on my leg from one of the buggers. The rest of the tour for us turned out to be the same as the previous year.

After the tour had finished Simon and I decided to have a beer at the nearby café situated next to Fort Thüngen. Most of the café area is in the woods, making it an ideal retreat for a drink or meal. It can get packed at the weekends when the weather is fine. However, I guess that it's a more seasonal café. The place has that log cabin feel to it. You have to sneak through the edge of the kitchen to the loo. The indoor seating is very cosy. As it turned out most of the tour turned up and it was only then that we realised the tunnel trip was catering to a large party of French people. The sun was shining and I sampled the delights of an orange juice and lemonade. On our way into the café we had noticed a delicious looking custard and apple pie, Luxembourg style. Neither of us could resist it, so when the waiter came over, the pie was ordered. As it turned out it was delicious, especially after a three-hour tunnel trip to help recharge the batteries. The custard here is called Crème Anglaise and is normally cold.

On the edge of the patio area was one hell of a large frying pan, which was slowly being prepared for the night ahead. I sat there and watched. The size of the pan must have been a metre across! Small, eh! As we left to move on they had placed an incalculable amount of sliced potatoes in it. There were many small barbeques nearby. I can only imagine what followed.

Simon and I wandered down towards Fort Ober-Grünewald. We were aiming for the stairs down to the valley below. However, we stopped en route to have a look up one of the stairways, which has been renovated. This particular one went up to an area known as the *Ravelin*. This is a newly restored area, and once both of us had climbed the stairs, we surfaced onto a triangular area of the old fort where there is a modern, largish square glass board that had something written on it in four languages. What it had to say was most interesting.

The board tells the story of some Luxembourg farmers who emigrated to Transylvania about a thousand years ago. This is the area now covered by Romania. Anyway, the farming community grew and Luxembourgish still thrives in the region today.

"There you are, I told you Dracula's Ancestors came from Luxembourg," said Simon. He added, "No one believed me, now here's the written evidence." It's an interesting thought if nothing more! However, the language a thousand years ago was very different to what it is today. I would guess that it would be more of an original tongue, what with the infiltration of foreign words in today's language.

We headed through the tunnel in the fort wall, crossed the bridge, and down the steps to the valley below. Once again the two of us were aiming for our Caribbean and Latin bar Tainos which is in Pfaffenthal. To our delight, it was open. However, before either of us went in we walked up the street to look at the restoration that was being done on an old property on the left-hand side. It's a very old building, dating back over two hundred years, and is only now being restored. Next to it, I admired one of the Vauban Towers and walked through its arches. The whole area in the last few years is and has being going through a major renovation project. The results are impressive.

Simon and I wandered back to Tainos where several beers were downed as the Latin music played. We had decided to eat here and a tasty chilli con carne was enjoyed in the hacienda at the rear of the restaurant. Afterwards the two of us headed up the steep hill towards the old city, gasping for breath, but admiring the views en route of the countryside beyond. I was hunting for a glimpse of the secret statue of Christ. No, it wasn't to be seen due to the trees enclosing it.

Two weary souls headed though the archway of a very old entrance gate called the Three Towers that had been one of the original entrances in days gone by. Continuing our steep climb upwards on the cobbled street towards the old town, we walked past The Tube bar and upwards to the new Urban pub, continuing across the Place d'Armes to the bus station, where we hopped on a bus that took us to the Place de Paris.

The moment had arrived. It was time for a beer in The White Rose…

Several months later, in the autumn of 2003, Fort fever was happening again. In The White Rose various friends talked about the tunnel trips. One of them asked, "Was there going to be another one?"

Well, yes, actually, there was. I had found out there was another trip and we eager beavers were there ready for the action.

It was on a Sunday afternoon. Naturally, we all met up at The White Rose before taking a bus into the old town. This time there were four of us, three English guys and a Spanish girl. We were heading for the fountain, which is situated in the municipal park at the end of Avenue Amelie. We were warmly dressed and had our torches with us, even though it was hot autumn sunny afternoon.

Every time I went there before, I always found a fantastic display of flowers next to the fountain, its waters spurting out into the pool below. As it was autumn the flowers had all disappeared. The beds were being prepared for the next displays. We were greeted by our guide. The tour group today consisted mostly of Luxembourgers, but this time included some Germans, French and English. We set off.

Today's trip was to explore three of the Forts that were located to the west of the city.

"But, there aren't any?" I hear you cry.

"But there are!" I tell you.

There, right underneath where you walk the dog, right there where you lie on the grass, there where you go for a stroll. Yes, in the park that runs all around the west and north of the old town you will find quite literally under your feet the tunnels and remains of six forts! The forts we would be visiting would be Fort Berlaimont, Fort Vauban and Fort Lambert.

When these forts were dismantled, along with the other three located in this area, namely, Fort Marie, Fort Royal and Fort Louvigny, they were dismantled and then covered over. A municipal park was built over them. The French landscape architect Edouard André designed the park. He was a Parisian.

Several rich Luxembourg families built two prestigious houses on the site of the former forts within the park area. The two famous houses are the Villa Vauban and the Villa Louvigny. The Villa Vauban these days is an art gallery, which I knew already. The other Villa Louvigny we would discover more about later that afternoon.

The group headed through the park crossing the Avenue de la Porte-Neuve and walked down a path that took us past the Pescatore Foundation, which is an old people's home. As one of my friends called Eddie commented, "I wouldn't mind spending my retirement here, as it looks a really nice place." Indeed, it did look a very grand building—good enough to retire in, in a dignified way. The group walked further up the path. It found itself looking over the Alzette valley looking down on Pfaffenthal. The red bridge was to our left. The forest was opposite. The valley stretched away to our right. The view was spectacular in the autumn sunshine. The leaves were turning red and brown, making the view like a water-coloured painting.

"Didn't I hear someone call this country Leafy Luxembourg?" Eddie, one of the lads, said.

The name seemed quite apt as the paths around us were in the early stages of being covered with the fallen leaves. Nearby chestnut trees had conkers littered around on the grass.

In the corner of the park on the far right-hand side, away from the hustle and bustle of modern life, we came across the entrance of the tunnel which would take us down into out first fort—Fort Berlaimont.

This particular fort was begun in 1616 under the Spanish Governor *Count Florent de Berlaimont et de Lallaing* (1604-1626). The name was given to all the other works in front of the bastion.

The tour guide led the way, opening the green door. Everyone followed and walked oddly up some stairs and along a long tunnel. The further the group walked the more graffiti it discovered scrawled on the walls. Some of it was very old indeed, including some possible scrawl from World War Two. After maybe one hundred metres we found ourselves in the basement of the former *réduit* of the fort.

This area was quite large. It was well preserved and you could clearly imagine people staying here during the Second World War. There are arches and columns of sorts dotted around the room. In the centre is a very tall ceiling. Hanging from it was some form of very old air vent or heater. It was hard to tell. The room was lit with electricity so it did have some modern conveniences.

After exploring this room and paying our tour guide for the tour everyone followed him back down the tunnel. Torches were needed now. A little further up this tunnel he stopped by a tunnel that went to the right.

"You can go up and explore the area beyond on your own, but you have to come back to this to point," he said to everyone in Luxembourgish, French and German. This we all later did. In the meantime, we entered further into the tunnel system of Fort Berlaimont. The group split up and started their own explorations of the tunnels. The area spread out a fair way under the park area. I actually got detached from another small group I was with as I felt they were getting too deep down one particular tunnel system. I turned around and headed back. It does feel weird as you rush up the tunnel with just the light from your torch shining ahead of you and being the only one there. Most of the tour group by now had returned to the surface. In the excitement of exploring, one easily forgets that time is ticking away and everyone else might be waiting on the surface. One could easily spend hours exploring all these tunnels. But getting locked in was not a pleasant thought. Eventually everyone came out of the tunnel and back into the park. The group was ready to move on.

The tour group walked back, crossing the road and continued their walk through the park. We walked past the fountain and, staying in the park, we came out a little further along on the corner of the Boulevard Prince Henri and the Avenue Emile Reuter. Here the pavement lasts for about ten metres before it turns into a set of steps that took one down to another green door, which the tour guide unlocked and opened. This was the entrance to our second fort, which was Fort Vauban.

This fort was named after Marshall Sébastien Le Prestre de Vauban who was responsible for much of Luxembourg's fortifications. Once we had entered the tunnel we straightaway turned left, and headed down. In the dark our torches casting a beam in front of us, we reached a crossroads of tunnels. Splitting into smaller groups gave everyone the chance to explore by themselves. Some of us went down some steps and continued along a long tunnel. We were now right under the park. Turning around we retraced our steps and, going back up the steps, we could either go left or right. Whichever way we took would take us in a circular tour around the lower part of the former fort.

At one point I discovered a small cave that looked as if it might have been used as a solitary confinement cell years ago. It could have been used as anything, even a storage area, but it stirred our imagination.

Another interesting sight in one of the tunnels was some very unusual old fashioned stairs. These stairs looked as if they were built for soldiers and were reinforced more than the other stairs we had seen. The top of them was sealed off by the modern world.

It was a maze of passages and in the torchlight we discovered many tunnels and sub passages. We all had a good session looking around. One could easily get lost or get detached from the now split up group. This time some of the children were late back. After checking everyone was back, the group moved on.

We crossed at the junction and walked further round the park. We passed another tunnel entrance in the Boulevard Prince Henri that leads to the tunnels of Fort Louvigny. This fort was named after *Charles Chrétien de Landas de Louvigny* in 1673 who was a General and an engineer. From here we walked across the park to where the group entered the grounds of the Villa Louvigny. I was expecting to see a villa much like the Villa Vauban, so was surprised to see a building like a very grand office block that looked as if it had been built in the 1930's. It turned out this grand old building was built in 1933 and is the former home of RTL, the radio and television station. It was from this building that the English service of Radio Luxembourg used to broadcast. In 1998, RTL moved up to a new modern building in Kirchberg. These days the Villa Louvigny houses the ministry of Health—which isn't quite so glamorous, is it?

Our tour group was actually there to see the base of a rather tall tower that looked like an old water tower, but is in fact a large office block. The base formed part of Fort Louvigny and was of Spanish origin. The rest was destroyed as part of the dismantling process. But it was strong enough to build the tower on it. The base's original features remain intact and it was this that we were looking at.

We retraced our steps and found ourselves back in the park. We were heading for our final fort, Fort Lambert.

All these western forts were much of the same design, a wide V-shape formed the fortified walls, behind which lay the fort. The fort building housed the soldiers. The shape of the fort building or *réduit* was pentagonal, i.e. the walls have five sides. Around it was also a courtyard, which was also pentagonal. Surrounding that was the envelope, which had high walls. Below these were what is now part of the tunnel network.

If you put the seven forts (of which only six can be visited—Fort Peter being the seventh) together, you got a west and north facing impregnable wall. All of them were transformed during the Austrian period.

We retraced our steps and found ourselves back on the edge of the park where we crossed the road heading southwards past an old-fashioned hut and back into the park. We ended up almost on the pavement of Boulevard Henri. We were actually behind a small wall. Here was located a covered mesh entrance, which, once undone, led the tour down to yet another green door and the tunnels of Fort Lambert.

Fort Lambert was named after the French Governor, Duke of Lambert (1684-1688). Fort Lambert had only recently been excavated. In fact, it wasn't until they decided to excavate and build what is now the Monterey underground car park that they came across the *réduit* of Fort Lambert. Until then only insiders knew it was there.

You can actually drive through part of Fort Lambert if you choose to park in the new underground car park that has recently been built next to it. As we discovered later, the tunnels underneath have been carefully preserved.

We were extremely lucky to be able to go into these tunnels, as very few people have been down here. We went around the various narrow passageways, one of which led upwards. It split into two. One led into a tiny tunnel, which led to a sealed window. Here you could catch a glimpse of the car park from a most unusual angle. The other passageway led to some steps where there was a sealed gate beyond which was also the car park.

Later we wandered around the passageways that took us all around the fort. It was quite eerie looking up into the modern world from the inside of this fort, especially as the views we had were in darkness for all this time. The group went outside into the courtyard area of the former fort. Here you could clearly see where the modern world meets the past. We were standing under part of the Avenue Monterey. Next we explored the remains of the inside of the *réduit*.

There is still more work to be undertaken to clean up and restore Fort Lambert. After all, for the last one hundred and fifty odd years it had been completely covered in mud and had trees, flowers and grass growing on top of it. It will be interesting to see in the future if any more forts are uncovered and restored. It's an expensive business uncovering the past and, unfortunately, so much has been lost. No one would have realised back then how valuable those forts would turn out to be today. The excavated fort, or what's left of it, can be seen from above in the Avenue Monterey.

One thing we all learnt on our tunnel trips is that no new fortifications were built during the Napoleonic period.

Overall everyone had found the trips fascinating. The comment I keep hearing was, "When is there another tunnels trip?" Only time will tell…

It was time to head off, our party by now needing refreshment. The White Rose was beckoning and the chief barfly would be in the chair. The other barflies would be hovering nearby, waiting for those immortal words, "What are you having?"

32

At the Movies

Now most people like to go to the movies. Here in Luxembourg City there's quite a choice of films to go and see. The main cinema is up at Kirchberg where there's one of those out-of-town cinemas. It's called the Utopolis and is a ten-screen cinema complex that shows all the main new movies.

Up at Limpertsberg is the Utopia. This is a five-screen complex, which has two big screens and three others in various odd shapes and sizes. This cinema also shows new movies, but these tend to be more specialised or not the top ten films. They also show more worldwide films here. Utopia also has seasons of films, for example from Italy and Spain that are interesting to see.

There is also the Cinematheque Municipale (formerly the Vox) in the Rue Beaumont. It shows every night 'for one night only' some real classics.

Regretfully in the early part of 2004 the two-screen Ciné Cité that was just off the Place d'Armes closed. The site is going to become a modern municipal library, made of glass and concrete! In this instance, the scheme I think is a good idea.

Alas, all the other old cinemas in the centre of the city have long since shut, killing bar trade in the process. Years ago Luxembourg City, like other cities, used to have more than its fair share of in-town cinemas. There was the Marivaux in the rue Dicks. This is now a church, but it still retains its wonderful art deco. Nearby this was the Yank, which stood on the corner of the Memorial gardens. I'm told it was a fleapit. It was knocked down and is now a bank. The Eldorado was popular and in the same building was the Europe. Both stood next to the station in the Place de la Gare near to where the number 18 bus parks. The site is now an office block. Further up in the Avenue de la Gare on the right was the Capitol. These days it's a Chinese restaurant on the first floor and a bakers on the ground level. Round the corner on the right was the Victory, which still stands. It still looks magnificent, but empty, in the rue de Bonnevoie. I even discovered there used to be a cinema in the rue de l'eau called the Ciné de la Cour. All these cinemas have seen better days. Now people expect comfort, spacious seats, and modern trendy places to enjoy a movie. Time has moved on.

In case you're wondering, the old boarded up building with its front in yellow and white next to the HSBC Republic building on the Avenue Marie Therese was not a cinema. It was originally a dance palace and was called Pôle Nord (North Pole). In later years, it became a disco. During their time, both were extremely popular along with the busy restaurant upstairs. Alas, it has been closed for many years. Why someone can't restore it both inside and out to its original form and reopen it I don't know.

By the way, the intersection that's called the Place de Bruxelles is still referred to by many Luxembourgers as 'Beim Pole Nord', which is a much better name. It was, and still is, a focal or meeting point in the *heart* of the city. Let the owners of this building take note!

Quite a lot of people come from across the border to watch films here in Luxembourg. Severine, a French girl I know who lived in France, once commented, "I like to watch a film in Luxembourg as you can watch a real American movie in English." This is very true as in France they are dubbed into French and likewise in Germany into German. Luxembourg is special in the sense that you can watch the original or in the dubbed language version. Some are also subtitled into French and Dutch. In Continental Europe, after Luxembourg, it's a long way to go to watch a movie in English.

Luxembourg also makes its own films and hosts a season of these every so often. The Minister of Communications is François Biltgen. He seems to be a well-known face who pops up every so often promoting the Luxembourg film industry, which in recent years has really taken off in a big way. It might be a small country but Luxembourg is fast becoming a place where movies are made. Tax incentives help attract film companies. The scenery is varied and it's good for the economy as it helps stimulate jobs.

I first heard about locally made films after I had been here a while. One night I was having a pint in The White Rose when I heard some people talking about 'The George and Dragon.' I thought they were talking about the English pub of this name here in Luxembourg City but they were actually talking about a film being made locally.

One Tuesday night—some considerable time later—I was sitting in the Foyer bar with some friends when my Danish friend Jasper came up to me and said, "Why don't you become an extra in a film?"

"Why not indeed," I replied.

After all, I had nothing to lose and plenty of time in-between my studies. The thing was, I didn't know anything about it. Well, there was only one solution and that was to find out!

He then showed me some information that he had found on the internet whilst himself looking for a job. The advert had been on the www.jobsearch.lu site and was sitting there among all the other jobs. It said 'Figurants' wanted for the film 'Bye Bye Blackbird.' With a name like that, I thought it was something to do with a Blackbird. I rang the number and spoke in French to a charming Russian lady who asked me, "Could you come down to our studios in Dudelange and bring your picture with you." So I did. It was actually my first visit to this town and I decided to go there on the train. Before I went one of my friends advised me, "Watch out! There are four stations in Dudelange."

I changed at Bettembourg and after taking a shuttle diesel train found that my friend was right. I found out later that I actually needed to get out at the third station. However, it was my first time so I went to the last one. This actually is the end of the line. Once there I asked the stationmaster for directions. He was most helpful and to cut a long story short I found the place.

Samsa films are in Rue de la Liberation in part of the old steel works. The site is owned by Arcelor, the steel company, which, as I discovered later, rents parts of it out. Apparently, some of the site is still active. This at the time wasn't visible to me. What was, though, was a sign on the gate saying, 'Bye Bye Blackbird'.

I went in and found the casting office. Inside it I met the lady I had spoken to on the phone. I found her most helpful and polite. She said to me in French, "Please fill in a form and then attach your photo to it." I had brought with me one of those small passport size pictures. "Great," I thought. Then I saw the pile of forms on the corner of her desk. On each form were large pictures of people in all sorts of poses. My heart sank. I was obviously doing something wrong, so when I got home I selected a variety of photos and sent them off to the Samsa agent. It dawned on me that they don't want you dressed up looking smart. It helps, but they want to see what you look like in different clothes, at different angles, what your face looks like and how much hair you have, or in my case, not.

Well, time went by and I heard nothing. In the meantime, I had been told of another film company in Luxembourg called The Carousel Picture Company. This name conjured up one of those old black and white movie companies they used to have back in the 1920's. I went to check them out. I found out where they were and one day took the number 11 bus to Beggen. The bus driver wasn't exactly helpful when I asked him, even in French, to let me know where I had to get off.

This lack of help I have actually encountered on a number of occasions now. The bus drivers have this blank look on their faces. Surely, they should know some landmarks on the route they drive? Maybe not. I can dream!

After walking a kilometre or so back from where I had got off I eventually found the place. Again, it was in what looked like another old industrial factory in rue de la cimenterie. I found out later the site is in Dommeldange and is also owned by Arcelor. Again, it is a working site with parts of it rented out to various companies. At that moment it looked deserted to me. To add to the fun the security guard advised me that, "They are closed as it is the holidays."

About a week or so later I did somehow get the number of the Carousel agent, so I called her. As it turned out, I discovered she's a Dutch lady who speaks good English who again I found most helpful. The procedure I found to be much the same as before. I asked her, "What should I do?" She replied, "Could you send me some photos and details? Please."

They all like to know your shoe size, waist, weight and shirt size, so that the costume department can plan accordingly.

Some time later I got a call from this new agent at Carousel who at the time was helping out with a movie at Samsa. She asked me in English with a Dutch accent, "Are you free for three days to be in a Dutch speaking movie called 'The Preacher'?" Naturally, I jumped at the chance. "You're going to be a prison guard," she said, adding, "The movie is a Dutch movie set in the seventies and eighties. It is loosely based on the life of a former Dutch mafia boss." In the winter of 2003, the Dutch Royal family featured in the news when one of the Princes announced he was getting married to an old girlfriend of the former gangster. This caused a constitutional problem in the Netherlands whereby the Prince was forced to abdicate his position for the Dutch throne.

Well, the day arrived for the start of filming. I managed to get a lift down with another extra, Shamus, from Ireland. The weather that day was bitterly cold with full cloud cover. It was a grim autumn's day. We were to report to somewhere in a place called Rodange. I discovered when I looked on a map that this was in the west of Luxembourg, right on the border.

The set was actually in a disused warehouse or factory. It may have said administration building on the gate. Anyway, inside was a hive of activity. People were rushing round everywhere. They had built the inside of a prison and would be filming the scenes over the next few days. We discovered that this movie was on location for four weeks, so it was moving around to different sites every so often. The two of us were ushered straight to costume where we were fitted out in some Dutch prison guard uniforms.

"This is fun," I thought.

Afterwards we went to the makeup wagon and had various things done to our faces. I had to laugh as for me it put a completely new meaning into the ladies phrase, 'powdering your nose'! Grabbing a snack and a coffee, we were ready to start.

There was a Luxembourg girl with a very English accent coordinating everyone into place. She had a Jack Russell dog that followed her around but was very well behaved.

The Preacher is a Co-production between Samsa Film and Theorema Films. It is aimed at the Dutch speaking market and is directed by Dutchman Gerrard Verhage. The main stars are Peter Paul Muller and Daphne Janzen. The crew is multinational. It was all very quad lingual.

On the set I learnt all sorts of phrases, like "Turnover" and, "Quiet please, Rehearsal." Then comes, "Roll Sound," followed by, "Background." This is where the extras start acting. There's also, "First and Second positions." Then, when the camera is rolling, is the sight of the clapperboard, which shows the date, time, act number, scene and take on it, before the person holding it says, "Take One, Take Two," etc…before those immortal words, "Action!"

At the end of the take someone yells, "And Cut," followed by "Check the gate," which is the viewfinder. If the director is happy then they go onto the next camera angle or next scene. Finally, at the end of the day is "The Wrap."

I learnt a lot on the set of my first movie and my stint as a prison guard will probably be seconds in the movie. Overall, it felt like being in a Dutch version of the English TV programme 'Porridge' that was made in the late seventies, but without the comedy.

My second movie was 'Bye Bye Blackbird.' I got a call from a French guy who was the assistant to my agent who sorted out some dates with me. Great! I was told that "Bye Bye Blackbird is a movie about the story of a circus in the period 1900 to 1910, based in London, Paris and Venice." In fact, as I discovered later, it is also based in the period just before and at the start of The Great War. The main stars in it include Derek Jacobi, Michael Lonsdale, James Thierree and Izabella Miko. It's directed by the Frenchman Robinson-Savary.

I had to go down on the train to deepest Dudelange for a costume fitting a couple of days before the filming using extras started. I discovered that I was to be a middleclass gentleman in what I would describe as the Edwardian period. I must say that I found the whole experience fascinating as I learnt so much about the period, simply by the clothes we were fitted out in. Dressed as a middleclass gentleman, I actually felt my 'class'. Some people were being kitted out as upper-class or aristocrats, others as working class. I felt like I was on that famous English TV programme made in the early seventies called 'Upstairs Downstairs', which was set in the Edwardian period. Looking the part, I wore a bowler hat, a brown jacket and trousers, held up with braces, the cloth and cut being what typical middleclass people would have worn. I had an Edwardian tie and the shirt had a stiff collar, which was separate and was fastened at the front and clipped on at the back. It was the style in those days. I also had an overcoat on top of that and I wore light brown gloves, again typical of the period.

I was assisted and dressed by the costume ladies. I can now understand why people had servants in those days, some of whom were 'dressers'. You needed someone to help you get dressed! The clothes we all dress in today simply slip on and are light. The Edwardian clothes I had on were heavy to wear and were fiddly and difficult to dress.

I was sent over to the makeup department that, seeing the beard I was growing for another movie, promptly told me to "Shave it off."

"But I'm growing it for another movie," I protested!

"Yes, well, this is *our* movie, so please shave it off."

It was absolutely no problem and as I discovered made me look right for the part. The thing I found funny was that most of the older men had beards, goatees and moustaches stuck on.

I was now ready to step out onto the Edwardian set. I must say that it felt like stepping back in time. Outside everyone was milling around the yard or in the extras' tent. It was a lovely hot sunny day, even if it was winter. I could now begin to understand a little better the period my grandparents lived in.

One of the everyday interesting things about Edwardian life, I soon discovered, was going to the toilet. A simple task normally. Not so if you want perform anything more than a pee. Wearing all the heavy clothes and braces means you have to literally undress. Afterwards I had to literally redress with the help of whoever was in the washbasin area of the loo. There was no other way. Braces are not my standard ware. They are bloody awkward!

If you're a woman and dressed in Edwardian clothing, then going to the toilet causes even more problems. Well, think about it. The ladies were all wearing long dresses with multiple petticoats and undergarments. They also all wore corsets, which was normal in those days. The corsets made the waist thin and pushed the boobs up. They also wore large hats, generally flat and sometimes with feathers. Well, when you have these carefully clipped onto your hair, going into a toilet cubicle is an experience.

One English lady who had this experience told me, "I couldn't get in the door without twisting my head."

You get the idea.

The lavatory subject remained the main talking point of the first day as it affected everyone. After all, when you have to go you have to go. It doesn't matter what class you are! The corsets did cause a few of the ladies trouble. One girl practically passed out on the set several times during the first day of filming. When I saw her the following week she told me she threw up afterwards. I've heard of a few stories of women that used to faint because of their corsets. Another lady I met complained that her corset made her nipples hurt. Apparently, the corset pushed her boobs up and, stopping where her nipples were, caused her moments of friction! It did give us all a clearer idea of what women had to go through all those years ago.

It wasn't just the ladies who had problems. One guy told me he was originally given braces a size too small. He nearly became a member of the Bee Gees and it put a whole new meaning into the phase 'crushed nuts'. This minor problem was quickly solved.

I thought all the ladies looked beautiful in their costumes. Their hairstyles were elegant, the hats looked stylish and their pixie boots were magic.

The first few days of filming were on the London set after which the circus 'moved' to Paris. For this I gained a moustache to give me that Parisian look! On this set certain ladies wore some very aristocratic costumes that looked delightful.

All the extras joined in as part of the crowd in the circus tent, which was inside the old abandoned steelworks. The French co-ordinator kept us extras organised. We all owe him a lot. On set, the French director moved everyone round. We all did what we were told to do, including sitting in the seat of your class. That was very important and made it feel like the original travelling circus probably once was. The whole thing gave you a better understanding of the past right down to the real liquorice sweets in their brown paper bags, to which I became addicted.

We all did various crowd scenes, including one outside in a street. Meanwhile, inside the circus tent, one exciting scene had us all yelling "Assassin!" in French at one of the stars. Why? Well, you'll have to watch the movie to find out.

There was even a local Luxembourg band in the bandstand. Interestingly, the piano player in real life is blind. I thought it was brilliant he was given the opportunity.

At the end of the day's shoot or 'Wrap' everyone could get changed and go home. As there are many extra's those first in were first out. I will never forget one night when it was a little foggy; a long queue had formed outside the office where you get your pay. It snaked its way round towards the costume building. It reminded me of the hundreds of steel workers who would have probably done the same all those years ago from the same place.

My next film was with the Carousel Picture Company. My agent there rang me up and asked me, "Would you like to be an extra in a film called Retrograde?" Of course, I didn't say no.

I had to report to the film set which this time was in Esch-sur-Alzette at one of the old steel works down there. This particular one was closed back in the eighties and has remained part of the landscape ever since. Its vastness hovers over the whole town. It's an industrial relic from the past.

Soon the whole site is going to be redeveloped. Part of it is going to be the new University of Luxembourg. This will certainly rejuvenate Esch-sur-Alzette after the big loss of part of the steel industry.

On the winter's day I arrived on the set the sun was shining and there wasn't a cloud in the sky. As I walked through the open gated entrance, the great industrial relic stared across at me. I ventured across the vast openness of disused land now overgrown, the disused rail lines that used to run right into the steel works still there in part.

Inside the steel works I found it fascinating, later, to nosey around. It is its own tourist attraction, if you're into old industrial relics.

Again, I was only an extra in the movie. Blink and you'll probably miss me. The big star in 'Retrograde' is Dolph Lundgren who was in 'Rocky IV'. Other stars include Gary Daniels, Joe Montana and Silvia de Santis. The movie is directed by Christopher Kulikowski from Los Angeles.

In the first day's shoot I was a crewman on the deck of a boat in Antarctica. One of my parts was scraping the ice off the deck of the ship. I also walked through a doorway a couple of times. It'll probably all be edited out. But hey! It was fun.

I was then asked to do two nights of filming on this movie. Well, this was my first time working at night and I can tell you that takes a bit of getting used to. To be honest, it gave me side effects afterwards, so God knows how everyone else felt. Still, I wouldn't have missed it for the world and it was great experience.

As I walked up to the costume van the Japanese coordinator said, "Did you know you're going to get wet tonight?"

"No," I replied.

I didn't mind. It sounded interesting. The extras were told that "The engine room of the boat is going to be flooded and you're going to get rather wet."

Soaked, to be precise!

That night the extras had several scenes in the engine room of the boat. Sometime during the night we were all kitted out in wet suits under our engine room clothes. Our big flood scene was to be the last one of the night. Before we went on set the Japanese coordinator tipped six cups of extremely cold water inside my wetsuit.

"To get you acclimatised," she said with a smile on her face.

That water was bloody cold even before we started!

On set there were special effects everywhere including smoke, steam and fire all around us. Oh, and I mustn't forget the water. Loads of it! This arrived from above and was itself an experience. After several 'takes' the director was happy. This was followed by one more final take and involved all of us getting absolutely soaked with the water. To say it was cold was an understatement. We acted our parts magnificently, working and hanging on to try to save the boat. It was a great moment which all of us thoroughly enjoyed. Afterwards we were taken directly to an indoor tent that had been specially prepared for us that had warm air blasting out inside it; thereafter we headed back to the trailer to get changed. It had been an experience.

My final night there involved a long seven-hour wait in a dining bus. In it were tables and seats where at meal times all the crew including extras ate. Later we slept a bit until we were called at four in the morning. This time we found ourselves in a warehouse full of scientific equipment. Our bit was just that—a bit. We were in the background, acting, doing our small part as part of the crewmembers in the warehouse.

DeLux Productions are another film company here in Luxembourg. They are based in Contern, which is about nine kilometres from Luxembourg City on an industrial estate in brand new buildings. The place is in the middle of nowhere, so unless you've a car, getting there is frustrating as there's only one bus an hour, which is the 163.

In the winter of 2003 DeLux were filming two movies. One was 'The Merchant of Venice,' the other 'The Golden Man.' They wouldn't take me for the 'Merchant of Venice,' as after I had been in to see them and had given them some photographs the agent said to me, "You don't have enough hair and we don't have enough wigs for everyone."

"Charming!" I thought.

291 ...

Nevertheless, I did get a part as an extra in 'The Golden Man.' This is a story set in the sixteenth century. Part of the story involves a playwright and the school of the night…What I do know is that they were advertising on Radio ARA for women who didn't mind bearing their breasts in the movie. The rest I have yet to discover myself.

I went for a costume fitting for this movie. This again was an experience as I was kitted out in the clothes of the period, this time as some religious character. However, this time I was going to be one of many in a crowd scene. My hat looked ridiculous and I was told to grow a beard. 'The experience ahead should be interesting,' I thought.

I'll give DeLux credit as they had a couple of adverts up for film extras in ADEM, the local government job centre, which I thought was a good idea as it is a bit of work for the unemployed.

Incidentally, many of the costumes come from BBC costumes in the UK who appear to have a massive library of costumes they rent out to movie companies worldwide. Both Samsa and DeLux use them in their productions.

Making a movie takes forever. They film with mostly one camera. This is very much to do with the quality of picture, the right light etc…In fact, the correct lighting is a very important part of the shoot together with the camera angle and length of shot. I'm amazed how long it takes to film each shot. Each scene has to be filmed from different angles and has to be re-shot each time. The camera has to be rebuilt for each shot.

There are many tricks used in the making of movies. There are also many unexpected things that only become apparent at the time of filming. Sometimes there are cock-ups, which are highly amusing, others just mundane. First aid is on hand in case of accidents.

Being an extra involves a lot of waiting around. In fact, you can be waiting a very long time. You await your call, which could be between ten minutes and seven hours! As I discovered later from others, sometimes you aren't called at all so you wonder if it's all worthwhile. The average day is twelve hours.

Most extras are people who want to be in a movie, or they're the unemployed earning a few bob. Why do they want to be in a movie, you may ask? Well, it's fun. The pay, though, is appalling. My mother reminded me, "When I was involved in the theatre and TV I was paid a pittance." So nothings changed!

Some people do do it for the money; others do it for the fun and ego of being in a movie. I've also met a few extras who take a day off work to do a movie. After all, it's a good way to spend a few days of one's holiday time. One of these told me, "I've done twenty-three movies." Another, a baker in real life, said, "This is my tenth." An unemployed French girl I met on a set said, "I need the money." That was very honest of her. Incidentally, many unemployed and employed people from France and Belgium work in the movies here in Luxembourg. There's also many unemployed actors about who do the rounds, even famous ones.

At the end of the day we all have different reasons why we do it. However, once more, I've met a rich mix of people on set here in Luxembourg and I've worked with many different nationalities, including Japanese, French and Chilean friends, which has thankfully forced me to utilize my French.

They do feed you as an extra and the food is varied and good. All sets are different and the caterers prepare to the needs of the number of people on site. On all the sets there is a constant supply of hot and cold drinks together with snacks for those that feel a little peckish, so you never go without.

On the set of 'The Preacher' Dutch chefs freshly prepared the food. It was typically Dutch and the meals were delicious. I ate my first English fry up or 'Greasy Joe' as I call it on location on 'Retrograde.' The chefs were New Zealanders and English and were very good cooks. On the 'Blackbird' set there was also a good variety of food, which everyone tucked into.

All the chefs had a great sense of humour. The English chef on the 'Blackbird' set, on the first day of filming after England defeated the French in the World Cup Rugby tournament in 2003, scrawled in chalk on the menu board, "France 7—Jonny Wilkinson 24!" I thought that was great. Even better when England won the tournament.

On some sets (not all), everyone eats together whether they're a film star, an extra, the backstage crew or the director. All the crew and stars I found friendly and when they had a moment in-between takes you could have a chat with them. On days when there were many extra's on the 'Bye Bye Blackbird' set, when the snacks arrived it was like being in a scrum of the England Rugby squad. You had to fight your way forward. During one of these breaks one of my lady friends witnessed and commented on a French woman taking the fillings out of the remaining sandwiches and putting them all in hers.

"She was like a peasant and had the manners of a pig," she said in disbelief.

"Thank goodness my French girl friends aren't like her," I replied.

Many of the extras do the rounds. By that, I mean, they appear as an extra in many of the movies made here in Luxembourg. From the impression I get this is common in the film industry worldwide. The thing is, once you've done one film you'll want to do another.

Working in the movies sounds fun and it is, but as a friend of mine Russell commented, "You are here one minute, gone the next." He added, "As an extra it can be very disappointing at times, as until you are actually on the set nothing is guaranteed, and even then they can cut the scene out or re edit it." Shooting days are changed or cancelled and weeks of preparation altered literally in minutes. You can be cancelled at any time and I know of a few people this has happened to. There are also mix-ups with times and the language barrier has caught me out a few times. But at the end of the day, "That's show business!"

33

And finally…

I've been living in Luxembourg for nearly three years now. It's been an interesting experience, and I am glad I tried it. When I arrived I was going into the unknown. Now I'm a little older and wiser, but I've probably learnt more in the short time I've been here than in many years of living in the UK.

Simple situations that you can take for granted back home in the UK, have here forced me to recognise that the most basic things can be incredibly difficult to sort when living in another country. I'm not just referring to the language barrier, but the politics and beurocracy, the system. Once you've found the answer then it's easier, but it's making that first step.

There have been good, bad, harassing and frustrating moments. I'll also admit to have made a few mistakes on the way. Overall for me, it has been a steep learning curve about life.

Remember, I could have carried on with the same life as before. But I chose to try to do something different with my life, to try out new experiences. Most I have enjoyed, and overall it has been fun. I've met many new friends that I would otherwise not have met. I particularly like the experience of meeting and talking with many nationalities. The languages I'm learning—French and German—have improved, be it slowly, but I have given them a go. I have visited places that I would not have visited. There are still many more places to go, and this book reflects only some of the places I have been to in my travels across the border, but if I wrote them all down I'd end up writing another book. Overall, opportunities have arisen that I have seized upon and then enjoyed the moment.

The idea hopefully is to have given you a taste of what it is all about here in Luxembourg and what you can do through the eyes of an expat.

A girl friend said to me, "As a result of your book you've inspired me to try something different." I thought 'inspired' was a good word. To me that's what this book is all about—inspiration—and if you've learnt or identified with anything, then it makes it all worthwhile. Everyone's life is different but we all go through many similar experiences, which I hope is where you may empathise when reading this book.

I'm still searching for a job, which is incredibly difficult at this time, but I've not given up or wasted my time. I've done some part-time work and continued my languages. Writing this book has taken me a while to compile and has taught me a few things that I would not normally have found out myself. By sharing with others my experiences, both good and bad, I hope to encourage others to give living abroad a go. Just remember one thing, every country is different.

One thing I discovered whilst writing this is that I'm amazed just how many expats have similar stories to tell me about their experiences, once they've read or heard about this book. It appears there are as many horror stories to tell as there are good stories.

What happens next? Well, I don't know. Maybe I'll be lucky and get a job, or perhaps I'll write another book...

Updates Page

Time moves on and since I started writing this book one or two changes have taken place. There will be further changes, of course, long after this goes to press.

1. The Centre on the Route d'Arlon has since changed its name to FlashDance and has new owners.

2. César and Louise have moved to another dance studio.

3. Tainos has tragically closed for the moment but is rumored to be reopening!

4. The new development on the Plateau du Saint Esprit is under construction. A giant design of the development was there in January 2004, for all to see, on the large coverings in front of the building site. I have to admit the design is not as bad as I thought it would be. Much to my surprise, the development is not all concrete and glass and is quite cleverly integrated with the buildings already there. However, knowing what has been lost I still have mixed reservations on it.

5. El Compañero has salsa nights on Fridays and Saturdays.

6. My language classes have continued. I'm struggling, having stalled on level 6 French. I'm up to level 3 German. However, this is also struggling. It could all have something to do with me spending time writing this book—or I'm "a bit thick." Probably both.

7. The city administration and not the Catholic Church pay for the hospice's gardens near the youth hostel.

8. Since December 2003, signing on at ADEM has altered for those people who have done their full year unemployed from fortnightly to every three weeks. The number of chairs has more than doubled on the first floor to cope with demand and people at times are still there at 12.30pm from 10am. I also heard regrettably that volumes of people through the door are still increasing. Let us hope that alters in the near future.

9. I am pleased to advise that the curries at the Tahj Mahal Indian restaurant are now much improved and hotter than they used to be! Why? Well, many curries used to be spicy and mild. However, some money brokers demanded them hotted up to UK standards. One restaurant started this trend, the others followed!

10. If you are interested in going down the secret tunnels in Luxembourg City and would like more details—The friends of the Fortress Association e-mail address is: ffgl@pt.lu.

11. The old Jenisch dictionary that I saw in the National library has been reprinted for the first time in ten years. It is now on sale in local bookshops.

12. The Golden Man film was cancelled. To date it is, 'on hold.'

13. The newly refurbished underground supermarket at the Nobilis Centre at 47 Avenue de la Gare has now reopened.

14. The Foires Internationales at Kirchberg has changed its name to 'LuxExpo'. Details of events can be found at www.luxexpo.lu

15. City Concorde's big hypermarket has changed from Match to Cora

16. Yesterdays bar is now Casemates bar

From the Author

I hope you have enjoyed reading this book. It is the first one I have written.

I would welcome any comments you have, be they positive or negative, or any corrections you may find. You might also have had some experiences yourself that you may wish to tell me. These I would be particularly interested in.

My e-mail address is

expat@internet.lu

Thank you.

David Robinson.

Bibliography

Books:

Martin Dunford and Phil Lee, _The Rough Guide Belgium & Luxembourg,_ 1999
André Bruns, _Luxembourg as a Federal Fortress 1815-66,_ 2001
Joseph Tockert, _Das Weimerskircher Jenisch auch Lakersprache oder Lakerschmus genannt,_ 1993
Richard Nichols, _Radio Luxembourg; The Station of the Stars,_ 1983

Periodicals:

Revue
Telecran
Luxembourg City Tourist office, various brochures including, _Summer in the City,_ Welcome to Luxembourg, _Luxembourg the city_
Service Central de la Statistique et des Études Économiques, _Statec_
Le Jeudi
The Times
_352_

Primary Sources:

Frënn vun der Festungsgeschicht
The Internet
Office du Tourisme, _Verdun_
Mousel's Cantine
Asia Market, Luxembourg
La Commission Indépendante de la Radiodiffusion

Maps:

Inside

Plan of the countermine system of the fortress of Luxembourg (1814).
Origin: KOLTZ, Jean-Pierre: Aus der Kartothek der Festung Luxemburg, in: Société des Amis des Musées, Annuaire 1931, Luxembourg 1931.

Plan of the fortress of Luxembourg in 1867.
Origin: KOLTZ, Jean-Pierre: Baugeschichte der Stadt und Festung Luxemburg. II. Band: Beschreibung und Schleifung der Festungswerke. Luxembourg 1946.

Back Cover

Plan of the country of Luxembourg
Origin: Market Development International SARL plans.

Inside pages

Plan of Europe
Origin: Market Development International SARL plans.

Plan of Luxembourg City (David Robinsons version)
Origin: Market Development International SARL plans.

Photo's

David Robinson

0-595-31485-6

Made in the USA
Lexington, KY
06 February 2013